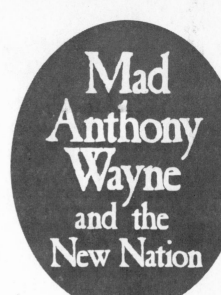

Mad
Anthony
Wayne
and the
New Nation

Major General Anthony Wayne from an engraving and painting by Edward Savage, who published it on June 1, 1796, a little more than six months before Wayne's death. *(Photo from National Archives)*

Stackpole Books

Mad Anthony Wayne and the New Nation

THE STORY OF WASHINGTON'S FRONT-LINE GENERAL

GLENN TUCKER

Maps by Dorothy Thomas Tucker

973.34
T 892
A-1

Copyright © 1973 by
Glenn Tucker

Published by
STACKPOLE BOOKS
Cameron and Kelker Streets
Harrisburg, Pa. 17105

Printed in U.S.A.

Library of Congress Cataloging in Publication Data

Tucker, Glenn.
  Mad Anthony Wayne and the new nation.

  Bibliography: p.
  1. Wayne, Anthony, 1745-1796. I. Title.
E207.W35T82   973.3'44'0924 [B]   72-13438
ISBN 0-8117-0958-2

To the memory of the late Judge B. Fain Tucker
of the Cook County Circuit Court of Chicago,
my much admired sister, a good scholar,
always generous with her viewpoints and books

Books by Glenn Tucker

POLTROONS AND PATRIOTS, 2 vols.
A Popular Account of the War of 1812

TECUMSEH
Vision of Glory

HIGH TIDE AT GETTYSBURG
The Campaign in Pennsylvania

HANCOCK THE SUPERB

CHICKAMAUGA
Bloody Battle in the West

FRONT RANK
(North Carolina in the Civil War)

DAWN LIKE THUNDER
The Barbary Wars and the Birth of the U.S. Navy

ZEB VANCE
Champion of Personal Freedom

LEE AND LONGSTREET AT GETTYSBURG

THE WAR OF 1812: A COMPACT HISTORY
(in collaboration with James R. Jacobs)

MAD ANTHONY WAYNE AND THE NEW NATION
The Story of Washington's Front-Line General

Contents

Acknowledgments

AMONG THE SOURCES consulted for this book, first mention should be made of the large collection of Wayne papers, mostly of military character, at the Historical Society of Pennsylvania in Philadelphia. The writer is indebted to Nicholas B. Wainwright, Director, and Conrad Wilson, Chief of Manuscripts, for guidance in the use of the Wayne and related manuscripts. Appreciation is expressed also to the New York Public Library for permission to work with the Wayne papers there.

Valued assistance has been obtained and much time saved by the volume containing Wayne's correspondence with Secretaries of War Knox, Pickering, and McHenry during his Northwestern campaign. This correspondence was transcribed and edited by Richard C. Knopf, Historian of the Anthony Wayne Parkway Board, and published in 1960 under the title of *Anthony Wayne: A Name in Arms*. The last four words are a quotation from Wayne, who felt, toward the end, that it had been his fortune to win such an addition to his numerous sobriquets.

Among the books mentioned in the condensed bibliography, the writer is indebted for direction on the progress of the war to John Marshall's, Washington Irving's, and Douglas S. Freeman's biographies of George Washington (with less frequent reference to several others); while among the histories of the American Revolution used, special mention should be made of Henry B. Carrington's, Benson J. Lossing's, Christopher Ward's, and the splendid and time-saving compilation of original source documents by Henry Steele Commager and Richard B. Morris entitled *The Spirit of 'Seventy-Six: The Story of the American Revolution as Told by Participants.* Of major importance both for the scope of its research and its graceful style is Carl Van Doren's *Mutiny in January*, a gripping story of one of Wayne's supreme travails.

Guidance has been obtained from the several Wayne biographies that have preceded this book, the most helpful being that of H. N. Moore (1845), who did research beginning in the 1820s and wrote with the cooperation of General Wayne's son, Isaac, who himself had written a biography of passing value. Others are John Armstrong (1845), Charles Janaway Stille (1893), John Hyde Preston (1928), who minimized Moore's value because Moore smoothed out some of Wayne's English; Thomas Boyd (1929), and of less interest to this writer, Harry E. Wildes (1941), and John R. Spears (1905). Wars have come and gone since these biographers wrote and there is occasion for fresh review of Wayne's conduct in the light of military practices given later ratification.

Willard B. Willcox's *Sir Henry Clinton's Narrative*, the correspondence of the British commander in the late stages of the war, is of value. I am appreciative of the assistance given by E. Richard Cole, curator of the Sondley Collection, Pack Memorial Library, Asheville, N.C., who obtained books from other libraries and listed numerous magazine articles about Wayne.

Special thanks are given to the Yale University Press for permission to quote brief scattered extracts from *The American Rebellion: Sir Henry Clinton's Narrative, etc.*, William B. Willcox, Editor; and to the University of Pittsburgh Press for a similar use of extracts from Richard C. Knopf's *Anthony Wayne: A Name in Arms.*

Finally I express appreciation of my association in this volume with Stackpole Books. The late James Rietmulder, President, made valuable suggestions for condensation of the narrative, eliminating digressions I in the first draft considered intriguing. His company, publisher of military and other books, was long conducted by the late Lieutenant General Edward J. Stackpole, soldier, author, and publisher, and was a companion interest to that which General Stackpole maintained in the progress of the popular historical journals, *Civil War Times Illustrated* and *American History Illustrated*. To these periodicals, founded and edited by Robert H. Fowler, the author of this book has been privileged to contribute articles over many years; it is now gratifying to have a biography of a leading American military character published by a company having a similar background and headquartered in the same building.

This book, like earlier efforts, is intended for lay readers interested in the development of the American story. The epoch it deals with has been plowed over and harrowed in almost innumerable books, treatises, and specialized studies but it will always remain fresh and vital because of the desperate task confronting Washington and his generals and their resourcefulness and at length triumph. The secondary sources available in vast array are fully as enlightening, at times more so than original documents and eye-witness accounts that often are so partisan as to be grotesque. One concerned with only the primary source material of the American Revolution is fairly certain to be misled; the long processes of reflection and seasoning over the last two centuries have contributed to a much better understanding of this bitterly fought war and of the capable officers on both sides, and to a more tempered view of the Loyalists, and of the once despised Redcoats, and the even more disdained Hessians.

The notes have been condensed as much as is feasible. They are of more special than general interest. I immerse the reader lightly in the brackish waters of the *supra* and the *ibid*. My thought has been mainly to show a student where the material might be augmented most readily and not necessarily to evidence where it was first encountered.

Since virtually all of Anthony Wayne's adult career was devoted to the army, this book is mainly a story of his battles. It has been written out of a profound admiration of the soldiers and officers who sacrificed so unstintingly to create a new nation. Wayne was preeminent among them. He was, as he hoped, and as Richard C. Knopf has quoted him, "a name in arms."

Introduction: A Glimpse
at Mad Anthony

As A FIGHTER Anthony Wayne rated with the best. Often blocked for promotion and deprived of opportunity by lack of seniority, he emerged nevertheless from the Revolutionary War as one of its most striking, romantic, and successful generals, following, perhaps, only Washington, Nathanael Greene and Lafayette.

His battle actions flashed with the gleam of naked steel. His last spectacular campaign, fought against the Indians after the Revolution, which culminated in the battle of Fallen Timbers, reaffirmed his vigilance and capacity for independent command, and gave the infant Republic firm possession of the vast Old Northwest.

Wayne was a true combat type, perceptive, decisive, often courageous to a fault, scrupulously obedient to his chief, idolized by his men. Some who followed him and learned from him in the Revolutionary War and in the Northwest went on to later military fame, and one, surely not the most talented among them—William Henry Harrison

11

—to the Presidency. Yet, striking as was Wayne's performance during the struggle for independence, it was not until after its conclusion that he reached a rank higher than brigadier general.

One is not likely to become an outstanding general unless he possesses an intense, transporting eagerness to win, a trait as manifest in obstinate Ulysses S. Grant and restless George S. Patton as in the renowned Ferdinand Foch or the Duke of Wellington. Wayne's will was such that it cast aside all doubts of victory and made him essentially a general of the offensive. When Washington before Brandywine was confronted by an army superior in discipline and numbers, Wayne urged not the defensive, but attack. Counseling a flanking movement, he almost impudently instructed Washington that the outcome of a battle was controlled by "the irresistible impulse of the human heart."

Ordinarily the first question asked about him is how he gained the incongruous but indelible sobriquet of "Mad" Anthony. The name implies indiscretion, heedlessness, or irrationality, qualities as foreign to Anthony Wayne as to Washington. But Wayne could fly into a passion, as could Washington when his orders were flouted or when confronted with a grave dereliction. The "madness" in Wayne was temper, not impetuousness. He accumulated a host of nicknames in his long military career, some denoting extreme caution—"the blacksnake," "the chief who never sleeps,"—others, "Mad" Anthony, the "Big Wind," "Dandy," the "Hotspur of the Revolution."

Much more is known about Wayne than about Hotspur, but the skeleton of that choice character has been filled in by Shakespeare and others with the flesh of a headstrong Percy who died with an arrow in his brain at Shrewsbury. The similarity between him and Wayne appears in their intense zeal. One cannot read English history without lingering over the intriguing Hotspur any more than, in a study of the American Revolution, one can avoid being inquiringly arrested by the "mad" as attached to the flamboyant Wayne.

That inappropriate designation came to Wayne from a nondescript character known only as Jemy the Rover, a shadowy figure in Revolutionary War campaigning, who flitted in and out of the Pennsylvania Line with Wayne's tacit approval because during his absences he sought and procured information of military value. He acted, in truth, as Wayne's principal spy during the Valley Forge campaign and often thereafter. Much longer remembered than the spy and rover was the title he fixed on the stern disciplinarian who commanded him with uncommon tolerance.

In Wayne's Virginia campaign shortly before Yorktown, Jemy, whom the general at times affectionately called "the Commodore," apparently because of his wandering habits and long absences, vanished. Wayne wrote to Pennsylvania friends that "Jemy, the Rover, alias the commodore, has absented himself from this detachment of the army." He requested that if Jemy passed that way, comfort and hospitality should be extended to him, for: "I am convinced that, whether in his hours of sanity or insanity, he would cheerfully lay down his life to either me or any of my family."[1]

Jemy at length returned to camp but became unruly, by one account from a spell of derangement, but more likely from rum. A file of soldiers escorted him to the guardhouse. Wayne meantime had been wounded severely in the leg by one of Lafayette's impulsive sentries and was not in good spirits. At the guardhouse door clamorous Jemy caught his senses sufficiently to ask by whose orders he was being incarcerated. Informed that they came directly from headquarters, he inquired if Anthony—he always called the general by his first name—were angry, or just in fun. The answer was not reassuring: as an additional savor of the general's disposition he was to have twenty-nine lashes across his back. General Wayne was "much displeased by your disorderly conduct." Twenty-nine lashes was a fairly moderate sentence in Revolutionary War armies.

Jemy exploded. "Then Anthony is *mad*, stark mad," he exclaimed. Again and again he repeated the remark: "Mad Anthony Wayne! Mad Anthony Wayne!" He was bitterly aggrieved over his beloved general's uncommon rebuke and lashing. When he had paid for his obstreperousness he sullenly parted company with the Pennsylvania Line and was heard of no more, but the memory of him lingered as long as any of Wayne's veterans survived, and the name would abide for centuries.

Though Wayne gloried in combat, his was no harebrained impetuosity. He was conspicuous for his valor in all of his battles, but a general of discretion and sober judgment. These qualities were displayed dramatically in his bold and resourceful attack on Cornwallis at Green Spring, Virginia; in his assault at Germantown; in his intrepid storming of Stony Point; and in his skill in extricating his command at Paoli after a subordinate had permitted the British to bayonet some of his troops in a night attack about which he had been warned and had sought to guard against. There was a wartime saying that "where Wayne went there was a fight—that was his business."[2]

Thus this cautious, usually victorious general carried through life and has retained in history an appelation that marks him as headstrong or irrational, when he was neither. The reiteration caused some of his compatriots, who did not understand the origin of the term, to pause at times before awarding him their full confidence. Even the discerning President Washington, after the new government had been formed, would hesitate, wonder, and counsel with others before entrusting to him the remote, independent command in the Northwest. Understandably he has been termed "the sanest brigadier general in the army."[3]

Even more properly it may be said that his generalship was prudently aggressive, which is perhaps as ideal a combination of qualities as can be found for military command. At times when Washington might seem unaware of some opportunity that his subordinate considered precious, Wayne was ready with a memorandum of urgency and explanation. His frequent insistence causes one to wonder at the great man's patience. But Washington came to appreciate him for his eagerness. From his first Revolutionary War combat in the fastness of the Canadian forests to his last campaign in the swamplands of Georgia and the vaporous, miasmal banks of the St. Mary's River, he was a bundle of vitality, and a leader always pushing.

Washington in his heart never doubted Wayne. He admired the younger man's zest, which shone in his shortest but most famous speech, delivered at a council of war on the night before Monmouth. The question was whether or not Sir Henry Clinton should be attacked as he crossed New Jersey to Sandy Hook. One by one the higher ranking generals counseled caution, advised against the hazard of battle.

"What would you do, general?" Washington inquired, when he finally reached Wayne.

"Fight, sir!" was the quick response. Washington cast his weighty vote with Wayne. Fight they did, with Wayne leading the attack, only to have a clear victory snatched from the army by the impudent disobedience of Washington's ranking subordinate, General Charles Lee.[4]

Wayne understood the importance of a soldier's neatness and cleanliness. Contemporaries described him as foppish and tried to ridicule him as a dandy. The plea was guilty! His explanation to Washington reeked with exuberance: "I have an inseparable bias of an elegant uniform and soldierly appearance, so much so that I would rather risk my life and reputation at the head of the same men in an attack, clothed and appointed as I could wish, merely with bayonets and single charge of ammunition, than to take them as they appear in common with sixty rounds of cartridges." He understood that neatness and discipline were inseparable. Almost at the outset, in his Canadian campaign, he issued orders that a barber should be assigned to each company to shave the soldiers and dress their hair, and reinforced it by

Waynesborough, the Wayne family home near Paoli, Pennsylvania, built in large part by Isaac Wayne, the general's father. It stands today much as it was when Isaac completed it in the early 1740s. Here Anthony was born. He inherited the valuable estate with its pastures, herds, and tannery, when he was twenty-nine years old. *(Courtesy the Historical Society of Pennsylvania)*

saying he would punish every man who came to parade with a long beard, or was dirty, or slovenly dressed. He told his officers it was their duty to make certain their men always appeared "washed, shaved, their hair plaited and powdered, and their arms in good order." The regiment had just emerged from tough Canadian fighting and might have expected a season of relaxed discipline. About the only thing they retained was their beards, and now Wayne ordered that they be sacrificed. Consequently, the Pennsylvania Line under Wayne was always noted for its esprit de corps and polish.

Any biographer with such a subject as Wayne is in danger of caressing the favorable incidents and adorning the worthy traits. The normal biographer writes of one he admires. He is not likely to anticipate and mollify his critics by discovering a character whom he wishes to berate. One must search in vain through the Wayne records to find a biography of denigration; the wonder is about the unnamed man who stood more than a century and a half ago in the Radnor, Pennsylvania churchyard, and, pointing, said, "Here is the grave of a scoundrel." One of Wayne's veterans was at hand to knock him down.[5]

Wayne would have been puzzled—he could not have remotely understood the moral reproach and repugnance of warfare involved in much present-day thought; he had the uncomplicated belief that wars were fought for great causes, that though they involved death and carnage, the soldier's aim was to win. He may have seemed at times eager, even lustful for combat. All of that he was, to a degree. He was frankly a tradesman in slaughter, a devotee at inflicting death. He was a progenitor of the "expanding torrent" theory of warfare, the quick concentration and impulsive explosion of superior energy. But if one dismisses Wayne for glorying in warfare, and risking all for victory, one must likewise draw a blue pencil through the American Revolution, which was no less brutal than other wars. Manifestly it could not have been won without the shock of battle such as Wayne schooled his men to deliver, and battle is coarse and savage.

Wayne's campaign methods and battle tactics may now be viewed in the light of two world engulfing modern conflicts and the devastating twentieth century revolutions, "police actions," and bush wars, climaxed by the prolonged Indo-China involvement. Against them his military principles remain sound. Good fighters are not developed in over-abundance in the higher echelons of any wars. Theodore Roosevelt, whose opinions as a scholar and historian are entitled to some respect, rated Wayne the best fighting general of American history. He clearly stands in the forward rank.

With his abundant acres of choice Pennsylvania farmland, he could have had wealth and ease but, like Washington abandoning Mount Vernon, he chose the service of his country, suffered from mediocre to poor management of his fields and tannery, and was able merely to carry them along. He did not choose public service for any tangible advantages he could get out of it. His quest was for fame, power, glory. But he was at heart an entrepreneur, a doer; he could see that a great nation was being built and wanted to share in it. Throughout the war he used his own money to maintain himself, and, as far as it would go, to outfit his soldiers. "When I was first called upon by my country to defend her rights and liberties," he wrote to his daughter Margaretta, "in [that] hazardous task I spent my prime of life, nor was I sparing of my blood." Again, in command of the army in the Northwest, he gave added years to the rigors of the frontier camps, on guard through near sleepless nights against the constant danger of surprise.

Wayne was one of the "reading generals," who set a pace for study among the Continental soldiers. A picture is provided by Captain Johan Ewald, leader of a company of Hessian chasseurs of Knyphausen's Corps, who took note of the character of the baggage captured from the Americans between his arrival in 1776 and the surrender of Yorktown. In "every wretched knapsack" he found a quantity of military books: "For instance, 'Instructions of the King of Prussia to His Generals,' Thielke's 'Field Engineer,' the partisans 'Jenny' and 'Grand Maison' and similar books." These, he commented, had all been translated into English, and they came into his hands through his soldiers "hundreds of times." He continued: "This was a true indication that the officers of this army studied the art of war while in camp." That was not the case with the "opponents of the Americans," whose portmanteaus were loaded with bags of powder for their hair, with boxes of "sweet-smelling pomatum," with playing cards in lieu of military maps, and (mentioned with apparent contempt) "some novels or stage plays."[6]

Wayne was an officer who ransacked history during his spare hours, while some of his fellow generals, like many in other wars, looked with contempt on old methods, not recognizing that one is unlikely to see the next forward step without coming into tune with the past, studying each improved weapon or tactic or form of organization, ascertaining what it contributed, and concluding what was left still wanting.

With him often in his campaigning went the haunting vision of a brown-eyed Delaware girl, Mary Vining, whose breath-taking beauty had stirred the French officers with Washington, and come to the attention of Marie Antoinette through Thomas Jefferson. Lafayette and the other young Frenchmen were drawn to her in Wilmington and Philadelphia because of her faultless beauty and her near faultless French. Lafayette introduced her to Wayne when Washington's army was in Wilmington in preparation for the Brandywine campaign, and the response, when their eyes met, was soft, anxious, enduring.

Meanwhile, Anthony's letters to his wife, Polly Penrose Wayne, were dutiful, informative, at times affectionate, but most of them might well have been written by a brother—not by a loving husband. One must wonder how long or deeply the love that marked their early years retained its ardor.

At Legionville, Pennsylvania, in 1792, when preparing to launch his hazardous campaign against the Northwest Indians who had destroyed the army of his predecessor, St. Clair, he wrote to his neighbor, Captain William Hayman: "It is now seven months since I left Waynesborough, without having received a single line, either from my own family or you—you may reply that this is the first from me, but that is not the case with Mrs. Wayne." He went on to explain the severe illness he had suffered, the bilious vomiting and weakness, his ability to ride only an hour or two a day to inspect the fortifications he was building, and the task of shaping an army out of recruits "who have yet to learn the dreadful trade of DEATH."

Was Mary Vining as inattentive during this period of stress? It will never be known. Though beseiged by suitors during the weary years of war and the heady days of triumph, she rejected them all and never married. Wayne's correspondence was voluminous. There are fifty-seven volumes of it in the collections of the Historical Society of Pennsylvania alone, additional volumes in the New York City Public Library, and other correspondence is in scattered repositories, but apparently there is not in that vast assortment, military, governmental and personal, one line from the charming, adoring girl who was destined to spend her life in Wilmington, waiting. Nor is there an affectionate line to her from Wayne.

One wonders. When Wayne in 1796 followed his wife in death, the effects at Waynesborough passed to his son, Isaac. The son wrote a biographical sketch of his father for a magazine whose hapless name, *The Casket*, forewarned that it would soon be buried. Those who read it were not held spellbound by Isaac's literary effort, but he must have looked on it as both exemplary and altogether adequate for posterity, because he thereupon burned an indeterminate amount of his father's correspondence and papers, and left the future deprived and biographers despairing when traversing blindly over some areas of Anthony Wayne's spectacular but in some respects not quite satisfying career. What remains is largely official army correspondence.

Still, there is enough information, plus much shadowland tradition and an abundance of impressive deduction, to establish that Mary Vining was the genuine love of Anthony's life. His wife died while he was in what was then the far Northwest. He and Mary were at length betrothed. On his next return they had some weeks of happiness together, planning their nuptials that were set for February 1797, when Anthony was due back again in Philadelphia and Wilmington at the end of a final assignment Washington and Congress had given him.

But Mary was destined to disappointment. Anthony never returned.

ONE

Assignment from Dr. Franklin

ANTHONY WAYNE'S SELF-DIRECTED military education was the outgrowth of his times and his boyhood drilling, his father's sporadic soldiering, and a strong Wayne family tradition in arms. Boys of his era, with meager athletic outlets, were usually involved in mimic strife as the world about them reverted again and again to warfare. What was more natural than for boys to engage in marching and make-believe battle?

His first reading of military history was Caesar's *Commentaries,* a good and bad beginning. As exciting as were the triumphs of the legions, the author's self-esteem so pervaded the text that Wayne must have caught a store of it to add to the goodly quantity gained from his own family heritage. Marshal Saxe's memoirs, *Mes Reveries,* published posthumously in 1757, a military classic, stirred his fervor as well, though he could not, of course, emulate the powerful Marshal's feat of bending a horseshoe double in his hand. Carlyle might say the Saxe memoirs were "a strange military farrago" and that they must have been composed under the influence of opium, but they did have a place in the self-education of one of America's leading combat generals.[1]

As a result, by the time he had become an important officer in the Continental Army, Wayne was perhaps better versed in the history and methods of warfare than any of his brother generals, even the book-store keeper, Henry Knox. He discovered in early years what William Cobbett described as the "joy of reading," though Caesar must have been a bit more dull for Wayne than Jonathan Swift's *Tale of a Tub* was for Cobbett. Unfortunately for Wayne, books were not readily obtainable when he needed them later in the Georgia and Ohio forests. Although the quantity of one's "common sense" is presumed to be innate, there can be no doubt that the capacity to judge soundly in military matters quite as much as in lay affairs often is nourished and brought into fuller flowering by the extent of one's reading.

Anthony Wayne's ancestry was English, though the family tarried some time in Ireland. The Wayne family had long lived in Yorkshire, and tradition places its members in a plenitude of English wars. At about the time of the "Bloodless Revolution" of 1688, Anthony Wayne, grandfather of the American general, secured land and moved his family to Wicklow County in East Ireland, a mountainous region south of Dublin. His move is unexplained, as are his other apparently impetuous migrations. He is at times alleged to have served under one of the greatest of the English generals, John Churchill, later Duke of Marlborough, but more authentic is the record that he was a captain of a company of dragoons in King William III's campaign in Ireland against the deposed James II that culminated in the battle of Boyne, July 1, 1690.

Riding alongside him at Boyne in a charge that distinguished them both and should have endeared them to the stiff new monarchical succession, was his neighbor, John Hunter, of Wicklow County, his companion through later life. This was the phase of the battle in which King William, who commanded in person his army's left wing, crossed the Boyne River, launched a cavalry assault against the right rear of the Jacobite army, and routed it, causing King James to abandon the field and his cause to collapse. The matter is of some speculative interest because of the uncertainty that surrounds the sudden departure of the Wayne family for the American colonies.

Since he was "about thirty" at the time of Boyne, his birth date was therefore around 1660. Sometimes it is given as late as 1666. He lived in Ireland after Boyne and secured from the cold, cynical, and stingy William III a tract of confiscated land near Rathdrum, situated in one of the valleys near where the mountains of central Wicklow rise. Here, during his stay of about 32 years, he saved some money. He married a Dutch girl and was above the age of sixty when life erupted for him again. With no more explanation than why he had gone to Ireland, he suddenly gathered his belongings and with his Dutch wife, Hannah Faulkner, and large family, took ship for America in 1722.

The question naturally occurs of why Anthony Wayne parted company with Ireland and thereby gave the oncoming western republic one of its esteemed military leaders. Surely it was because he had hoped for more from his charge at Boyne. Seeing the German favorites enriched at court after he had waited long, he had learned not to put his faith in princes. Being a Protestant, wholly inculcated, it was averred, with the "republican doctrines advocated by the Puritans" who for a century had been settling the New World, he grew restive, with only his companion John Hunter to worship with him in their Protestant enclave. In addition—and this seems paramount—he found that after more than thirty years of trying to be a landed squire in a mountainous country devoted mainly to mining and sheep herding (potatoes, which were to become one of the main crops of the county, had not yet been introduced) he suddenly felt the call of the Western World with its domains of virgin land and its buoyant promise.[2]

His Irish-born sons came with him, as did Hunter. The sons explain best why a man in his late years would remove to a strange, new land. The family cast about for a time making investigations, and in 1724 Anthony and Hannah purchased from Thomas Edwards a tract of 386 acres in Eastown, Chester County, Pennsylvania, near what became the town of Paoli. They added by purchase thirty-nine acres more, then conveyed fifty acres to their eldest son, Francis. On February 20, 1739, they conveyed the balance of the plantation to their third son, Isaac, who was six years later to father another Anthony, the Revolutionary War general. Isaac had been born in Ireland in 1699 and was forty years old when he took the estate. The condition was that he pay an annuity to his parents for the remainder of their lives, which he (and afterwards Anthony to his mother) did.

Captain Anthony Wayne, the veteran of Boyne, died before the end of 1739 and was buried in the St. David's Protestant Episcopal church yard at Radnor, where he and John Hunter had been pewholders and vestrymen. Isaac began at once the improvement of his property by building, first, a magnificent stone mansion of the type that beautify the Philadelphia back country, which stands today much as when he completed it and named it "Waynesborough." Many cities, towns and counties scattered over the country, populous cities and great counties, and a university and a college would bear that or a related name or would be content simply with Wayne. As the years passed, the house acquired a patina of age and, with its roses and honeysuckle, learned to smile.[3]

Isaac, the general's father, likewise a vestryman and pewholder at St. David's, grew restless at times, living a conventional squire's life. He was offered little opportunity to pursue the Wayne fortunes in arms. He was a man of industry and considerable spirit, and a cragginess that some termed crudity, a combination that left him admired by many, detested by some. He went to the provincial legislature for eight years as a delegate from Chester County and gained a commission in the local militia. He made money, built up the largest tannery in Pennsylvania, possessed herbs, grew grain and feed-crops. His militia commission enabled him to go out when the Indians rose or threatened, as he did to Forts Nazareth and Allen in the east central part of the, state, where the town of Nazareth and city of Allentown now stand.

He found better opportunity for combat, though, in his celebrated feud with neighbor Colonel William Moore of Moore Hall. The precise cause of the feud was lost as its vehemence grew. Isaac was a planter of the strictest integrity. Money matters do not appear to have been involved. Leadership and prestige were more at stake, perhaps. Two men who should have been most distinguished in the otherwise peaceful Philadelphia back country, though both somewhat obnoxious in their inordinate self esteem, stormed at each other lustily. They did not resort to swords or pistols, but they did at times wantonly employ their fists.

Isaac in the main lived in reluctant peace, as had his father before him. Boyne, as a battle, had not been markedly more dangerous than the marches to Fort Nazareth or the bouts with Colonel Moore. Like his father, he married late. When he was reaching toward forty he took as his bride a Philadelphia girl, Elizabeth Giddings, probably ten years younger. She was of a good colonial family, about whom information is scant, and remains a hazy, retiring figure during her life of more than thirty-five years with her stern, honorable, industrious, quarrelsome husband.

Isaac Wayne died at the age of seventy-five, in 1774, leaving one son, Anthony, and two daughters, Hannah, three years Anthony's junior, and Ann, born when he was six. Anthony succeeded to the estate when he was twenty-nine years old. Isaac had not been entirely pleased with Anthony's progress toward manhood. The boy was born just after midnight as the new year of 1745 arrived, at Waynesborough. This was to be the year of the Young Pretender, Bonnie Prince Charlie, who after landing first in the Hebrides reached Scotland in August. He won battles and captured fortresses right and left until in the next year his exhausted army met overwhelming defeat at Culloden. Wayne, in remote Pennsylvania, seeking no crown, had better prospects.

Isaac Wayne envisioned for his only son the country squire life he had sporadically enjoyed with his wealth and copious drafts of stout.

Benjamin Franklin in a half-length portrait by Joseph S. Duplessis. Franklin gave Wayne his first important assignment. *(Photo from National Archives)*

But from the very beginning it was clear that Anthony had decided he had no future in agriculture or stout or whiskey either, though he learned to enjoy rum in moderation. He took no interest in the farm and its labors, preferring the mimic warfare with neighborhood boys marching with hickory sticks, playing Long Knives and Indians. He was bright, alert, but worthless for farming. Gilbert Wayne, Isaac's brother, also Irish-born, had become one of the learned men of Chester County and a country school teacher. Smothered in books, he did not know how to handle an intellect a little out of the normal mold. After a time he wrote to his brother Isaac saying that Anthony's progress, if any, was quite unsatisfactory.

The nub was that parental affection might have blinded Isaac as to the lad's capacity, then: "What he may be best qualified for I know not. One thing I am certain of, he will never make a scholar. He may perhaps make a soldier. He has already distracted the brains of two-thirds of the boys under my charge by rehearsals of battles, sieges, etc. They exhibit more the Appearance of Indians and Harlequins than Students. . . ."[4]

Wayne's father happened to be home from the forts, where he won acclaim from his home community but took no arrow wounds, when his pedagogical brother was threatening the boy with expulsion: "I must be candid with you, brother Isaac—unless Anthony pays more attention to his books, I shall be under the painful necessity of dismissing him. . . ." Isaac's recourse was to admonish the boy that unless he knuckled under he would be assigned to the most onerous farm tasks his father could discover. The old man ruled more with harshness than manifest love.

Smart young Anthony, showing the prudence that characterized his later "mad" career, yielded and suddenly discovered the intriguing challenge of mathematics. His interest became so acute that he devoted eighteen months to the intense study of all the mathematics his uncle could offer. Gilbert again reported to the father, this time saying that the boy had passed beyond his capabilities to instruct and should be sent to Philadelphia for a more advanced education.

There is a close parallel in the educational progress of Washington and Wayne in their abrupt interest in surveying. When Washington advanced from Sexton Hobby's open-air school into that of a teacher, Henry Williams, at Bridges Creek, he dropped all concern over languages, rhetoric, classical studies, and entered with zest into mathematics and business subjects, but in particular into land surveying. So it was with Wayne when he was sent to the Philadelphia Academy, now the University of Pennsylvania. As Washington, through his surveying, gained assignment from Lord Fairfax and began the journey toward prominence in his state, so surveying brought to Wayne one of the significant events of his life, an assignment under Benjamin Franklin.

Franklin was among the first to recognize the opportunities for profit and development opened to the American colonies by the British acquisition of Canada in 1763. A year later he was organizing an association for the purchase, settlement, and development of an extensive parcel of land in Nova Scotia. Several leading citizens of Philadelphia took shares. By the time the deed was acquired for two tracts aggregating 200,000 acres, the number was twelve, of whom the most active participant was the youngest, Anthony Wayne, just turned twenty.

Anthony left the Philadelphia Academy before he was graduated. Prior to the age of twenty he had acquired a compass and chain and set up in Eastown his own surveying business, which quickly took him into the seemingly endless tracts of Pennsylvania timberland and across the vast acreage already under cultivation in this rich and extensive commonwealth. Behind the Quakers and a spot or two of Welsh settlers lived the Germans, termed "Pennsylvania Dutch," though they were in no quantity Hollanders; they had been induced by beguiling promotion to settle on what became some of the world's most choice farmlands, in order to provide a buffer against the Indians. Already the westward march was sturdily under way. Pennsylvanians, Virginians, and others were passing over the ranges and soon were pressing into Kentucky and Ohio.

Wayne was a good surveyor, industrious and accurate, and business came to him. His work took him to far off Westmoreland County, washed by the Allegheny and Youghiogheny Rivers, not far from where Braddock had met disaster only ten years before. Anthony could never have guessed that three of the state's western counties would be named after three of his companions in arms, Washington, Greene, and Fayette, and that another county at the other end of the state would bear the name of Wayne. He surveyed in Cumberland County beyond the Susquehanna, a fertile expanse that stretches across one of the richest and most beautiful of the great eastern valleys. His reputation spread from woodland to city and his surveying business became well known in Philadelphia.

Meanwhile, Dr. Franklin was departing for England on what was to prove one of the longest and most significant journeys of his career, which marked his transition from a stanch loyalist undertaking to strengthen the British Empire, to a firm Continental at heart, and ultimately into a separatist. Before riding horseback to take ship at Chester in November 1764, he gave an assignment to one of his favorites, John Hughes, who appears but briefly and a trifle unhappily in the Wayne and Franklin stories. Franklin used his influence to have him appointed the next year as distributor of stamps in the Philadelphia area, and soon the angry mob was storming at his door.

Franklin told Hughes to be on the lookout for a surveyor of intelligence and quality who could appraise the Nova Scotia lands, set up the rudiments of a settlement that would attract others, and make a report on the various characteristics of the area. Not unlikely Franklin mentioned Wayne, who had come to be admired by most of the younger group and Franklin was acquainted with virtually everyone in the city. More recently Wayne had been paying court to Mary Penrose, daughter of a prominent merchant, Bartholomew Penrose, who, before his early death, had been a friend of Anthony's father and representative of a family that had been acquiring wealth in Philadelphia since the times of William Penn. Hughes likewise was acquainted with Anthony's father and had heard of the young man's surveying adventures in the settlements. He invited Anthony to come to Philadelphia, and Wayne arrived the day after he received the letter. He made a favorable impression on Hughes.

Meantime, while the colonies were in an uproar over the threatened imposition of direct taxes by a far distant Parliament that was extending the levies to no others, Anthony Wayne assembled and equipped his expedition, loaded his supplies, and in the brooding spring of 1765 sailed for Nova Scotia. His instructions had been prepared by Hughes. He was directed to learn if the land in question could be reached readily by navigable water; to find the head of navigation and of the tides of the usable rivers; to determine the convenient places where ferries might be located; to ascertain where there were passes through the mountains; to locate any deposits of iron ore or coal and calculate where mines might be opened; to find good mill sites and other useful waterpower locations; to note road crossings and junctures; to mark the beaches and islands; and firm land, good meadows, the existence of any mineral springs, the quantities and quality of timber. All these, with other things, went to make a comprehensive assignment for so young a man with a limited number of helpers, and he the only surveyor.

Wayne's work was thorough and rapid. He not only had to do a great amount of surveying and some correcting of surveys already made, but he had also to take out the warrants for the land; supervise a small group of settlers; procure land patents; and attend to a host of matters that fell to the position of the general superintendent—and

Anthony Wayne was not yet twenty-one. He organized his work well. In little more than ten months from his departure, he was back in Philadelphia in late December 1765. He presented charts of the lands acquired and a full report on all he had done, plus a detailed description of the area that would answer the questions propounded at the time of his departure.

The prospects for colonization appeared splendid, and Wayne had exercised his authority to obtain for himself and friends grants from the province, 100,000 acres on the Piticoodzack River and 100,000 acres on the St. John's River, the grants being made to a number of names, including those of Dr. Franklin and Wayne. He left the rudiments of a colony behind him in Nova Scotia under the charge of an overseer. Wayne's association with a group headed by Dr. Franklin greatly enhanced his prestige in the Philadelphia area.

Speed in returning to Philadelphia was due partly to attractive Mary Penrose. Wayne had been a young man of many romances but was gradually won to Mary, known as Polly by her friends. She was stately, self-reliant, blonde, and slender. Her smile was warm, her manner refined and befitting one who had been reared in the large house of the affluent Penroses. Still, Wayne's first duty was to Nova Scotia. After a pleasant winter in Eastown and Philadelphia, with increasing attentiveness to Polly Penrose, he was preparing to sail again in April, 1766. This time he was taking a cargo of farm implements, provisions, and as many new colonists as he could recruit. One matter remained unsettled as he made his ship ready, however. As the days passed, the young man's heart turned to it urgently and joyously. He could not sail before he had won Polly Penrose. He proposed and was accepted by the girl of seventeen years, who had scarcely been outside of Philadelphia, and infrequently away from the home where she lived with her mother, Mary Kirll Penrose, and a brother and sister. Inexperienced, she was likewise young for marriage.

In order to meet Anthony's sailing schedule, the wedding arrangements were rushed. The two were married on March 25, 1766, in Christ Church, just as spring was budding over Philadelphia. Many of the leading personages of the city were guests. Here, again, John Hughes had to represent the absent Dr. Franklin, but Dr. Franklin did send personal greetings to the happy pair. They left for Waynesborough after the wedding feast at the Penrose home and stayed there until Anthony again sailed for the northern wilderness.[5]

Polly Penrose Wayne remained behind at Waynesborough, and Anthony's marriage was notice that he did not intend to become a permanent part of the settlement he was cutting out of the wilds. Nevertheless, the expedition was of marked significance to his career. Neither he nor Dr. Franklin, nor the others of the association, realized any wealth from it, nor did they even retain possession of a proprietory colony such as those that had been set up here and there in early America. But the venture gave Wayne self-assurance and experience in leadership. None could scarcely have expected to receive such responsibilities and discharge them so well in and before his twenty-first year. In addition, it brought him to the favorable attention of Dr. Franklin.

The Nova Scotia colony was visionary from the beginning. It was too remote at a time when there was promise of the opening of vast virgin tracts beyond the mountains. Philadelphia people did not want to live permanently in the cold climate of the North. And conditions were too unsettled between the colonies and the mother country for families to venture far from home. Wayne was in Philadelphia again before the winter of 1766–1767. He did not make another trip. Because he had performed ably and had at his finger tips all of the matters regarding the colony, he was appointed its director at the Philadelphia headquarters. But as the war came on, the settlers came home, the office was closed, and the dream was forgotten.

TWO

Committeeman and Continental Colonel

ANTHONY WAYNE'S CHIEF DANGER as war loomed was that his might not be a combat role, for his acquaintance with Franklin was both an opportunity and a threat. Franklin was still abroad but he was coming home and he knew Anthony's organizing abilities. The situation between colonies and crown had not yet hardened but rigidity was setting in and Franklin might well try to cast Wayne in some vital—though hardly exciting—civilian position.

From the standpoint of Pennsylvania and Anthony Wayne personally, the most cataclysmic event in the sundering of peaceful relations and the approach of conflict was the seizure and burning of the schooner *Gaspee*, one of His Majesty's warships, in Narragansett Bay. Rhode Island had become a haven for smugglers with whom public opinion was in sharp sympathy. They piled brazenly into Newport and Providence, and were tolerated by the crown authorities after a tax collector had been mobbed in Newport without any punishment being meted out to his assailants by the courts. When the *Gaspee* was dispatched to extirpate the smugglers, Rhode Island citizens boarded and burned her.[1]

The *Gaspee* incident, a forerunner of the Boston Tea Party, led the Virginia House of Burgesses in 1773, to suggest the creation of Committees of Correspondence that were to become the cohesive agency among the colonies. Samuel Adams already had organized such a network in Massachusetts that soon extended over New England. When the Committees of Correspondence reached Pennsylvania, Anthony Wayne became the leader in Chester County. More and more he was working toward the front among the aspirants for American autonomy.

At Waynesborough, meanwhile, all was calm. Anthony, despite his early revulsion against farming, reluctantly became a good manager. The rolling farmlands were the scene of intense activity in the spring, the plow moving on each favorable day, and no open day was to be lost, because, as any farmer knew, a good plowing day came infrequently enough and it never returned. He had cattle—not many, but sufficient for his family's needs of meat and milk. His horses were the finest that could be bred or procured in the Pennsylvania country. His flock of sheep was reputed to be the largest in the colony. Yet the principal business of the plantation was the tannery, for which hides came in abundance. The finished leather was shipped to colonial markets, to the West Indies, and to the mother country when the lanes were open. But blockades imposed as a whip to lash out of the colonies the spirit of dissent and potential rebellion seemed inevitable, another reason to encourage Wayne's growing commitment to the infant Patriot movement.

When the Pennsylvania Assembly of 1774 gathered to consider the colony's course in the growing crisis, Wayne was a member from the beginning. More than this, he spoke out boldly of breaking ties completely with the mother country, at a time when such assertions should have been whispers. And outside the public halls, he was showing proficiency as a drill master of the young men who came to him for advice and remained for training. Apart from the Assembly, he served as a member of the Pennsylvania convention that debated lustily the abrasive course the ministers in London seemed bent on pursuing— debates that gave inspiration to some of the other colonies puzzled in their search for proper measures. Pennsylvania was a large colony, strong in population, prosperous in resources, already the keystone, a colony that might properly give guidance.

Such were the uncertain conditions in Pennsylvania as the winter of 1774 wore into glorious springtime in the Philadelphia back country. Almost every courier from the north brought news from Boston—news about General Thomas Gage's regiments, of friction, of the tenseness in New England. Wayne was busy with the spring planting and with drill on the Chester meadows, but mainly he was waiting.

The Committee of Correspondence stood in session in Philadelphia when at 5 o'clock on the afternoon of April 24, 1775, an express rider galloped up to the City Tavern. His haste, his aura of excitement and the firm compression of his lips, plus the train of people who noticed his mein and followed him for the reading, showed that he carried news of ominous portent.

Few, if any, messages have been as fateful. He had dispatches from Watertown, Massachusetts, inland from Boston, telling succinctly how General Thomas Gage's Redcoat regiments marched out of Boston, fired on and killed many of the Massachusetts militia assembled on Lexington Common, marched on to Concord and destroyed provisions and stores there, and, at the time the dispatch bearer departed, were hastening back to Boston, hotly pursued by the Minute Men. Growing groups of farmers and militia were rushing to the scene while the country behind them was rising. The long awaited hour had arrived. War!

Though it was late and the people were at home when the first dispatch came, word of its contents spread from house to house in the darkness. By early morning, 8,000 persons gathered on the State House commons and on Chestnut Street, where the Committee of Correspondence, the main revolutionary body then in existence, took charge. The rolls were at once opened for the enlistment of volunteers.[2]

Franklin reached Philadelphia May 5, 1775, well after the news from Lexington had spread and companies of recruits were drilling on the meadows along the Schuylkill River. Even though some of his attitudes while in London had been questioned, his own people and the other colonies quickly took him into their hearts. He was promptly made a member of the Pennsylvania Assembly and the very next day after his arrival home was named one of the Pennsylvania deputies to the meeting of the Second Continental Congress, scheduled to convene in Philadelphia May 9, 1775. More than that, he was designated by the Assembly to head the Committee of Safety that in a general way superseded the Committee of Correspondence and controlled the defense measures of the colony. One of his early acts was to summon Anthony Wayne, and it was beginning to appear that Anthony would have a governmental role—a desk job—under the guidance of his old patron, Franklin.

The membership of the Committee into which Wayne was drawn was impressive. Among those seated at the table was Robert Morris, whom all looked on as the most astute financier of the town, as ardent as any other man in his championship of home rights, and who would become Wayne's devoted friend. Many of the younger man's letters were addressed to him when Anthony turned to his writing table at night after the exactions of the day's campaigning. Another was John Dickinson from Wayne's Chester County—a "piddling genius," John Adams called him—who had been writing much about the cause of the colonies, but in too conciliatory a vein for Wayne's taste. John Cadwalader and Benjamin Bartholomew were there, along with others of note. They dealt with the all-important matters of raising troops, giving them arms and equipment, providing ammunition that from the outset seemed always in short supply, and of the utmost importance, fortifying the Delaware River to prevent a sudden seizure of Philadelphia by the British Navy. With most of the great men of Pennsylvania around him, Wayne was still easily the best versed on military matters. He would find himself stirred deeply, like most others at this hour, when a detachment headed by the fife and drum marched down Chestnut Street.

He had little time after Dr. Franklin's return for supervision of the farm. The happenings in Philadelphia were too thrilling and stimulating. Committee sessions seemed interminable. What could he look ahead to? In the midst of transcendent events, the management of the farm and tannery did not seem appealing. Perhaps his uncle-schoolteacher had been correct in telling his father that he would never be a farmer. He might aspire to a political career through service on the home front while the issue was determined on the battlefield. His thirty years would admit of that, or so it appeared at the beginning.

As a committeeman Wayne rode occasionally back and forth over the twenty miles from Waynesborough to town, but remained frequently with his city friends, Sharp Delaney on Second Street, with whom he would continue a long correspondence from camp; Dr. Benjamin Rush, the eminent surgeon, whose correspondence would become even more voluminous; Richard Peters, long his link with the Pennsylvania and Colonial governments. On afternoons when the Committee of Safety adjourned early he would attend the drill session of companies that could hold their own with his Chester trainees, or surpass them, and were in sharp competition with each other. As he watched them on the fields where the Schuylkill glided smoothly, he could dream, perhaps, but could not truly expect that many of these men would some day be the followers of Anthony Wayne and would be merged into that glorious organization, the Pennsylvania Line.

One of the most striking was called the "Quaker Blues," which was in uniform prior to the incident on Lexington common. Though the Quakers officially undertook to hold aloof from the promised conflict, many of the young men found the tenets of the church too restrictive in the swirl of such high emotions and exciting events. They donned uniforms and boldly announced that their lives were offered to the common cause. The "Greens," composed of young men of some of the leading Philadelphia families, were commanded by John Cadwalader, wealthy native of the city, whose standing would take him quickly to the command of a division. He was always stanchly loyal to Washington. Quaker-born Thomas Mifflin, later a major general, called the Greens "aristocrats." After they completed their drills, held twice daily in the spacious Cadwalader grounds, they were treated with choice Madeira out of the Cadwalader cellar.

All of this was no mere sudden emotional gushing or ebullition. Thirty companies were drilling morning and afternoon in supreme earnest in and around Philadelphia. Observers felt that the men were being whipped into soldiers rapidly. Some who saw the drills used the word "elegant." There is no doubt these first Pennsylvania soldiers moved grandly at close order. The belt crossed over the shoulders was held by Philadelphia observers to "give an agreeable appearance viewed from the rear. . . ." "They are, without exception, the genteelest companies I ever saw." Such was the achievement of Wayne's committee.[3]

The break for Anthony Wayne came out of the most foolish of American adventures, the invasion of Canada in the fall and winter of 1775. Washington opposed it but Congress was in the saddle and was demonstrating at the very outset of American self-rule what is frequently not remembered, that legislative bodies are clumsy military leaders. But Congress had grown impulsive as a result of the showy triumph of Ethan Allen and Benedict Arnold in the May surprise and capture of Fort Ticonderoga. Memories of the importance of the Lake Champlain route between the St. Lawrence and the Hudson lingered from the French and Indian wars. That, plus much misinformation about the attitude of the Canadians, prompted the invasion, for which Washington not only had to sacrifice from the army in upper New York 2,000 well-trained men under Major General Richard Montgomery, but also was compelled to detach from his forces in front of Boston some of his best combat regiments. These included Colonel Daniel Morgan's formidable rifle corps brought up from Virginia. The whole force of 1,500 detached from Boston was under Colonel Benedict Arnold, who worked his way through the Maine forests and effected a juncture with Montgomery in front of Quebec. There the small British garrison repulsed them in a blizzard the night the old year 1775 ended.

Washington's sacrifice of 3,500 men for the ill-starred invasion left him recruit-hungry and soldiers could be obtained nowhere more readily than from the sprawling, industrious commonwealth of Pennsylvania, settled by William Penn for peaceful reasons but now the heart of the maelstrom of a war that after bloody Bunker Hill promised to be desperate and protracted. Restless Anthony, diligently performing his civilian tasks, had constantly kept an ear tuned to the north, listening to the armed clash around Boston, the shout of the Green Mountain boys as they burst into the ramparts of "Old Ti" and headed on toward Montreal, and the slashing of Arnold's and Morgan's men cutting through the virgin forests along the Kennebec River. Here was Wayne, a true fighter at heart, consigned to talking around a table and passing papers when he could hear the voice of destiny calling.

Wayne's chance came when the Second Continental Congress, toward the close of 1775, combing the colonies for reinforcements for Washington, asked Pennsylvania to recruit and equip four battalions for the Continental Army, to replace the troops detached for Canada. They were to be regulars, not militia. The esteemed Dr. Franklin presided at the meeting of the Committee of Safety where the decision was made to organize the four battalions, or regiments, and select the four colonels. Franklin by this time must have been altogether sympathetic with Wayne's ambition for a military career and confident of his military ability, which had been amply demonstrated over half a year at the preparedness sessions. Franklin's attitude was evident when it developed that the first man selected, the first Pennsylvanian to be a colonel of these Continentals, was Anthony Wayne. The other three were John Shee, a prominent Philadelphia merchant, Arthur St. Clair, large landholder from the western part of the colony, and Robert Magaw, a militia major.

Wayne returned at once to Chester County to begin raising his battalion. So strong was the confidence inspired by his character, sturdiness, and military talents in the young men of the neighborhood that almost without an effort he had his quota. His commission as colonel was dated January 3, 1776. As he put on the colonel's uniform Anthony had just reached the age of thirty-one years. He stood about five feet ten inches but his erect posture and commanding presence gave the impression of greater height, unless in the presence of Washington, who was six feet two in his stockings. Anthony's high forehead and the manner in which he carried his head, plus the alertness of his countenance, reflecting a sharp intelligence, easily made him an outstanding figure in any ordinary gathering. All—men and women—regarded him handsome, as much because of his vivacity as for his clear-cut features. His hair, dark brown in the Revolutionary War years, would gray in his later campaigns. His nose was high-ridged and hooked, almost eagle-like. His innate disposition was to be friendly. The word amiable, sometimes used in describing him, seems inappropriate, though, because it does not reflect his firmness nor the passions into which he would occasionally fly, not unlike those of his father, Isaac, in the feud days with Colonel William Moore. His eyes were a "dark hazel," which would be close to brown, a color not generally associated with military leadership. One early quasi-official account rated his morals as "chaste," which likewise invites clarification, if not doubt, because it varies sharply with Washington's comment that he was a "roué." It is easier to accept the affirmation, still too general, that his manner was refined, which goes with his courtly habits and elegant dress. One noticeable physical feature was his muscular compactness. This, with his sturdy health, explains his ability during the Revolutionary War years to sustain the severities of continual campaigning and life in the open, often in the cold, stormy winters of Pennsylvania, New Jersey and upstate New York.

Undeniably Wayne was vain. All his companion officers were aware of it, but it was the vanity of a performer and not a cloak of incompetence. It did not defeat the natural warmth of his greeting and conversation, or the charm of his ready smile. In camp he was almost invariably clean shaven. His uniforms were as spotless as he could keep them in the field, the ruffles of his shirt impressively white. He could not require his men to dress their hair without careful attention to his own. He had an affection for lace.

Wayne with his high confidence never doubted that the colonial cause would prevail. Captain Alexander Graydon, writer and, early in the war, an officer of a battalion of Pennsylvanians, conversed with Wayne at his headquarters before the battle of Brandywine and found him utterly contemptuous of the enemy. He stated "in his confident way" that the British and American armies had changed their modes—that the Americans had thrown away their shovels and the British had picked up theirs; that they did not dare to face the Americans without entrenchments. Graydon found Wayne, though unquestionably brave, "somewhat addicted to the vaunting style of Marshall Villars." Villars was one of the ablest soldiers and most unabashed braggarts in all the history of the French army.[4]

At last, preparations done, there were the leave-takings with Polly, his children and his mother. When it was time for Wayne to go, he departed.

Washington, while besieging Boston, had not neglected lower New York, which many expected would be the next object of British attack. He had collected a substantial army for the defense of Manhattan and Long Island and placed it confidently under the command of the most highly rated of his subordinates, Major General Charles Lee. Fortunately for two of the new Pennsylvania battalions, Wayne's and St. Clair's, they did not remain long in New York, where they probably would have become involved in the Fort Washington disaster, as were Magaw's and Shee's. The call for reinforcements for the American army in Canada was another urgency. Wayne's and St. Clair's battalions were dispatched up the Hudson to Albany and on to the St. Lawrence River to join the army commanded by Brigadier General John Thomas, retreating up the St. Lawrence after the unhappy experiences of the winter campaign against Quebec.

Now Anthony Wayne, the student of Caesar and Saxe, the drill master of the Chester County meadows, the colonel of the Pennsylvania Line, was to hear the longed-for cacophony of enemy musketry at last.

THREE

Confidently In, Hurriedly Out of Canada

WAYNE'S PART IN THE Canadian campaign was mainly that of extraction. Only lack of experience in war, to which Washington himself frankly confessed, could have induced the colonies to invade Canada when they were not yet possessed of military cohesiveness or even a semblance of a central government. Only skillful work, principally by junior officers, with Anthony Wayne and Benedict Arnold in the forefront, saved the army of invasion from encirclement and capture in the northern woods and brought the remnants back to the soil of the revolting colonies. From beginning to end the invasion of Canada was a costly mistake.

The invasion had rolled northward through New York and Maine, crested in front of Quebec, and when it began to subside, Congress sent a commission to Canada headed by Franklin. The commissioners went in the spring of 1776, when an American army was still making a pretense of besieging Quebec. They reached Montreal, where Benedict Arnold entertained and some English-speaking sympathizers met them, but among the French Canadians they encountered nothing but hostility. By that time the ice had broken on the upper St. Lawrence and British reinforcements were momentarily expected. When intelligence was received that fresh regiments had reached Quebec, Franklin left Montreal on May 11, 1776 and the other commissioners followed, with nothing but a long trip to their credit. Wayne reached Canada soon after Franklin departed.[1]

Conditions there had changed abruptly. The large British fleet that entered the St. Lawrence in May, 1776, brought an army of about 2,000 Hessians, and one British and seven Irish regiments. Governor-General Sir Guy Carlton thereupon assumed the offensive. General John Thomas, who commanded the Continental army around Quebec, scarcely had time to retreat. The army determined to depart on its own volition, when five newly arrived ships began discharging British soldiers. Much artillery, equipment, gunpower, and flour was abandoned. The disorderly withdrawal continued to Point Deschambault, sixty miles up the river, where Thomas stopped with 500 men while the bulk of the army went on to Sorel. There the Richelieu River, the outlet of Lake Champlain, with its heavy current and swirling rapids, enters the St. Lawrence.

The site was of strategic importance for guarding the natural route the British might employ in invading New York along the line of the lake and Hudson River, cutting the colonies through the middle. Consequently, when Carleton lifted the siege of Quebec, apprehension spread through New York, reached Congress in Philadelphia, and led to the prompt formation of a succoring force. This consisted of Colonel William Maxwell's 2nd New Jersey, followed by Brigadier General William Thompson's brigade of four regiments, about 2,200 men, sent by Washington, and by a division from New York, of about 3,300 men, under Brigadier General John Sullivan. Sullivan was ordered to supersede Thomas in command of the army in Canada. Wayne's regiment was a part of Thompson's Brigade.[2]

The American army concentrated at the mouth of the Sorel River after the retreat from Quebec numbered around 5,000, while the British, who selected Three Rivers (Trois Rivières) for their concentration, below where the St. Lawrence broadens into the expanse of Lake St. Peter, had a rapidly expanding force which the Americans vastly underestimated as less than 1,000. Thus, the audacious campaign in which Wayne had his baptism of fire was conducted on scant and faulty information for, back on the Sorel River, Sullivan felt himself in sufficient strength to think of marching toward Quebec again.

At this juncture Colonel St. Clair picked up information that the enemy had an exposed force of about 800 British regulars and Canadian militiamen at Three Rivers, forty-five miles down the St. Lawrence from Sorel. He reported this to General Thompson, who directed him to attack it with a force of about 700 men. Sullivan arrived shortly and approved the movement but was not satisfied with the size of St. Clair's party. He told Thompson to follow St. Clair with support, which would bring the little army to a strength of about 2,000. The main components were Continental regiments from Pennsylvania under Colonels St. Clair, Wayne, and Irvine, and Maxwell's New Jersey regiment. Sullivan instructed Thompson not to attack the British camp at Three Rivers unless the chance of success seemed most inviting.

Sullivan wrote confidently to Washington, saying the Canadians were "flocking by hundreds to take a part with us," and forecasting that within a few days he could "put a new face on our affairs here." He left the letter unfinished in order that he might report the success of Thompson's expedition.

In the darkness of early June 8, 1776 Thompson landed his men on the south bank of Lake St. Peter at Nicolet, where he picked up St. Clair's command and remained under cover. On the following night he stealthily crossed the broad expanse of the St. Lawrence at Lake St. Peter, intent on surprise, for which he debarked three miles above Three Rivers, a little below Pointe du Lac. Naively he and his men believed they were undetected, but at daybreak June 10 the British frigates close offshore opened an unexpected cannonade that pushed the Americans farther inland, into the forest that extended along the river some distance from the bank.

They advanced in four columns under St. Clair, Irvine, Maxwell, and Wayne, the last blithely exuberant over the prospect of battle. They had a poorly selected guide, a French Canadian named Antoine Gautier, whom the Americans came to suspect of either abominable ignorance of the country or else clouded loyalty. He guided them, to be sure, toward the forward elements of the large British army concentrating at Three Rivers. They were hunting Three Rivers and he surely led them there, but by a route perhaps none had ever taken before. He took them through a wooded morass in which they floundered frantically for four hours. The four regiments became separated and acted on their own, without cohesion from brigade headquarters. The slime in the bog sucked off some of their shoes but they slogged ahead desperately.

At length the venturesome little command, now nearly exhausted, emerged and saw directly in their front, between forest and river, a formidably posted line of British regulars supported by artillery landed from the ships, commanded, they soon learned, by a capable, veteran officer, General Simon Fraser. Other regiments under General Carleton were in and below Three Rivers while a strong force was aboard the transports at the foot of Lake St. Peter. The ships protected Fraser's left while his entrenched line was securely posted against the swamp on his right. A stretch of firm, cleared ground in his front provided an ample field of fire from his earthworks. Thus, instead of finding a town inadequately defended by 800 militia, Thompson and his four regiments encountered a third of the British regulars in Canada, concentrating for a major effort by Carleton to drive the Americans back across the border and open the invasion route up Lake Champlain and down the Hudson.

Irvine and St. Clair were on Wayne's right, Maxwell on his left, when they approached Three Rivers and the British defenders. Lacking prudent regard for his orders not to attack without good prospects of victory, General Thompson thought his men were entitled to some sort of combat after marching all day from Pennsylvania and New Jersey. Besides, Thompson had little opportunity to extricate himself, coming upon Fraser's strong line suddenly as he burst out of the swamp and woods. He was intent on the offensive, but almost immediately the attackers became the attacked, and soon the pursuers the pursued. Despite Thompson's efforts to rally the men and make a vigorous stand, his forward units, with the exception of Wayne's, were thrown into confusion and speedily routed.

Wayne's regiment had pulled out of the morass first. When it was on firm ground and Wayne saw the strong enemy line, he sent ahead a detachment of skirmishers and began a scantily supported effort at an advance. He did manage to drive in the first line of skirmishers thrown out by Fraser. The disorder elsewhere became calamitous when the British not only fired heavily from their entrenchments, but also began to land men from transports up the river in Lake St. Peter, now in Thompson's rear. This flank attack cut off Thompson and Colonel Irvine with 250 men and left them Fraser's prisoners. Colonel St. Clair, next in line under the Continental ranking, injured his foot at this critical stage by stubbing his toe on a tree root. With Thompson a prisoner and St. Clair appearing to be incapacitated, Wayne suddenly found himself in command of a debacle, the breakup of an army.

No situation could have offered him a more severe test. He had no intention of retreating. He shouted to his own men and to front line wanderers from other commands to stand firm with him. Some of them responded. As the balance of the army disintegrated, Wayne's little force was gradually depleted until not more than a score remained. Holding courageously by his side was Lieutenant Colonel William Allen, of the 2nd Pennsylvania Line Regiment, scion of a wealthy

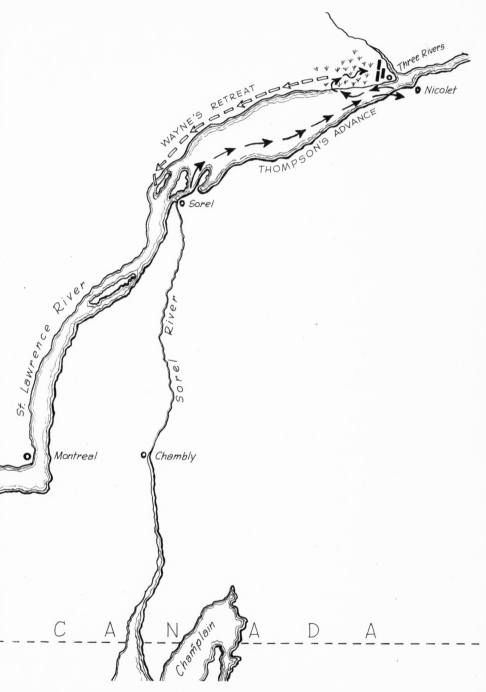

THREE RIVERS CAMPAIGN
June 8–13, 1776

Philadelphia family, always known in the army as Billy. His father, a thoroughgoing Tory, would in a darker hour lead the family, with Billy trailing, into the British cause. At this moment, under a hail of British bullets, he was Wayne's faithful brother-in-arms.

There was glory for few on the American side but it is fair to say that when the troops left Sorel they had anticipated no heavy opposition at Three Rivers. Wayne, sword in hand, did his best to maintain some sort of a battle line. His efforts proved hopeless when the British left their entrenchments and advanced. His own men, with all the others he now commanded, broke and ran. On the fringe of the woods, Wayne picked up portions of Irvine's regiment and a detachment Thompson had held in reserve and led them rearward through the woods, toward the boats that had been left on the north bank at the landing point near Pointe du Lac. Finding the boats gone, he struck up the river through the woods. Fraser, unprepared for a general forward movement, did not pursue, but returned to his fort and entrenchments.

Being now thoroughly routed, the American army disintegrated into small bands making their way up the north bank of the river. Possibly Carleton did not want any bigger bag of prisoners. His food supplies were inadequate and he had no buildings for jails. Being satisfied that he could advance at will as soon as his full force was concentrated, he allowed the defeated enemy to find their way through the forests and swamps. Wayne had taken a painful leg wound but paid no attention to it.

Meantime the bateaux that had landed Thompson's army had been menaced by the approach of two British frigates. The major left in command found himself about to be cut off and captured. He took the boats and army baggage up the river until nightfall, then stopped, hoping to gain contact with the wandering army. When the frigates again appeared he continued the forty-five miles up the river to Sorel, bringing with his empty bateaux deep apprehension about the fate of the army. General Sullivan, at Sorel, had heard the guns from the ships and, concerned, he sent a scouting party of riflemen down to the north bank and crossed the river himself to await word. On the second day the scouts encountered the first elements of the retreating army, if it might still be termed an army. They were part of Irvine's regiment, leaderless after the capture of their colonel.

At length the stragglers came in, singly and in bands, over a two-day period, worn out, famished, depressed. Much credit went to Wayne, whose regiment, the most compact of any in the army, acted as a rearguard. His troops were harassed on their retreat by no more than some unorganized Indians and vast swarms of mosquitoes. Most of the men had returned to Sorel by the end of four days, with a loss of perhaps a third of their numbers from battle casualties, capture, desertion, and illness.

Sullivan completed his letter to Washington telling him of the repulse, of the arrival of heavy British reinforcements in Canada, and of the distressful condition of his own command, with both officers and private soldiers discouraged. Smallpox was raging. Sullivan entrenched his camp. He told Washington he would hold it "as long as a person will stick by me," but on June 15, on the recommendation of his council of war, he dismantled his batteries and began a retreat toward Lake Champlain.

By the time the army had left St. John's the British were close behind. Wayne, with customary but justifiable pride, was not unmindful that he had played an honorable role in the battle and retirement. Nor was he forgetful that Colonel Billy Allen had stood with him in front of the British regulars while a large portion of the American army was in flight. As quickly as he got his men ferried across the St. Lawrence he wrote letters, one to Benjamin Franklin apprising him of the affair and containing a line over which the great man must have mused, and would have known it came from Wayne, even had there been no signature: "I believe it will be Universally allowed that Col. Allen and myself saved the Army in Canada." He may have been right. Wayne's leg wound was much worse than St. Claire's stubbed toe, but he stayed on his feet during the march of anguish through the woods. His conduct was not forgotten by the rank and file and word of it spread through the army. Pennsylvania soldiers found new pride in having served under Anthony Wayne.

Wayne commanded the rear guard during Sullivan's disordered march from Sorel and Chambly to St. John's and on to Fort Ticonderoga. After the battle of Three Rivers Arnold evacuated Montreal. He feared he might be intercepted and hemmed in; so he sent an aide to Sullivan requesting help. The bearer of the message was a slim, personable youth, Lieutenant James Wilkinson, who was destined to appear from time to time in the Anthony Wayne story, to the very end. Sullivan, who had no disposable force at hand, directed Wilkinson toward the rear with an order for 500 men to be sent by the Prussian colonel, Baron de Woedtke. Search as he would, Wilkinson was unable to find de Woedtke.

Farther back he encountered Lieutenant Colonel Billy Allen. Allen was about to tell Wilkinson the quest for men was hopeless, when he suddenly remembered Wayne. The army, said Allen, was conquered by its fears. He doubted that Wilkinson could draw assistance from it, but Wayne was in the rear, and if any man could help, he was the man.

Wayne listened to Wilkinson's story of Arnold's need. He read Sullivan's order to de Woedtke. He knew Arnold was a fighter and would not abandon his men, and might, indeed, accomplish something that would dull the pain of defeat. Nearby was a bridge. Wayne took post at one end, stopped all comers, and soon had a detachment of about 500 men and was marching, with Wilkinson as guide, to the relief of Arnold. Then word reached him that Arnold had slid through the encirclement and joined Sullivan. Wayne turned and marched to the army's rendezvous at Isle aux Noix. This crowded, near barren island was anything but a haven and the army continued its withdrawal up Lake Champlain to Crown Point, then Ticonderoga, reaching "Old Ti," where the soldiers found shelter, on July 17, 1776.

Wayne's men immediately became part of the Ticonderoga garrison. However, when Washington's reverses around New York in 1776 caused him to draw on the Northern army for reinforcements and a heavy detachment was sent to him, General Phillip Schuyler, department commander, issued an order which reflected the esteem in which Wayne had come to be held because of his conduct during the Canadian operations. Schuyler placed him in command of Fort Ticonderoga and Mount Independence on the opposite side of the lake, his force to consist of his own and five other regiments, including Irvine's, plus an artillery complement and some light infantry companies, aggregating at the beginning about 2,500 men. In the order, Schuyler wrote: "I have the fullest confidence in your vigilance, attention, and foresight to guard against surprise, and to do everything that may have a tendency to secure your post, and promote the weal of the service." Congress approved the assignment and on February 21, 1777 promoted Wayne to be a brigadier general of the Continental Army.

FOUR

Winter Ordeal at "Old Ti"

THOUGH GENERAL SCHUYLER did not fully appreciate it, Wayne had been inured to difficulties such as those that in the severe winter of 1776–1777 attended the Ticonderoga assignment in a wooded wilderness stretching alongside a frozen lake. His winter in Nova Scotia serving as superintendent of Franklin's real estate and colonizing venture acquainted him with life in a cold, remote, and sparsely settled land. The experience had told him how to ward off boredom and deal with men who were likely to lose any veneer of civilization they might have possessed, when thrown into primitive conditions with scant rations during heavy snows and bitter winds sweeping down from the frozen north.

Wayne was at Ticonderoga about ten months, from July 1776 until May 1777, a stretch of time that covered one of the darkest periods of the war and perhaps the dreariest days of his life. Conditions for the soldiers were not good, with irregular supplies, scanty clothing,

45

and mounting boredom. But on July 28, 1776, eleven days after Wayne brought his wearied little command back to Ticonderoga, something happened. He had the drums beat an assembly. The soldiers of the garrison came to attention on the parade ground, and all knew that something of portentous nature was transpiring. Colonel St. Clair came to the front with a document and in a low, uninspiring voice, read the lofty statement of resolve beginning "When in the Course of human Events," mentioning "created equal," and ending with "we mutually pledge to each other our Lives, our Fortunes, and our sacred Honor."

Congress had ratified Thomas Jefferson's eloquent rhetoric. The war had taken a new turn. In the long winter ahead, the soldier now knew what he was drilling and fighting for. As with the armed forces elsewhere when the document was read, there were cheers for independence in which all seemed to join, but some forgot them and went home when the autumn days told that winter was approaching. Wayne, later writing to his wife Polly, dashed off a line: "The Blessings of Liberty can not be purchased at too high a price." He had known long—ever since the Committee of Correspondence days in Chester County—and had said so, that the looming war was for the creation of an independent nation.

Undoubtedly Wayne's letters—and he was a vigorous, trenchant, and indefatigable writer—were the reasons why some notice continued to be focused on Ticonderoga and the Northern Theater as the colonial cause endured a series of crises wherever it fronted against the British. Disease, the tedium of camp life, the temptation to desert, homesickness, and at times near famine, made Ticonderoga worse than most other stations. Desertions were heavier in autumn and spring. In midwinter most preferred such comforts as the fort and camp provided, meager as they were, to a tramp through the snow or across the ice of Lake Champlain, a gamble between freedom and possible death from exposure or before the firing squad as a deserter.

Wayne was not impulsive in doubtful cases. He wrote a letter to one of his colonels saying he was sending along "a Certain John Millage taken upon suspicion of being a Spy." Wayne had confined him for several days but now instructed the colonel: "You may let him make his Escape with Orders never to be seen in this Quarter again."

In the early part of his stay at Ticonderoga, before he was in command, Wayne shared the officers' mess and drill ground with two of the craftiest, most unscrupulous marplots of the Continental service, Major General Horatio Gates and by now, his deputy adjutant general, James Wilkinson. Gates was the more foxlike in appearance but proved to be among the most incompetent in action of the general officers, as was evidenced at the battle of Camden, South Carolina, where he had no Arnold or Morgan to fight for him.

Arnold was at Ticonderoga and still devoted to the colonial cause, but disgusted that an officer of the diminutive endowments of Gates should be appointed to command him. Another member of this unprepossessing group was St. Clair, who had been promoted to brigadier general ahead of Wayne, for no apparent reason except that with the army, as is often the case in politics, the western district had to be accommodated. Clearly Wayne was the more competent soldier, but he was so devoted to the cause that he would wait.

Before winter set in or Wayne took command, varied assignments tore the group apart, much to Wayne's comfort. When Billy Allen introduced him to Benedict Arnold as they were retreating from Sorel in front of Carleton's advance after Three Rivers, they must have taken each other's measure as they shook hands, because here were two of the tough combat generals of the war. Neither could remotely know that Anthony Wayne would die as commander-in-chief of the United States Army, and Arnold, a man who lacked not for courage but for stability, as an outcast in one and a virtual outcast in the other of the two warring countries for which he employed his sword and genius.

James Wilkinson, a lad on the way up by devious methods, wrapped his fortunes around St. Clair and Gates and accompanied them when, in Washington's emergency in New Jersey, Gates took reinforcements of eight regiments to the commander in chief. Restless Arnold could not be expected to settle down slothfully for the winter. But before he or Gates departed from Old Ti, Arnold, Wayne, and John Trumbull, son of the governor of Connecticut, who had served a short time under Washington at Cambridge, then had been appointed colonel and aide-de-camp to Gates during the Lake Champlain campaign, made some tests of the fort's defenses that disclosed Gates's indifference to the obvious.[1]

Trumbull, one day to become a great painter, was about to begin topographical sketching around Ticonderoga, accompanied by Arnold and Wayne. That fort had become a symbol of strength and victory in Great Britain and the colonies. It was the citadel between the St. Lawrence and the Hudson, the possession of which, it was commonly believed, would control the outcome of the war.

The ramparts around the old fort had more psychological than physical significance. Ticonderoga was situated to command the juncture of Lakes Champlain and George. It looked out from a point of land jutting into Lake Champlain. The name itself, a corruption from the Iroquois, means "rushing waters," indicative of the two falls over which Lake George discharges its waters thirty feet down into Lake Champlain. The French, who were splendid fort builders after the era of Vauban, constructed here a barrier with walls and ramparts of great strength, which they called Fort Carillon because the waters around them in the spillway seemed to riot and sing. The Iroquois name, originally "Cheonderoga" prevailed and was confirmed by Major General Lord Jeffrey Amherst when he finally captured the fort for the British in 1759.

The walls and bombproof barracks were of limestone. From general appearances the fort seemed impregnable. That was what Gates thought when the wretched and defeated army hastened back to security there from the Quebec and Three Rivers campaigns. Water all but surrounded the fort. On three sides were the lake or its arms and inlets; the fourth fronted on a swamp through which ran an easily defended roadway. Neither Arnold nor Wayne was satisfied that the fort was unassailable from land, if approached by an opposing army with an artillery train or with ships having guns that might be landed. Gates, who commanded at this stage, scoffed at their apprehensions.

To the south, across the outlet of Lake George, is a rocky eminence 600 feet above the lake, called Mount Defiance, referred to as Sugar Loaf Hill in British and some American accounts. Across from Ticonderoga, on the eastern side of Lake Champlain, in Vermont, is another elevation named Mount Independence.

From the standpoint of the Ticonderoga defenders, the more important summit was Mount Defiance, or Sugar Loaf Hill. In order to demonstrate to Gates the vulnerability of the fort from that eminence, Wayne and Arnold had Trumbull double load one of Old Ti's cannon and aim it at the top of Defiance. The shot reached more than half way up the height, almost to the crest, as some observed it, but Gates still regarded the whole idea of a bombardment from the hill preposterous. Thus challenged, the two generals and the colonel—Arnold, Wayne and Trumbull—procured a boat, crossed the arm of Lake George, toiled up the obdurate side of Mount Defiance, and viewed the wild, surrounding country, the swishing outlet of Lake George beneath them, Ticonderoga on the promontory jutting out from the west bank, off to the east the Green Mountain range, while far to the northwest the blue sky was broken by the gentle summits of the lordly Adirondacks.

Their attention was fastened on the huge stone fort beneath them. Gates had arbitrarily thought, without making an examination, that it would be impossible to haul artillery to the height on which they stood. Earlier at Quebec, the French defenders felt safe that Wolfe could not scale the cliff at Anse du Foulon to reach the Plains of Abraham in the

Dr. Benjamin Rush. This most distinguished of Revolutionary War physicians was professionally skillful according to the standards of the day; ardently patriotic, provocative, and controversial, and among Wayne's close Philadelphia friends. Their correspondence during the war from Canada to Georgia was illuminating and always cordial. *(Courtesy the Historical Society of Pennsylvania)*

city's rear. Winfield Scott at Cerro Gordo, the key battle for the capture of Mexico City, in 1846, broke down his artillery and drew the sections up the mountain with ropes, and won a scarcely expected but overwhelming victory. Certainly cannon could be hauled over a road, even one hastily cut, up the steep side of Mount Defiance.[2]

That was what Wayne, Arnold and Trumbull concluded as they surveyed the grand prospect before them. With Defiance in enemy hands, Old Ti would be untenable. Such is the essence of what they again told Gates, who unhappily had a ponderousness in his thinking and a mulish obstinacy once a conclusion was lodged in his head. He again rejected the recommendation that Mount Defiance be garrisoned and fortified. Even with a road to the summit, the height could have been held by a few hundred men and half a dozen cannon against a heavy assault.

The emergency that then existed passed, for Carleton decided that winter was too close at hand for an investment of the fort, and returned to Canada, while General John Burgoyne, his new superior, an impulsive gambler who enjoyed the London tables above the piddling Canadian garrison stakes, returned to England, until he could again exchange his eager love of cards for the more heady hazards of war with the Americans. But Gates's refusal to heed the warning of Wayne, Arnold and Trumbull left Old Ti a ready prize for the invaders when they came again.

And the autumn wore on. Wayne wrote to Dr. Benjamin Rush in October 1776 describing an incident contradicting the impression that has worked itself into history: that virtually everyone in the army wanted a discharge or a chance to desert. Instead, there was an abundance of stanchness. One hundred Pennsylvanians had arrived at Ticonderoga October 21, 1776 from the Lake George hospital. They had heard that Carlton's British fleet had defeated a hastily built flotilla under Arnold on Lake Champlain a week before and immediately demanded their discharge—not from the army, but from the hospital of Dr. Jonathan Potts, the physician in command. They wanted active duty in the ranks.[3] As Wayne told Dr. Rush, they swore "they were determined to return to this place and conquer or die with their countrymen and brother soldiers. These poor emaciated worthy fellows are entitled to more merit than I have time or ability to describe."

His militant patriotism and vehemence rang from every angered line of a later letter to Rush, on November 5: "We hear upwards of 150 militia from Tryon [now Montgomery] county [New York] and about Fort Edward are marching to join the enemy against their native country; what punishment, what torture can be adequate to so horrid a crime. Would to God I could meet them *with only half their numbers*. The sword should be drunk with blood—and mercy stand suspended. . . ."

The matter of promotions rankled with Wayne, though he held his calm demeanor and performed his duties. A sentence in the letter of November 5 to Rush shows this clearly: "I believe was I to ask General Gates to write in my favor, he would most cheerfully comply—but

Sir this is what I can never do, any more than submit to being commanded by an officer whom yesterday I commanded."

Insubordination, quarreling, and gambling were frequent derelictions among some of the men, who toughened mentally as the winter continued. Wayne kept them well drilled, always aspiring to have the best disciplined men in the service. Still, in such instances, idleness usually triumphs. One of the teamsters looked them over and concluded they were the most "profligate" set of men he had ever seen brought together. Wayne had moments of disgust. He wrote to Franklin that God must have made Ticonderoga in the dark because it was such a confused jumble.

When the army had come back from Sorel with its heavy number of sick soldiers it had established the general hospital at Lake George. Colonel Trumbull, writing to his father, the governor of Connecticut, soon after, told how the army had been 10,000 strong in the spring, then, in midsummer, had "three thousand sick and about the same number well." What happened to the other four thousand? "Of them the enemy have cost us perhaps one, sickness another thousand, and the others God alone knows in what manner they were disposed of!" Large numbers were of course deserters, men wearied of the war who had simply gone home.[4]

During the winter's cold Wayne made the regular sentry shifts only a single hour in duration. Considering the poorly clad condition of the garrison, even an hour was long. He gained some comfort from inner warmth. Writing to his Philadelphia friend of long standing, Sharp Delaney, he told how, after an inspection of the fort and sentries, he was not half thawed out by sitting three hours before the fire. But he corrected the condition: "I put one Bottle of wine under my Sword Belt at Dinner." He wrote that he has toasted his friend but could not toast himself: "for by the time that one side is warm the other is froze."

In another letter to Rush at the beginning of the winter, he described his "poor fellows in a wretched condition . . . not a handful of straw for them to lay on or any covering other than their own ragged clothing . . . the dead and dying mingle together." He censured Congress sharply by explaining: "Add to this that one soldier will not attend another, but by compulsion . . . I answer the Congress—they have by a late Resolve ordered that no soldier employed as a nurse in any hospital shall receive pay." Also: "Misery becomes so familiar to the eyes and ears that they pass almost unheeded by. . . . I shall at all hazards make some better provision for the sick although cashiering should be the consequence. I will not be bound by rules and regulations that hurt humanity."

His letters to his wife Polly disclosed concern about her and the children back at Waynesborough. The demands of the service prevented him from seeking a leave of absence. It was in his mind, but he wrote on April 1, as faint touches of spring were beginning to show in the north, that a journey home was uncertain while a sudden visit from the enemy was more likely as soon as the ice melted on the lake.

In his instructions to her he ordered like a general: "You will cause every care to be taken of my affairs—and let me once more advise you not to let any mistaken fondness be a means of keeping my Little Boy and Girl from School. I would have my Daughter's Education suitable to her Rank in Life. Let it be protected and easy."

Of his son, he understood enough of life to know that one must be equipped to perform some useful function—that wealth alone is a frail and tenuous support. "My son must be the first of schollars. This will put him above the frowns of Fortune and enable him to make a figure in the World. And when ever his Country may Demand his Service either in Council or the Field, I trust he will not turn aside from Honor, although the path would be marked with his father's Blood."

He asked that they be kissed for him and that his "kindest love and respect" be conveyed to his mother, his sisters, and "all friends."

Of nearly everyone he knew in influential places he sought food, shoes, stockings, uniforms, blankets. As best he could, with such an aggregation, he kept the post momentarily alert to attack even while the lake was frozen and an approach by ships impossible. Ethan Allen with his Green Mountain Boys had shown how Old Ti could be carried by surprise. Wayne's order: "Every night at Sunset Shut and Secure doors. *In case of attack* Defend your Post to the last Extremity." When the thaw came he sent reconnoitering parties up the lake by boat and land, to Five Mile Point, to Basin Harbor on the Vermont side, and up Otter Creek. Unfortunately, Wayne did not have the men or equipment, and particularly not the cannon, necessary to turn Mt. Defiance into a bulwark against an invasion, as Mt. Independence was across Lake Champlain.

His force dwindled during the winter, mainly from illness and reassignments instead of desertion, to about 1,000, with 800 fit for duty, and they mostly lads, some as young as twelve years. After some of his units had been detached for other service, his garrison was heavy with New Yorkers. At length, at the beginning of 1777, the terms of all his Pennsylvanians expired. The men preferred waiting for an order, expected momentarily, that would take them south again, either to Philadelphia or to unite with Washington's army; they would rather not attempt the journey on their own resources.

He quickly quelled one near-mutiny, of a company that had arrived at the beginning of the winter. It formed in marching order to go away. He put a pistol to the breast of the sergeant who led them and the man cowed. Then the company obeyed his order to ground their arms. After he had talked to them they went to their quarters quietly. The incident was a little experience for greater mutinies he would have to face later in the war. One soldier refused to obey and grew insolent. Wayne knocked him down and sent him to the guard house. When a captain stormed in favor of the soldier, Wayne sent him to the guard house, too.

Wayne, even more than the men, wanted to join Washington. Many of his efforts and much of his correspondence were devoted to that paramount desire. Washington was conducting the main performance and Wayne wanted a part in it. His February promotion came in March but being a brigadier general did not appease his appetite for combat. He inveighed to General Phillip Schuyler, department commander, that his men would be of prime assistance to the commander in chief in New Jersey. Finally, the marvelous, coveted order came. It was May and Wayne was to join Washington. St. Clair was ordered to take command at Ticonderoga.

Before Wayne left his field officers presented him with an address that reflected their respect. They expressed "hearty thanks for your impartiality of command, your extreme Vigilance in Putting the Post in a State of Defense, your indefatigable attention to the instruction of Raw Troops." They spoke also of his "exemplary conduct" and "cheerfulness." Normally it probably would be difficult to think well of a commander after a winter with him in an isolated post, but Wayne had won the admiration of his subordinates. Now he would have his turn in the main theater of the war.

Burgoyne returned to Canada in May, about the time Wayne left Old Ti, and took the field in June, renewing the advance up Lake Champlain. He was a keen enough soldier to see at a glance what Wayne, Arnold and Trumbull had tried to drive home to Gates, that Mount Defiance, or Sugar Loaf Hill, was the key to Ticonderoga. The competent Fraser, who headed his advance, recognized it also. St. Clair, the disciple of Gates, commanded the fort on Burgoyne's approach, having a garrison of 5,000. Sycophantic Colonel Wilkinson, writing to Gates when Burgoyne's army had reached Crown Point and was menacing Ticonderoga, was sanguine: "What can be done, the great St. Clair will effect."[5]

Following Gates' strategy, St. Clair left Defiance ungarrisoned. Burgoyne and Fraser bypassed the fort, took the Sugar Loaf, and promptly placed a battery on its summit, the guns drawn up with difficulty by oxen and cattle. That night, July 5–6, St. Clair was forced to evacuate Ticonderoga and Mount Independence across the lake. He left large quantities of military stores, ammunition, and all his cannon. What Wayne and Arnold had foreseen had come to pass.

The impact was tremendous on both sides of the Atlantic. In London George III, apparently skirting near the edge of his later unfortunate spells of imbecility, considered the war won. He rushed into the Queen's room, dancing in glee and shouting, "I have beat them! I have beat all the Americans!"[6]

A shock of incredulity ran through the colonies. The widespread amazement was in tune with Washington's letter to Schuyler: "The evacuation of Ticonderoga and Mount Independence is an event of chagrin and surprise not apprehended nor within the compass of my reasoning." The cry of the public and in Congress was for a scapegoat. Soldiers said they would not defend any fort anywhere until some general had been shot. St. Clair and Gates, who, to say the least, had been negligent, even though, as St. Clair maintained, it was "better to lose a fort than an army," were ignored by the clamorers, and the ire fell on Schuyler because he commanded the department. Congress charged him with neglect of duty. He was tried by court-martial, which discerned that he was in no manner culpable and acquitted him with high honor.

Wayne, Arnold and Trumbull had conducted a necessary reconnaissance and made prudent recommendations. Had they been followed, they would have slowed Burgoyne in the 1777 campaign. Possibly it was all for the best. Burgoyne was compelled to surrender at Saratoga in October, 1777. Had he become involved in a long investment of Ticonderoga, he, too, like Carleton, might have considered the season too far advanced for a march to Albany, and turned back, and the great victory that brought France into an alliance with the colonies and was a profound help toward independence would not have been won that year. The war would have taken some other course, one that can only be speculated about and not vaguely determined.

F I V E

Sparring with Howe in
New Jersey

WAYNE BROUGHT enthusiasm and confidence to Washington's army at a moment when the cause of independence faltered and friends in Great Britain despaired that a raw aggregation of men from scattered colonies could ever stand against British regulars in open combat.

For Washington and Wayne it was not a season for despondency, but for renewed effort. In the spring of 1777, the army was reorganized and strengthened by hosts of newcomers. Wayne was assigned to take command of the large body of troops lately recruited and now officially designated the Pennsylvania Line of the Continental Army—troops with whom he would be associated through arduous campaigns and exacting trials. Along with the greenhorns having no acquaintance with camp and battle hardships were many veterans who were reenlisting, among them men he had drilled in Chester County or on the banks of the Schuylkill. Nearly all would be his stanch friends and, on most

55

occasions—an angry and impellent mutiny being a marked exception—faithful followers.

Congress was building a substantial foundation for a more reliable military force. Although it was not yet able to produce or acquire the arms, equipment, uniforms, and military stores so urgently needed, it was creating a national army to replace the militia systems of the separate colonies that had provided the first armed resistance against the British. After two years of combat, much of it ineffectual, the militia was consigned to a less consequential role. Most of the original fifty-three regiments from the different colonies had, by the spring of 1777, been discharged. They had responded at times more to the colony than to the Congress in Philadelphia, or, in turn, to General Washington.

The change was of the first significance and without it Washington could not likely have faced the large British armies that were being assembled under Howe in New York and Burgoyne in Canada. In the newly recruited Pennsylvania regiments assigned to Wayne were many lads from the back country who had never seen a British Redcoat but were first rate shots at squirrel and deer. His thirteen regiments, aggregating about 1,700 men, were sufficient to form a division of two brigades and to call for a major general to command it. Since they were all Pennsylvanians, the general should appropriately be of that state. But Pennsylvania already had two major generals in the Continental Army, the full allotment allowed one state. Both had been elevated in February, 1777, at the time Benedict Arnold had been passed over, along with Wayne. One was Thomas Mifflin, devout Quaker merchant, thirty-three years old, who had been active in the cause from the beginning as legislator and then as an officer under Washington at Cambridge. The other was Arthur St. Clair, who rejected the request of John Hancock, President of Congress, made with Washington's concurrence, that he become adjutant general of the army. He preferred the independent command at Ticonderoga at a time when the spring thaws suggested another British advance up Lake Champlain.

Leadership of the first two Pennsylvania Line brigades therefore devolved on Brigadier General Wayne, newly arrived from the north. His devotion to the army was so imperious that though he had been absent from home for sixteen months, he did not take time on reaching Morristown to visit Polly and his family at Waynesborough. The ride there would not have been difficult. With good mounts the distance, less than 100 miles, could have been covered in less than two days. Polly was becoming a more trifling factor in his view of the universe.

Neither then nor afterwards did he complain about his rank and the oversight which in the later stages of the war became apparent to the entire country. The only reference he ever made to the subject, as far as can be discovered, was his letter at Ticonderoga saying he could never ask Gates to recommend him.

Washington's army of about 7,300 was composed of forty-three regiments organized roughly into five divisions, each of two brigades. All at this period were from states below the Hudson River. As commander of a division, Wayne had risen to one of the five most important combat positions in the army, following that of the commander in chief, not because of personal observation and approval of his battle conduct by Washington, but by the ardor he always carried with him, and the influence of a growing reputation.

Pennsylvania provided one other line division for the Continental Army. It was commanded by William Alexander, or Lord Stirling, a solid and usually reliable major general. He was Wayne's superior officer at times, which was not surprising, because he had under his command, at one time or another, every brigade in the Continental Army except those of South Carolina or Georgia troops. He and Wayne worked effectively together. The title of Lord Stirling he employed, though not fully authenticated, was by no means spurious.[1]

Wayne suffered during the spring and early summer because his beautiful blue coat, white breeches and ruffled shirts had been casualties to the Ticonderoga winter. He reported to Washington wearing an old, faded, red jacket. His cravat was a rusty black and his three-pointed hat was battered and tarnished. His sprightly air of confidence and enthusiasm after a dull winter in the North, at a time when the Colonial cause elsewhere had seemed to many to be falling apart, impressed the commander in chief and quickly overcame any surprise at the apparel. Wayne's men were in large measure wearing butternut colored field tunics. Until they could all be better uniformed he would have been a little out of place supervising their drill in the ornate garb he preferred. Washington in the succeeding year came to know Wayne intimately and to hold him in high esteem. After his first operations with the main army, the Pennsylvanian became a favorite with the commander in chief when assault operations were in prospect.[2]

Early activities in New Jersey in 1777 were a part of the maneuvering between Howe and Washington as spring passed into summer. After Washington's triumphs at Trenton and Princeton as the year 1776 had turned, he had retired belatedly to winter quarters at Morristown, a position selected as a convenient base because it was on the British flank in any overland movement between New York and Philadelphia. Washington now felt strongly that the next British project would be to capture the American capital. Morristown was ideal for his strategic purposes. The surrounding country was wooded, the terrain was rough, with passes and defiles that gave protection in front, while avenues for retreat into a fertile, productive country were open in the rear.

Wayne came to know almost every acre of the northern Jersey hills and plains, from the heights and difficult approaches to the encampment that reached from the village of Pluckemin, near Somerville, through Bound Brook and Springfield. The position had an immediate advantage in that when Howe retired to New York for the winter after the battles at Trenton and Princeton, he left strong outposts at Brunswick, Amboy and Newark, which Washington at Morristown might watch and harass, a duty on which he employed Wayne.

Howe after a delightful winter in New York, got his army underway in June, when grass was long enough for grazing. The delay was not wholly due to indolence. He had the dual object of engaging Washington in open combat in New Jersey and capturing Philadelphia. He had a magnificent army of 30,000 which appeared sufficient, even if employed half heartedly, to crush almost every vestige of colonial resistance. Whether moved by personal ambition, or being poorly advised by Lord Germain and the British Colonial office about Burgoyne's timing in coming down from Canada—or whether, as some have believed without much warrant, he was governed by a latent fondness for the colonies because of his political antipathy to the cabinet and King—he neglected Burgoyne, about whom he knew well enough, and Canada, and looked south instead of north. In mid-June he appeared in heavy force at Brunswick, moving to all appearances on an overland campaign against Philadelphia.

During these days when Washington was more procrastinator than tactician, and when it seemed confirmed for many that Howe's heavily reenforced, competently officered army would be unassailable in the field, Pennsylvania fully as much as any other colony was harrowed and torn with dissension. Wayne's corresponding friend, Dr. Rush, whom he regarded as "one of the greatest and best men who have adorned his country," felt urgently that the handsome and articulate brigadier general could help the patriot cause, reduce partisanship, and check a drift back to the crown, by a visit to Philadelphia. Undoubtedly Wayne had come to be the most affectionately admired of Pennsylvania soldiers. His well-remembered confidence and aplomb would be a lifting tonic to a population where many had grown disheartened, wondering what good was coming from all the sacrifice of life and the personal hardships that are the inevitable toll of war.

Caesar Rodney. Cousin of the beautiful Mary Vining, his ward, who presided over his social affairs when he was a delegate to the Continental Congress and later when president of the Delaware Republic, Rodney gained fame by riding through the night from Wilmington to cast the deciding vote of the Delaware delegation in support of the Declaration of Independence. The charming, talented Mary Vining, who spoke near flawless French, caused his home to become a rendezvous of Lafayette's and Rochambeau's officers. Lafayette introduced Wayne to her at Rodney's house and thereafter she spurned all suitors and waited. (Courtesy the Historical Society of Pennsylvania)

In addressing Wayne, Dr. Rush showed that he could wield words as well as the scalpel: "Come, my dear sir, and let us weep together over this dear nurse of our childhood, the protectress of our youth, and the generous rewarder of our riper years . . . Let us unite our efforts once more, and perhaps we may recover Pennsylvania from her delirium. . . . Your timely prescriptions may yet save her life."

Wayne, the devoted soldier so dutiful that he did not even visit his home, could not leave the army in the midst of a campaign that on any day might determine the outcome of the war and the fate of the colonies. He told Rush the visit was out of the question, and, to explain his constant drilling, wrote: "The enemy do not seem fond of meeting disciplined troops. My brigade offered Gen. Grant battle six times the other day; he as often formed, but always on our approach his people broke and ran, after firing a few vollies, which we did not return being determined to let them feel the effects of a close fire, and then give them the bayonet under the cover of the smoke." Wayne continued that "this hero" who had proclaimed he would march through America at the head of 5,000 men "had his coat much dirtied by artillery fire, his horse's head taken off, and himself badly bruised, for having the presumption, at the head of seven hundred British troops, to face five hundred Pennsylvanians." He reassured Rush that he might rest confident that the Pennsylvanians could stand before "any troops on earth."[3]

Wayne's reference was to a widely quoted vaunt that Major General James Grant, a combat leader along with Cornwallis and Knyphausen in Howe's army, had made before the war. Of similar nature was Grant's reassurance to Colonel Johann Gottlieb Rall, just before Washington struck the Hessians in Trenton: "Tell the Colonel he is safe; I will undertake to keep the peace in New Jersey with a corporal's guard." Grant, a good soldier, had been an active factor in the British victory over Putnam and Lord Stirling on Long Island. Wayne skirmished with him and found him chary about giving battle. They exchanged only long-range firing. They would meet on other fields.

Washington established in New Jersey the practice of giving Wayne the post nearest the enemy, and this he did now, when the army moved from Morristown to Middlebrook. The British were only two hours march away at Brunswick (New Brunswick). Here, on a forward road heavily employed by scouts and skirmishers, Wayne continued the diligent drill of his men, intent still on having his command known through the service for its precision, neatness, discipline, and instinctive response to orders.

Howe's feints to dislodge Washington were readily understood. The British commander could not cross the Delaware and march on Philadelphia, leaving Washington in his rear. He tried to lure Washington toward him. He appeared to be abandoning an overland campaign and suddenly began a withdrawal toward Staten Island, hoping that Washington would follow and expose himself.

Washington moved to Quibbletown (a position many generals

have reached without marching) and threw forward scouting parties. Judging that Howe might actually be retreating, Washington detached a pursuing force under General Nathanael Greene, which brought Wayne finally into a small but spirited action. Wayne long had an unbounded admiration of Greene as a general, an esteem that deepened into personal affection. His respect and fondness, formed in this small operation, endured until Greene's death.

Greene took four brigades plus Morgan's rifle corps, formed a reconnaissance in force, and intended, if the opportunity offered, to strike Howe's rear guard heavily while it marched toward Amboy. With three of the best Continental officers of the war involved—Greene, Wayne and Morgan—some sort of a battle was almost inevitable. The brunt of the action fell on Wayne and Morgan. The latter reached the Raritan River in the early morning darkness of June 20, 1777 and drove off the Hessians guarding the south side of the bridge at Brunswick, and struck the British rear. Wayne came up and the two vigorously assailed the retreating British, pressed them across the Raritan, drove their rear elements out of their entrenchments, and in a running battle chased them five miles along the road to Piscataway.

There Greene, becoming far removed from Washington's army, felt he was closing in on the main body of the British, who might turn on him. He sounded a recall and rejoined Washington at Quibbletown. Washington was highly pleased with the affair and so reported to Congress on June 22, 1777. He said of Wayne and Morgan: "They displayed great bravery and good conduct; constantly advancing on an enemy far superior to themselves in number, and well secured by redoubts." The retiring British fired houses along the way, apparently hoping to stir Washington's anger and cause him to come down for vengeance.

Before Howe renewed his campaign against Philadelphia, this time by water, Wayne made the acquaintance of two distinguished volunteers from afar who became his companions in arms, friends, and vital parts of the magnificent struggle for independence which at this juncture was entering into another of its disheartening hours. One was the Marquis de Lafayette, nineteen years old, of a stirring ambition that impelled him to be a part and eventually a leader of the aspiration beginning to sweep across Europe for personal freedom and popular institutions. The other, equally captivating at this stage, was the Polish cavalryman who appeared at Washington's headquarters when the army was still at Morristown. He was the handsome Count Casimir Pulaski, famous over Europe for his command of the Polish forces in the last abortive uprising against Russia, about whom there was a subtle atmosphere of charm, poise, and magnetism that won Washington in a twinkling.

Lafayette was to become Wayne's commanding general in one of the decisive campaigns of the war, which harassed and drove Cornwallis into Yorktown. At the time of his arrival in America he had never heard a shot fired in anger, while Wayne was well tested in the rigors of combat and the ordeal of command in camps of rough and famished men. But Wayne served under the French marquis faithfully and ungrudgingly, as he did under all superiors.

Wayne and Lafayette were soon as warm acquaintances as they could become using different tongues. They acquired a mutual respect because the main characteristic of each was enthusiasm, which breaks through the barrier of language. Both, to use a latter day expression, were supreme activists, both were combat-minded, both were venturesome, willing to take risks for great ends, for the consummation of what brought the marquis across the Atlantic and took the Pennsylvania planter and tanner away from his peaceful acres, his wife, children, and friends, in quest of glory and the creation of a new nation.

Where Lafayette was a novice in arms, Pulaski was a veteran, steeped in all the bitterness of the ages-old warfare of eastern Europe. He was, after the tradition of the Poles, primarily a cavalryman. That was what distinguished him in the American army, where at the outset trained cavalrymen were few.

Washington needed all the help he could get. Ticonderoga was gone and a tide of Redcoats began rolling in from the north, just when he was confronted in the field with a disciplined army nearly three times the size of his own. Though the British commander, Howe, has been denigrated in American historical writing, even to the suggestion that he lacked firm loyalty to his cause, there is no doubt that he planned and fought his battles well, even skillfully. Washington, Greene, and Wayne were facing no idler or dolt. Howe had the attributes of a competent commander—experience, youth, a command of the logistics required to move armies, large for that day, over forbidding terrain through hostile populations, and a self-confidence that is an essential attribute to military success. His faith in himself and his men enabled him to launch his entire army into battle, and not to fight, as was so often the method of that and later days, hesitatingly, piecemeal, without the required audacity.

While Howe commanded the British, the American cause was at its bottom depth; when he departed British propsects never rose so high again. The statures of Washington and his competent subordinates— Greene, Wayne, Lafayette, and a few others—are enhanced by their

Mary Vining of Wilmington, Delaware, to whom Anthony Wayne was betrothed after the death of his first wife. This portrait, taken from an old miniature attributed to Major John André, who paid court to her while the British occupied Philadelphia, 1777–1778, fails to confirm Lafayette's description of her as "the most beautiful girl in America." *(Courtesy the Historical Society of Delaware)*

ability to remain in the field opposing Howe with less than half his numbers.

Howe's judgment, combined with that of Lord Germain, was not without fault, as Washington, Wayne, and Lafayette detected. Washington was baffled about Howe's intentions when the British fleet of 228 sail, carrying a splendid army numbering nearly 20,000, headed to sea from Sandy Hook on July 23, 1777. The fleet turned south instead of north, but that might be no more than a ruse to send Washington to protect Philadelphia, after which Howe could return and sail up the Hudson. The actual objective could be Boston, Charleston, Albany or other point.

Then Howe appeared on July 30 off the Delaware capes and a movement against Philadelphia seemed his clear intention. Washington moved his army to Trenton, crossed the Delaware River, and waited at Germantown, six miles north of Philadelphia. Again Howe disappeared and again Washington moved, but finally authentic word came that the British had passed the Chesapeake Bay capes and were sailing up the bay. Now it was clear that this aim was a land campaign against Philadelphia from the south. Washington put his army into motion to intercept him. Poorly conditioned as it was to meet such a foe, he could not allow the British to march into the capital unopposed.

Wayne's division was the most elite, though still far from elegant, as Washington marched his army down Front and up Chestnut Street, directly through the heart of Philadelphia. Since the Continental soldiers had no regulation uniforms, but were motley garbed, Washington sought to give them a tincture of homogeneousness by requiring each man to wear a sprig of green on his hat. They numbered about 11,000 but would be joined by scattered elements of militia before they met the British. Lafayette, fresh from the trim armies of the French monarchy, judged them "but tolerably armed, and still worse clad." The best clothed, he found, wore brown linen hunting shirts.

But to most Philadelphians they were indeed inspiring, brigade passing after brigade, arms burnished; squadrons of horse beautifully mounted; pioneers with axes in their belts; guns and caissons rumbling; trumpets blaring; and sounding heavily from every regiment the rolling battle call of that most martial of all music, the drums. Never before had Philadelphia, a city that has always loved parades, witnessed such a sight. Naturally eyes were fastened on the home boys, the attentive, neatly aligned regiments of Wayne's Pennsylvania Line, their handsome leader in a new uniform of deep blue coat with red lining, ruffled white shirt and light lambskin breeches. He was a veteran to the eager onlookers, but for him, in truth, the war was just beginning. His great battles were ahead.

Wayne had seasoned sufficiently to feel privileged to give suggestions and some elucidation of military principles to Washington, who was not as well read in military history as his studious subordinate. When the British were about to advance, he proposed that Washington detach "2500-3000 of our best animals and most disciplined men (he clearly was thinking in terms of his own division) to make a vigorous assault on their right or left flank. . . . This, Sir, I am convinced would surprise them much—from a persuasion that you dare not leave your works."

Then came some explanatory sentences. This was no new idea, he told his chief: "It has been practiced with success (among many others) by Caesar at Amiens when beseiged by the Gauls. . . . He practiced the same maneuver at Alexia." He gave Washington a pointer: "This is a General rule of war; that the Irresistible Impulse of the Human Heart—which is governed by mere momentary Caprice and Opinion, Determines the fate of the day in all actions. . . .

"I know you have goodness enough to excuse a freedom which proceeds from a Desire to render every possible Service in the power of your Excellency's most obedient and very Humble Servant, Anthy Wayne."[4]

Washington did not adopt the bold plan of driving against one or the other of the British flanks when their army was in column, nor did he reply. Clearly he felt he was in no condition to detach so many of his best men and sturdiest horses. There were some obvious points of merit about Wayne's proposal. It might have had the same result as did, Wayne's spirited attack against Cornwallis at Green Spring later in the war, where Wayne's boldness confused his enemy and deprived him of the initiative. Still, Washington's prudent generalship told him he was in no position to lose 3,000 top quality men, and that was a distinct possibility if he sent them charging into Howe's army.

One of the singular aspects of Wayne's conduct during this time is that he does not appear to have met Polly while in the Philadelphia area, nor did she witness his march through the city at the head of his column, his head up, sitting erect in his saddle. His gleaming sword threw back the sunlight as he moved his men down Front Street along the Delaware riverbank. He could not escape regarding this one of the supreme moments of his life. But there was no Polly.

His letters to Polly from New Jersey were ardent enough. Yet it was increasingly apparent that the colonial cause occupied the first and Polly a lesser place in his heart. He seemed to feel a premonition when he wrote May 26, while Howe was making his New Jersey feints. Telling her that the British commander had landed thirty miles away and seemed determined to "push for Philadelphia," he asked her to kiss his little girl and boy, and ended: "Adieu my Dear Polly and believe me with true affection, yours, yours Anthy Wayne."[5]

But indeed, where was Polly? One account has her bringing him a shirt. The correct version seems to be that Wayne had written Polly and set up a meeting place convenient to where he was rounding up militia. But shortly after writing, he received a peremptory dispatch from Washington calling him back to the army. Howe had landed his forces on August 24th, where the Elk River enters Chesapeake Bay. Anthony had to cancel his request for her to meet him. One thing appears certain—that while he campaigned from May until September within a hundred miles of his home, he did not find time to go there.

After passing through Philadelphia, Washington marched to Wilmington, where Brandywine Creek meets the Christiana River that then enters the Delaware. Here he established headquarters. He had detached Wayne temporarily from his command and sent him to Chester, on the Delaware twelve miles below Philadelphia, to form supporting militia units. This Wayne had done. Then he rode down the right bank of the Delaware into one of his momentous experiences. Lafayette introduced him to Mary Vining.

Mary Vining was joyous, debonair, intelligent, brown-eyed and nineteen, and by all odds, many accounted her the most beautiful girl in America. Thus the French officers, fresh from sojourns at the court at Versailles, judged her; they had not seen all the American maidens but when they saw her they looked no further.[6]

After the French officers discovered Mary Vining, they hovered near her at every opportunity allowed them away from their military chores. Most of the literature about Mary employs the word "flirt," which Dr. Samuel Johnson was just then endowing with the connotation of a frivolous young woman, a coquette. Her flirting was obviously a protection that allowed her to toy with the courtships and lighten the fall of the young men continually crowding her parlor.

The quality that appears and abides behind her pertness and dallying was one of natural charm and frankness, which shone in her eager, sparkling conversation, informed alike on public affairs and the classics. Her self-assurance allowed her to control gracefully any group that came her way. There is no doubt but that she was radiant, superb.

When her mother passed she went to live with her cousin, Caesar Rodney, who had rapidly become outstanding in Delaware public affairs. He had come up from his home "Poplar Grove" at Dover and taken a house at No. 606 Market Street in Wilmington. Wealthy, a Congressman, and, in turn, chief executive of his colony, he kept a lavish table open to all comers of quality. His Wilmington home during the Brandywine Campaign and after the British were hemmed up in Philadelphia became an informal but veritable French headquarters where Lafayette came frequently. In the basement he stored the small casts of gold from which he paid the French officers in his retinue.

Anthony Wayne, coming down the river from Chester, was soon thrown into the company of the Rodney household. Lafayette appears to have been smitten with Mary himself, for he corresponded with her until her death and visited her grave when he returned for his triumphal tour of the United States in 1824. Anthony and Mary met as often as

Wayne could contrive it during the brief period when Washington's army was at Wilmington and Howe was moving up from the head of the Elk River toward Philadelphia. While such engagements could not have been lengthy, since a battle was impending, he saw her enough to remember her always and to return to her and win her when the exigencies of his career permitted. That, too, would have to wait.

S I X

Brandywine—The Battle Rolls Off to the Right

AT THE BATTLE of Brandywine, fought for the possession of Philadelphia, Washington stationed Wayne in what he believed would be the key position on the field, but as Howe developed his attack, Wayne's task became that of holding and waiting while the main British army marched off to a distant quarter.

In the late phases of the combat Wayne fought stubbornly and acquitted himself handsomely. He held his command intact while the right elements of the army were crumbling, and along with Greene, formed a rearguard behind which the defeated divisions found security in their retreat. But this, of all his battles, was the most irksome to his high spirit and his devotion to the offensive.

Throughout most of the fateful day he had been held under the leash of Washington's orders, hoping that the British corps that momentarily threatened him in his front would loose its attack. All he could do was listen while some of the other divisions were fighting and losing the engagement several miles up Brandywine Creek.

68

Events had moved slowly and the summer was almost over when Howe, whose naval officers were unwilling to navigate the well defended Delaware River, finally landed on August 25 near the top of Chesapeake Bay, at Head of Elk opposite Cecil County Court House. The weather was seething hot. Because of heavy thunder showers and wet roads he did not reach Elkton until the 28th. There he found ample supplies of food, military stores, and highly valued salt, which the Americans had not taken time to remove. He divided his army into wings. The first, under Cornwallis, was composed of British and Hessian troops, and the other, likewise a mixed command, was commanded by the Hessian, Lieutenant General Wilhelm von Knyphausen. The British army advanced in two-wing formation up the Elk River, then waited almost a week while foragers rounded up supplies, including large herds of cattle, sheep and horses. Meanwhile the horses that had been transported on board the vessels recovered their strength on the lush Maryland pasturage. Here, as in most instances, there was justification for what has been termed Howe's inexplicable lethargy.[1]

Washington, who had generously sent Morgan's riflemen, among his best light troops, to assist Gates against Burgoyne, had been forced to organize a new light division. This he placed under Brigadier General William Maxwell, who had been Wayne's companion officer at Three Rivers and for a time at Ticonderoga. Maxwell harassed Howe's army and fought a small delaying action at Cooch's Bridge over the Christiana River. When Howe resumed his advance, Maxwell slowed him by fighting a running battle, taking advantage of wooded areas for sharp encounters. By this time Howe was driving 1,000 sheep and 500 cattle, slow-moving animals that gravely impeded his advance but were the main part of his commissary.

Washington took different positions as the British moved but finally decided to fight on what was, after all, the most easily defended line between Head of Elk and the approaches to Philadelphia, behind Brandywine Creek. On the early morning of September 9, 1777, he aligned his army along the stream, centered roughly on Chadd's Ford. Wayne guarded this ford.[2]

The Brandywine flowed south to southeast. It was more than ordinarily crooked among the eastern Pennsylvania creeks and in that day had no bridges, but an abundance of fords. The banks elsewhere were steep and the surrounding country rugged and often wooded. The hills behind the bottomland rose as high as 200 feet. Briars and matted vines were common along the banks, making the use of the fords essential for rapid crossing. The Brandywine took its name from a minor marine disaster of early times, the details of which appear to have been scantily recorded. A ship from France loaded with brandy and wine was sunk at the entrance of the stream which was promptly awarded the name of the choice cargo.

Howe brought the two wings of his army together on September 10, 1777 at Kennett Square, Pennsylvania. North of this point, then a village, Brandywine Creek has its source in the junction of two creeks worthy of no other names than East Branch and West Branch. From near Kennett Square the Lancaster Pike ran northwest, forded the West Branch, and intersected the road that crossed the East Branch. By using this second road it would be simple to turn the American position along the Brandywine and threaten the army's rear. That is precisely the plan Howe adopted, being similar to the one he employed successfully in the Battle of Long Island.

In aligning his army Washington gave Wayne the position of honor, the defense of the Chadd's Ford crossing. Maxwell's light brigade had returned to the American side of the Brandywine, in front of and to the left of Wayne's position, from where it could be thrown forward to hamper Howe's progress. As a reserve in Wayne's rear, Washington stationed Greene's division, composed of Muhlenberg's and Weedon's brigades and containing some of his best troops. Downstream, where the terrain made the likelihood of a crossing remote, he stationed Brigadier General John Armstrong with the Pennsylvania militia.

Upstream, composing the right wing of his army, Washington aligned on the bluffs his remaining three divisions, each of two brigades. They were commanded by Sullivan, Adam Stephen, and Lord Stirling, all major generals, with Stirling on the army's extreme right. The right wing was under the command of Sullivan. Pickets guarded all of the fords below the juncture of the two branches and were supposed to watch those farther up both streams. Washington was short on cavalry but a regiment of Virginia dragoons under Colonel Theodorick Bland patrolled sections of the western or British side of the creek.

Wayne entrenched his position at Chadd's Ford and established headquarters in the John Chadd house. Colonel Thomas Proctor had brought his guns down the Delaware River on flatboats, landed them at Chester, and had drawn them overland to Wilmington, whence he retired with Wayne to Chadd's Ford and stationed them where they commanded the crossing. Some were guns captured by Washington from the Hessians at Trenton.

Just before the battle was joined along the Brandywine, Wayne received a delightful addition to his command in the person of a soldier-preacher, Chaplain David Jones, sprung from the Welsh colonists of

Washington's headquarters at Valley Forge. The scene suggests the bleakness of the encampment through the winter of 1777–1778. Most of the army lived in huts strung along Mount Joy and protected by strong works. Wayne was among the stalwarts in helping Washington preserve order when there was much under-surface seething. *(Courtesy the Historical Society of Pennsylvania)*

the Philadelphia area, who had been a missionary to the Shawnee and Delaware tribes beyond the Alleghenies. He was at Crown Point and Ticonderoga, came to Wayne's brigade of the Pennsylvania Line in the early fall of 1777, and remained with it until the surrender of York-town, then accompanied Anthony on the campaign against the Indians in the Northwest. Nearly two decades later, when he was seventy-six years old, he became a chaplain with the army on the Canadian border in the War of 1812, and served until the end of that conflict.

The effectiveness of Chaplain David Jones's work in morale build-ing might be seen from Howe's efforts to silence him. Howe offered a reward for his capture and then sent a detail of soldiers to bring him in. They were unsuccessful. Chaplain Jones had better luck than his pur-suers during this Brandywine-Philadelphia Campaign. He was scouting in Chester County when he saw one of Howe's dragoons enter a house and carelessly leave his pistols in his saddle pockets. The pastor seized them, confronted the marauder, threatened him with his own weapons, and rode the crestfallen trooper ahead of him to Wayne's camp.

Wayne's laugh was hearty when he saw his pious chaplain bringing in a British dragoon at the pistol point.[3]

Washington established headquarters at the Benjamin Ring house, about a mile behind Wayne at Chadd's Ford, which he looked on as the focal point of the British attack, while behind him Lafayette set up his headquarters at the home of Gideon Gilfin, then followed Washington as an aide with the intention of entering the battle at his earliest opportunity.

The battle opened in the morning mists of September 11. When Knyphausen's advance toward Chadd's Ford was detected through the fog, Washington judged it to be the spearhead of the main British assault up the Philadelphia road. Maxwell again crossed with his light troops to the southwest bank of the Brandywine and sometime around 9 a.m. engaged Knyphausen from Kennett Meeting-house back to Chadd's Ford.

Knyphausen spread out along the heights west of the creek. The assault that Wayne momentarily expected degenerated into a peculiar defensive. Wayne had studied the long red column as it advanced on the dusty roadway, winding here and there behind the hills and woodlands, and found his own excitement mounting. Combat exhilarated him but he would have to wait for it. While Knyphausen was taking his position on the opposite heights, Washington was riding along his front receiving cheers wherever he came upon a new detachment. He had issued an address some days earlier telling the army the consequence of the impending battle to the colonial cause, saying that after their struggles of two years the prospects had brightened, and suggesting that if they were victorious, this campaign would be their last. Hopeful words —the war had some of its most despondent moments, as well as inspiring triumphs ahead. Wayne was perhaps even more sanguine. This was the occasion on which he exhibited to his caller and friend, Captain Alexander Graydon, the Quaker soldier-author, his feeling of utmost contempt for the enemy.

Part of Wayne's animation was due to the circumstance that the position of his troops, not far advanced from army headquarters, seemed to give assurance that he would fight under the commanding general's eye. When Maxwell recrossed to the American side at 10 a.m., pressed closely by Knyphausen, and took a position downstream from Wayne, the Hessian general put batteries on the western heights above the ford and opened on Wayne's entrenchments. Proctor's guns replied and a desultory battle began in Washington's center, where the commanding general still confidently expected the main British assault to be delivered.

Washington's army, reduced by sickness and absenteeism but augmented by some recruits, numbered about 11,000, substantially the size of the army he had marched through Philadelphia. About 1,500 were militia, the remainder Continentals. Howe, with reserves up, brought an army of about 18,000 into the action.

Several of the Continental officers recognized the imminence of a flank movement, which all the time was underway, but not Washington. An element of stubbornness seemed to dominate his thinking. The British had made a frontal assault under Howe at Bunker Hill, and that is what he was confident they would deliver in their march on Philadelphia. He surely could not have forgotten their strategy on Long Island, where Grant amused the Americans under Putnam and Lord Stirling in front while Cornwallis was on his long flank march to reach their rear, but that did not influence his calculations at Brandywine as the morning wore into afternoon.

All through the morning Washington was riding over the hills, reconnoitering personally, watching the dust clouds rising to the northwest. His question during Knyphausen's indifference was whether to stand firm and await developments, or to assume the offensive, cross the Brandywine, and launch an attack in force against Knyphausen's corps that appeared to be isolated. Each time the temptation arose to cross he resisted it and waited. When the early afternoon brought no new developments, an offensive move appeared more and more inviting. Knyphausen had about 5,000 men at Chadd's Ford, but where was the balance of Howe's combat troops, comprising some of Great Britain's finest regiments, led by Cornwallis, among the more capable officers the home government had sent to the North American war? Accompanied by Howe, Cornwallis was marching through the morning fog on a wide encirclement, undertaking to make the major thrust of the battle a total surprise.

Washington at length cast his decision in favor of the counteroffensive. Some critics of the battle have found merit in it. If the British had divided their forces, he reasoned, he would take advantage of it. Knyphausen would be assailable in front of Chadd's Ford. The waters were low and fording easy. He prepared his orders for Wayne and Maxwell, supported by Greene, to cross to the west side and attack Knyphausen.

Wayne was elated. He had engaged all morning in long range battle and wanted to close. Viewed in the light of the British overall strength and the lack of resolution of elements of the American army, the maneuver would have been hazardous even with Wayne to spearhead it. Knyphausen had his men well posted on the heights. Fortunately for Washington, intelligence was received from Sullivan in time to prevent Wayne from crossing. What Sullivan learned had come in dribbles; in the first instance from a Quaker youth, Joseph Townsend, who had observed the British on their flank march. While he appears to have been excited and inaccurate in one or two of his descriptions, he possessed a tenacity that eventually convinced Sullivan and, in turn, others, that the extreme right of the American army was in danger. When Townsend saw the British they were moving along the road from Kennett Square to Lancaster, termed the Great Valley Road.

Along with the Quaker lad's report, Sullivan was warned at 11 a.m. both by Colonel Moses Hazen, who guarded one of the upstream fords, and by Lieutenant Colonel James Ross, of a Pennsylvania regiment, that British troops were moving toward the American right. Ross suspected that they were engaged in a flank march. Sullivan sent his report back to Washington, who acted on it by dispatching Colonel Bland's mounted troops to investigate.

Then, while Bland was on his reconnoitering expedition, a whirlwind of information and assurance reached Washington's headquarters in the person of "Squire" Thomas Cheney, a self-appointed and highly patriotic spy, who lived close by. Stirred by all the activity, he was out early to scout and gather intelligence. He pounced upon the flanking column of Cornwallis' Redcoats so abruptly that both he and they were startled, but he recovered first and dashed away while the bullets whined behind him. He was off at top speed for Washington's headquarters, his mare flecked with foam. He told the commander-in-chief in explicit terms that the British were in his right rear approaching Birmingham Meeting House.

Washington still doubted. He said such a report had come in (the James Ross message) and subsequently had been denied. But the red-faced, angry squire insisted. He drew a map of the roads in the sand and showed the route of the British. When Washington remained dubious, he broke out: "You are mistaken, general! My life upon it, you are mistaken! Ask Anthony Wayne or Persie Frazer and they will tell you I am a man to be believed. Put me under guard until you find that my story is the truth." Someone overheard him mutter that he had the matter of winning the battle as much at heart as anybody else did, and that included Washington. His Whig sentiments were flamingly ardent.[4]

Washington did not doubt much longer. As the downcast old squire went away exasperated, the commanding general received another note from Sullivan, the result of Bland's reconnaissance. This compelling message was that the British were closing in rapidly on Sullivan's right rear. They were marching sharply in close order and

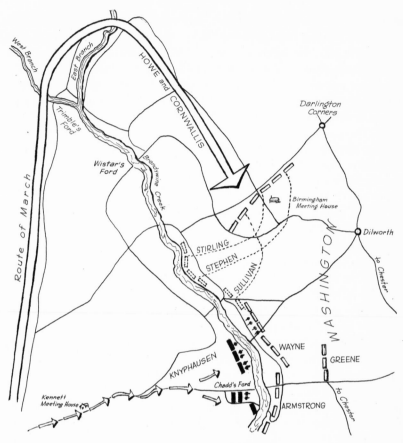

BATTLE OF BRANDYWINE
September 11, 1777

behind them a great dust cloud showed that they were heavily supported.

Lafayette gained permission and dashed off toward the menaced quarter. Wayne had to maintain his position at the bridge, certain now that Knyphausen would advance in earnest when the battle was joined on the American right. Washington had to rearrange his dispositions before following Lafayette. He told Wayne to stand fast at Chadd's Ford and ordered Greene to meet the onrush of the British from the right. Then he recruited another farmer, Joseph Brown, to ride ahead of him at top speed and show the most direct route to Birmingham Meeting House. They galloped across fields, jumped fences and ditches, plunged through woodlands, with Washington all the time shouting to the farmer, "Push along, old man! Push along." They were riding their fastest, with the head of Washington's horse at the crupper of the farmer's, but all the while Washington kept up his insistence for more speed with his "Push along! Push along!"[5]

It was 3:30 p.m. The approach of Cornwallis, plus orders from Washington, caused Sullivan to try to change front with his three divisions, his own, Stephen's and Lord Stirling's. They had faced southwest along the creek but now were called on to form a new line facing roughly northwest. Cornwallis struck them with his compact ranks while they were engaged in this movement and the two brigades on the extreme right hurriedly left the field. Other elements of the left began to give way at about the same time. The center held under Stirling until the concentration of musketry against it caused it to yield ground reluctantly through a wooded area. The British pressed into the timber, lost their alignment and found their advance momentarily weakened. Lafayette reached the wavering American lines at this juncture, followed soon by Washington. Both found that the time for rallying a broken army had passed.

Cornwallis' onslaught was devastating, irresistible. His mere appearance in an unexpected quarter proved a severe shock to the army's morale. He swept ahead, moving from north to south when all the while he had been expected from the south. He scattered the three American divisions, or such elements of them as remained on the field after his startling appearance on their flank and rear.

Back at Chadd's Ford Wayne could hear the rapidly mounting then diminishing musketry rattling far off on his right rear. He had orders to hold the ford and he did just that while the September day lengthened. Greene's division moved from its position in Wayne's rear and covered the four miles to Sullivan in the remarkably short time of forty-five minutes. It found the right wing already shattered and a large part of it in flight. Greene opened his ranks to allow the fugitives to pass through. Howe and Cornwallis, their battle won, did not pursue Sullivan or attack Greene with troops that had done a good day's work of marching and fighting.[6]

In front of Wayne, Knyphausen now stirred. He had heard Cornwallis' guns on the left then from his position on the heights had witnessed the departure of Greene's division toward the sound of the firing. He now advanced vigorously, the lead being taken by Major General Grant, who readily drove through the ford and pushed Wayne slowly before him. Wayne handled his men well and withdrew in good order. His danger was not only from Knyphausen and Grant in front, but from elements of Cornwallis' wing which, having pushed Sullivan's

three divisions off the field, moved down the east side of the Brandywine to cooperate with Knyphausen and gain Wayne's rear. Some of
the guns commanding Chadd's Ford had to be abandoned, but Wayne
lost none of his own brigade's artillery. Wayne, Maxwell on his left,
and Armstrong's militia units that had been farther down the creek, fell
back reluctantly to Chester. Knyphausen recaptured the guns of Proctor's battery that had been taken from his subordinate, Colonel Rall, at
Trenton.

No official report by Wayne on this battle has been preserved. A
letter from Colonel James Chambers of the 1st Pennsylvania line regiment serving under Wayne, written to General Edward Hand, under
whom he had fought earlier in the war, told how Wayne had ordered
him to cover the retreat of the artillery, which he had done. Some
fleeing artillerymen had left one howitzer behind. Though the British
advance was not thirty yards away, pouring in a heavy fire, the gun was
saved. "I brought all the brigade artillery safely off and I hope to see
them again fired at the scoundrels," Chambers wrote to Hand.

Wayne kept his men under his firm control in his withdrawal and
went into battle formation at times to check the enemy. Finally, when
he formed again, he found the pursuit ended. That night he camped on
the outskirts of Chester, where Washington was gradually reassembling
his army. Congress, on Washington's suggestion, moved to Lancaster,
then on to York.

Washington did not suffer severely at Brandywine except in the
loss of public morale. His casualties were light for a major battle fought
for high stakes: between 1,000 and 1,400 in killed, wounded, and
captured—casualties of about one out of eleven. Howe's loss, as he
reported it, was ninety killed, 486 wounded and missing, a small aggregate for such a victory. Wayne lost nothing in aggressiveness and
yearned for another battle before the British reached Philadelphia.[7]

SEVEN

At Paoli, the Surprisers Surprised

W AYNE WAS DEVOTED to the bayonet. For the type of warfare being waged in North America in 1776–1781 he favored that arm because muskets were erratic, rifles heavy, and because the bayonet struck more deadly fear in the heart of the enemy than the whine of bullets or the bark of artillery. Many who have studied the wars of the American Revolution and the Northwest Territory have been struck by Wayne's mastery of the bayonet and his use of it on every occasion when opportunity offered. His object in battle was to close and engage in hand-to-hand combat.[1] For this he trained his soldiers intensively. Nothing, in his view of warfare, gave more confidence to the infantry-man than a bayonet on his musket.

The bayonet was relatively new. It had not been in use by the leading armies for much more than half a century when Wayne formed an affection for it.[2] He had observed at Three Rivers that glistening steel on the barrel of a gun was like a ramrod up a soldier's backbone,

78

and though the thrust might never reach an enemy's abdomen, the gleam of it readily operated on his kidneys. Before Brandywine, Wayne wrote to the Philadelphia authorities requesting that the long, heavy squirrel rifles many of his men carried, which would not hold the ordinary type bayonet, be traded in for muskets around which bayonets could be fastened. As Napoleon found later, he wrote that "rifles are not fitted for the field." But he did want some of them retained for his true sharpshooters. He received the muskets and regularly employed the bayonet.

Wayne was now about to learn at the Battle of Paoli, often termed the Paoli "Massacre," that the bayonet was not exclusively his weapon, but could be used against him as readily as by him. Major General Charles Grey, an excellent soldier of Cornwallis' corps, disclosed that the British knew enough about the bayonet to go into battle without any ball or cartridges, or very few of them, and thereby gained in American history the title of "Cold Steel" or "No Flint" Grey. The night action, fought near Paoli, Pennsylvania, was the most controversial battle of Wayne's career.

The campaign following Brandywine developed slowly. After Brandywine Howe moved toward Philadelphia, his problem being mainly procuring supplies. He had sent his fleet back to sea and had to gather his food and forage from a population largely unfriendly. He could not move directly on Philadelphia up the Chester-Philadelphia road, because the Schuylkill River was unbridged and he had no boats, all being in the possession of the Americans on the Philadelphia side. He had to march upstream far enough that he could cross at one of the fords. The more important and most used were the Swede's Ford at Norristown, Fatland Ford at Valley Forge, Long Ford and Garden's Ford farther upstream in the Phoenixville area, and below Pottstown at Parker's Ford.

Washington's initial plan after his defeat at Brandywine was to cross the Schuylkill to the Philadelphia side, guard the fords upstream, defend the city on the line of the river, and try to prevent Howe from crossing. Philadelphia at that time did not extend west of the Schuylkill nor south to the juncture of that river with the Delaware, but reached only between the two rivers in what is now the midtown section of the city. Washington crossed the Schuylkill into Philadelphia on the night of September 12, the day after the battle, and camped at Germantown, six miles north. There he could contest the British crossing if Howe moved up the right bank of the Schuylkill and undertook to pass over by one of the fords.

The American army did not feel that it had been severely defeated in battle and was reluctant to remain on the defensive. Large numbers had fought in only a minor way, as had Wayne, and others had not fired a shot. The officers believed they had simply been outmaneuvered and not outfought and were anxious for another test, outnumbered as they remained. Wayne and his subordinates were among the most articulate in this urgency. These impressions had an impact on Washington. After reviewing his situation he recrossed the Schuylkill on the west bank on September 14 and waited close to Malvern, about two miles west of Paoli, which then consisted mainly of a well-patronized tavern.

Before the coming of war, Wayne and the young men of his Chester County neighborhood gathered frequently at the tavern to air their views about separation. They drank copious toasts. One night the talk was prolonged, the toasts abundant. The tavern keeper, who had been casting about for a name for his inn, appears to have become one of the boys. They toasted everyone they could think of who stood for popular rights and revolt against despotic or distant government. Finally, as the new day dawned, they hit on Pasquale Paoli, leader of the Corsican uprising against Genoa, then against monarchial France. "To Paoli," one shouted. They drank avidly, then departed or passed out. When the innkeeper awoke later that day the only thing he remembered vividly was the last toast to someone named Paoli. As a gesture to liberty and his good revolutionist customers, he named his establishment the Paoli Tavern, and the town that soon grew around it kept the appellation.[3]

While Washington waited at Malvern, Howe moved his army through West Chester, then called Turk's Head, in two wings, Cornwalls on the road a bit to the east. To meet Howe, Washington marched south, and on September 16 the armies again confronted each other, near Warren's Tavern, twenty-three miles west of Philadelphia on the Lancaster Road. Each felt ready to fight a more conclusive battle than the test at Brandywine.

Wayne had already been operating in front of Howe's advance. In conjunction with Maxwell and the new chief of cavalry, Count Casimir Pulaski, he skirmished with Knyphausen's Hessians under Colonel Carl von Donop, whom he momentarily threatened to capture, but the Hessians managed to reunite with Knyphausen's advance party and the exchange of fire was inconclusive.

As Howe's main army approached, Washington again ordered Wayne to head the attack. Wayne threw out skirmishers who were quickly engaged. A second large-scale battle appeared imminent. Then suddenly the heavens opened and torrents of rain fell. The violent

September storm lasted twenty-four hours. A cold, gusty northeast wind presaged the arrival of fall.

The weather advantage was on the side of the British. The hastily fashioned American cartouche boxes were not rainproof, while those of the British army were. The Americans' powder, wrapped into the crude cartridges of the day, became soaked and worthless. Rain also penetrated into musket locks that were not well fitted and the flints would not spark. By mere chance Washington's position was not as well drained as Howe's and although the roads over which both armies operated became difficult, those in Washington's rear were soon so muddy in stretches that the men sank halfway to their knees. The deep ruts that were quickly formed made the roads virtually unusable for artillery or heavy weapons. Washington, having the smaller army, had to be concerned at all times about avenues of retreat. Both sides suspended the engagement in the downpour but Washington was in no condition to renew it when the wind and rain subsided. He abandoned all thought of further battle until he could get to Parker's Ford on the Schuylkill for dry powder. There he had deposited his stores and left his baggage train when he was inviting battle. Substantially all of the action in this affair was Wayne's, Maxwell's and Pulaski's.[4]

Washington now dispatched Wayne to threaten the British rear. With him would go Brigadier General William Smallwood, who, prior to Brandywine, had been on the Maryland East Shore assembling a new brigade, with which he had followed Howe up to the approaches to Philadelphia. Colonel Mordecai Gist, who had commanded the Baltimore Independent Company, the first Maryland troops recruited in the war, and had fought at Long Island, was likewise to reinforce Wayne with the Maryland regiment he now commanded. Wayne was to have charge of the whole force.

While awaiting the coming of Smallwood and Gist, Wayne camped most of three days, September 18, 19, and 20, in a wood near Paoli which he regarded as secluded from the British. From this point he prepared to assail their rear when they moved toward the Schuylkill River. He was off the roads, two and a half miles removed from the British, and only about four miles from his own home, Waynesborough. The site was well selected for a surprise of the flank and rear of the British army. No one could have been more familiar with the country than Wayne. The fields and woodlands were those in which he had played as a boy and over which he had ridden so frequently as a young country squire.

Washington's general instructions to him were contained in a letter, written at 6 p.m. September 18: "I have this Ins. rec'd yours of 1/2 3 o'clock—having wrote twice to you already to move forward upon the Enemy. I have but little to add . . . Gn. Maxwell 'd Potter are ordered to do the same." Then he added: "I could wish you and those Gens. would act in conjunction to make your advance more formidable, but I would not have too much time delayed on this account. I shall follow as speedily as possible with jaded men . . . Give me the earliest information of everything interesting and of your moves that I may know how to go. . . . The cutting of the Enemy Baggage would be an easy [or a great] matter but take care."⁵

When Wayne had his division securely hidden, he reconnoitered the enemy position, approaching to within half a mile of Howe's camp. He saw the soldiers laundering their clothes and preparing their early morning meal. He felt they were off guard and could be severely handled if Washington would attack them from three directions simultaneously: Wayne, Smallwood and Gist from the west, Maxwell with his light infantry from the east, and Washington with the main army coming down from the north. His enthusiasm mounted.

On this early morning of September 19 he wrote a characteristic letter to his chief: "There never was nor never will be a finer opportunity of giving the enemy a fatal blow than the present. For God's sake push on as fast as possible. . . . We only want you in our rear to complete the Mr. Howe business."

There was one factor that neither Wayne nor Washington could calculate. This was the burning hatred of the American cause and the indefatigable energy of Joseph Galloway, wealthy, talented, long honored in Philadelphia. He had gone to Howe in New York, then became the British commander's principal pilot in the Brandywine-Philadelphia Campaign. When Howe and Cornwallis made their flank march at Brandywine, Galloway was close at hand to describe the roads and terrain and give invaluable intelligence on the position and strength of the Americans.

Through his network of informers he learned that Wayne's command, neither Smallwood nor Gist having yet joined, was lurking in the deep woods prepared to pounce on Howe's rear, disorganize or capture his trains, and perhaps engage him until Washington could come up and thwart him in his purpose to cross the Schuylkill and enter Philadelphia. He reported Wayne's position to Howe and then guided a British force under General Grey to attempt a surprise of the would-be surprisers.⁶

Wayne was pressing now because he had word that Howe would attempt to cross the river that night, at 2 a.m. on the 21st, and he was

Charles Grey, the British major general despised in the American Army because of his effectiveness in employing the bayonet in what was termed the "Paoli Massacre." At Paoli he gained the title of "Cold Steel Grey" and "No Flints Grey" by taking his men into action without balls, powder, or flints in their muskets. In historical perspective he seems one of the most capable of the British commanders. *(Courtesy the Historical Society of Pennsylvania)*

preparing to attack at about that hour. On the late afternoon of the 20th he felt assured that no enemy knew of his covert position in the nearby woods. He was counting on cooperation from Maxwell and Brigadier General James Potter coming from Potts Ford, as well as from Smallwood and Gist.

At this juncture one of Wayne's old neighbors obtained some critical information and rode through the early evening to pass it on to him. He came to Wayne's camp at 9 p.m. where the men were prepared for an early sleep, and told Wayne that one of the neighboring boys had been captured that day by the British, taken into their camp, and later liberated. While there he had heard a British soldier tell another that an attack would be made that night on the American camp in the woods. Wayne doubted the reliability of the story. He judged it unlikely that if an attack were contemplated a private soldier would know of it or confide it to another when a boy stranger was within hearing.[7]

Nevertheless Wayne, who had thrown out pickets and taken precautions against surprise, preferred to act as though the garrulous soldier knew what he was talking about. He ordered all of his men to sleep on their arms instead of stacking them in the customary fashion. They should be ready to form and march quickly, either to attack or retire. He directed them to put their cartouche boxes under their coats to protect their powder from the light rain that was still falling. He threw out extra mounted patrols and strengthened and increased the number of his pickets. His measures were well observed and recorded, because they were made the object of close investigation when he came to be accused of not taking proper precautions.

Wayne's division of two brigades and a four-gun battery aggregated about 2,000 men. The Maryland and Delaware troops who were expected to join him under Smallwood and Gist numbered approximately 2,600. If Maxwell and Potter should be added he would command an effective striking force. But the situation took a different turn. No supporting units reached him. Smallwood approached but bivouacked a mile away. The others were not due until he attacked, or until Washington put them in motion.

Howe, with his main army at Tredyffrin, detached Grey with a brigade of veterans plus some light troops, then ordered Lieutenant Colonel Thomas Musgrave, a brilliant young officer who would subsequently hold high rank in the British service, to operate against Wayne. Musgrave had the 40th regiment, of fame a little later at Germantown, and the 55th, with which he took position a short distance east of Paoli. His were stand-by troops that did not enter the main action.

Grey's attacking force consisted of the 42nd or Black Watch Regiment, the 44th Regiment, long a factor in the North American wars against the French, and an advance party of dragoons and two demi-brigades of light infantry. Grey was among the more capable of the British officers, regarded in colonial opinion as ruthless, but that appears to be mainly because he followed orders and usually was victorious.[8]

The night battle at Paoli has been treated in both British and American history as a surprise and given in America the name of "massacre." It was neither a surprise nor a massacre. Grey's column left the British camp at 10 p.m. and moved through the darkness. Musgrave waited until 11 p.m. Nearing the juncture of roads to Swede's Ford and Langford, the British under Grey were challenged by a party of Wayne's videttes, who fired and sounded the alarm. Grey proceeded as rapidly as night marching would permit by way of the Langford Road and at Warren Tavern turned east on the Lancaster road, with which the Langford road for a time coincides. When the Langford left the Lancaster road in a scant quarter of a mile and turned south, Grey's column was challenged again by a picket of twenty or more men, who fired a round in the direction of the British, then fell back slowly to Wayne's main body, the men loading and firing as they retreated. Here Grey rode to the head of his column and apparently in apprehension that it would be halted by the desultory firing, or that he was approaching Wayne's camp, shouted, "Dash on, light infantry. Dash on."

Major John André in his journal account explained that the firing of the American pickets served the British. Although it notified Wayne's camp of the danger, it disclosed to the attackers, who were uncertain as to the exact location of their enemies, the route to follow in seeking them. Having few, if any, charges or flints in their muskets, Grey's men were unable to reply and hence did not reveal their line of approach. As a further precaution Grey made prisoners of all the inhabitants he passed to prevent them from spreading the alarm. According to André's version, the British forced a blacksmith near the Warren Tavern to tell them where Wayne had his bivouac.

Wayne's troops, still half a mile distant from the British advance, were already in a state of preparation. When the first vidette gave information of the British march, Wayne had the horses harnessed for his artillery and trains and formed a line of battle in the woods, all the while listening to the firing of his pickets as it drew nearer. Seeing that the British assault would fall on his right, he ordered the artillery and trains to move to his rear, taking the King Road by which he had arrived at his present position. He then ordered his light infantry to form a line in front of his camp and oppose the enemy's advance.

Taking no chances, he went forward himself to see that the line was formed, and remained when this line opened on the British only thirty yards away. This little action was a diversion in order that his main body could clear the camp and move off by the King Road following the artillery.

Wayne had ordered his second in command, Colonel Richard Humpton, to form the main body and "wheel by sub platoons"—similar to the column of squads of later wars—to march via the King Road to some higher ground 300 yards west, and establish a line of resistance there. But from his forward position with the light troops he detected that his order was not being obeyed. He repeated it twice without gaining prompt compliance. Finally the left elements moved off. The right of the division, confused and clearly misled, moved in exactly the wrong direction, to the right, toward the Griffith farm house where the division had been obtaining its water. In this unauthorized maneuver, Wayne's little army suffered its heaviest losses.

The main action occurred after Wayne finally got his order through to Humpton. By one account he had to shake Humpton by the collar because the colonel was foggy with rum. He had lost time and the British were on him. He ordered the 4th Regiment up to the line of the light infantry and with these troops gave the British a momentary check. Then he ordered the 4th to follow the artillery on the King Road, which it did. When it departed he remained personally in command of the resistance. He fought a rear guard action with the light troops and the 1st Regiment, then fell back on the route taken by the 4th.[9]

Wayne's trouble was that he could not be everywhere on the dark field or know what was transpiring a few yards from his immediate front. His organized resistance ended when he got his light troops off the field, but only then were the British engaged in the mop-up.

Had the order to Humpton been obeyed with alacrity, Wayne's infantry could have been retired without much damage. Perhaps he was unwise to entrust such a responsibility to Humpton. When he said in his court-martial defense that he had to issue the orders three times, he added significantly that the delay was "owing to some neglect or misapprehension, which is not uncommon in Colonel Humpton." Wayne left that this "neglect or misapprehension" had delayed the division grievously; otherwise his arrangements would have been perfect. He said nothing about the liquor.[10]

The principal error was that when Humpton took some of his men, mostly the 2nd Regiment and part of the 7th, off to the right, they were silhouetted against the blazing camp fires. Some of the British light troops shot down a number of fleeing Americans outlined by the camp fires. Grey's main body, with no more than bayonets, cut through Humpton's feeble resistance, drove the Americans into their camp, and either with bayonet or cutlass dispatched any who offered fight. He cut down a great many more, including skulkers who had sought haven in the huts.[11]

Smallwood deserved no censure. He was thinking in terms of an attack the next morning and was unaware of Grey's approach. There was no foundation for the statement that Smallwood's men, who camped nearby at Sugartown, when they learned of Wayne's defeat and feared the approach of the British, broke and ran. Smallwood united with Wayne the next morning near Lionville and the two rejoined Washington's army. A bit of irony about the battle was that by the time it was fought, Washington had abandoned the plan to attack the British rear. He had already ordered Wayne to return to the main army by way of French Creek, whence he had gone to Paoli. The order never reached Wayne and was supposed to have been captured, as Wayne explained after the battle in a note to Washington.

As soon as he had collected his command, Wayne wrote at noon, September 21, from the Red Lion Tavern west of the battlefield, a report to Washington describing the action as candidly as a defeated and chagrined commander could. Crestfallen at first, he buoyed up his spirits before he wrote. He told of the alarm at 11 p.m. from the firing of one of his outguards, upon which the division was formed and at once "firing began on our Right Flank." He told of ordering the retirement to the left except the regiments nearest the attack, which would shield the retreat. The lines were not more than ten yards apart at this time and a "well directed fire took place followed by a charge of Bayonet." After numbers had fallen on both sides the Americans drew off and formed a new front, though the British "did not think it prudent to push matters further." At the time he wrote, the division, which had been a "little scattered," was "collecting fast." "We have saved all our Artillery, ammunition, and Horses, except one or two Waggons belonging to the Commissaries Department."[12]

That Wayne did not regard himself badly defeated was shown by his statement to Washington that Smallwood had now joined him and as soon as they refreshed the troops for "an hour or Two," they would follow the enemy. Washington had a different thought; he wrote to Wayne that "should we continue detached and in a divided state, I fear we shall neither be able to attack or defend ourselves with a good prospect of success." He recalled Wayne's force to the main army.

Major Samuel Hay, who had been Wayne's aide at Ticonderoga,

writing on September 29 to Colonel William Irvine, declared that "the annals of the age cannot produce such a scene of butchery." Irvine's old regiment was the most exposed when "the enemy rushed in with fixed bayonets and made the use of them they intended." He placed the loss at 300 privates, killed, wounded, and missing, but the reader must wonder at his statement that on the 22nd, a full day after the night attack of the 20th, he went over the ground to see the wounded. "The scene was shocking—the poor men groaning under their wounds, which were all by stabs of bayonets and cuts of Light Horsemen's swords." The statement is inconsistent with that of Major André that forty of the badly wounded were left in the care of residents nearby.[13]

The two prime factors accounting for the "massacre" aspect of the battle were a letter from a Hessian soldier, and the account of the affair in John Marshall's *Life of George Washington*. The Hessian was there but, though most private soldiers strive for accurate accounts, occasionally one is boastful, imaginative, and just whimsically unreliable. The last undoubtedly was the case with the Hessian private, who told about half-clothed Americans running about in their bare feet while the British killed 300 with the bayonet. The clinching line was: "I stuck them myself like so many pigs, one after another, until the blood ran out of the touch-hole of my musket." It is possible that he did do a little sticking, but the hyperbole is apparent.

John Marshall wrote early and established something of a pattern of Revolutionary War history. He dealt briefly with Paoli and not in any manner derogatory of Wayne, but he did state that "Major General Gray was detached to surprise him, and effectually accomplished his purpose." Instead of accepting Wayne's figure of a loss of 150, Marshall felt that it was probably twice that number. Howe put it at 500. The British took 71 prisoners, including the forty gravely wounded left at farmhouses. These, with the dead on the field, would make the casualties aggregate 124, to which the number of wounded who remained with Wanye or escaped should be added. A fair number of the American casualties appears to be 150.

John Armstrong, Secretary of War in the Madison Administration, in his review of this battle, took pointed exception to Marshall's use of the word "surprise," though he acknowledged Marshall's general accuracy as a historian. "To have made it such," Armstrong wrote, "it was necessary to show, on the part of the General, an ignorance of the enemy's intention, or a want of preparation to meet or avoid his attack. Yet it is in proof, that he [Wayne] was informed of the enemy's purpose between eight and nine o'clock in the evening, and that every part of the corps was under arms and in line, when the attack was made."[14]

As is not infrequently the case, the officer mainly responsible for the disaster was the one who felt most aggrieved. Though Wayne generously mentioned Colonel Humpton to Washington among the officers he commended, Humpton, seeking to clear himself of gathering censure after the fight, preferred charges against Wayne which led to much discussion in the army, where many were induced to believe Wayne had been guilty of grave neglect. Aware of criticism and the cloud that was being cast over his honor and career, Wayne wrote to Washington on September 27, saying he felt himself much injured and asking if the commanding general would be "kind enough to indulge me with an Enquiry into my conduct Concerning the Action of the night of the 20th Instant."[15]

He made a straightforward denial of guilt in this request: "Conscious of having done my duty, I dare my accusers to a fair and candid hearing; dark and insidious friends I dread; but from the open and avowed enemy I have nothing to fear. I have no other mode of showing them forth to open view, than through your means. I must therefore beg an immediate investigation by a Court-Martial."

Washington's army was in motion or alert for chances to attack Howe and a general court could not be convened until October 25, after the battle of Germantown. Sullivan presided. Testimony was adduced for three days with Humpton the prosecutor. Humpton's charge before the court was that although Wayne had timely notice of the enemy's intention to attack ". . . notwithstanding this intelligence, he neglected making a disposition, until it was too late either to annoy the enemy or make a retreat, without the utmost danger and confusion." Wayne then spoke in his own defense, outlining precisely what he had done that night. He took special pains to answer the complaint that he had not posted pickets properly, an absurd charge; he told how he had sent Colonel Chambers to Smallwood to guide him to the camp, and had taken every precaution the circumstances required. The court reflected only briefly, then announced its unanimous decision that "General Wayne is not guilty of the charge exhibited against him; but that, on the night of the 20th September ultimo, he did every thing that could be expected from an active, brave, and vigilant officer, under the orders he then had. The court do acquit him with the highest honor." The decision was approved by the commander in chief.

Meanwhile, relieved from Wayne's menace to his rear, Howe was able to cross the Schuylkill without further combat. He moved up the west bank of the river to Swede's and Parker's Fords, found them well guarded, then marched as if to capture Washington's stores at Reading, which caused Washington to move upstream. Then Howe turned suddenly, countermarched rapidly toward Philadelphia, crossed the Schuylkill at Gordon's Ford, now Phoenixville, and Fatland Ford near Valley Forge, and moved on the unguarded capital city that symbolized the independence of the thirteen American republics. He halted his main body at Germantown and sent ahead an occupying force. Cornwallis entered first, the band playing "God Save the King."

Credit was due Washington that he delayed Howe for two weeks in an advance of only 26 miles by a direct route from Brandywine to Philadelphia. As the British historian, John Fiske, remarked, not even Napoleon performed such a feat with an army that had just been routed.[16]

After the action had been fought at Paoli, a bit of sideplay took place at Waynesborough, which was so close at hand that the British assumed that Wayne, whom they knew commanded the division hidden in the woods, would be spending the night there with his family. They surrounded the house and searched it, but all the testimony agrees that they did so courteously and respectfully. They behaved politely to the women. They found no Anthony Wayne, for whom they would have given much, but they carried away two male servants.[17]

Polly Wayne, with the war so close at hand, knew what was occurring, and was deeply worried. Her lack of security was so intensified after the British entered Philadelphia that Anthony wrote on September 30, a trifle censoriously, saying he thought she was above "being depressed at a little unfavorable Circumstance." Then he radiated his usual confidence: "The enemy being in Possession of Philadelphia is of no more Consequence than their being in possession of the City of New York or Boston. They may hold it for a time but must leave it with circumstances of shame and disgrace before the close of the winter. Our army is now in full health and Spirit and far stronger than it was at the Battle of Brandywine."

He gave one order, but cushioned it so as not to cause alarm: "Remove my books and valuable writings some Distance from my House—if not already done—this is but an act of prudence and not to be considered proceeding from any other motive."[18]

E I G H T

Driving Ahead Through the Germantown Fog

ANTHONY WAYNE PLAYED one of the leading combat roles in the battle of Germantown and discharged it magnificently. That Washington assigned Wayne's division to spearhead the attack evidenced that he had not lost confidence in his aggressive subordinate after the unhappy affair in the woods at Paoli.

The sanguinary engagement on the outskirts of Philadelphia, one of the most desperately fought of the war, came about because Howe felt it necessary to divide his forces. Lacking control of the back country, he had to feed his considerable army with provisions from the fleet, which had sailed around from Chesapeake Bay, entered the Delaware River, and found itself blocked by the American fortifications below Philadelphia. The general's brother, Lord Richard Howe, who commanded the fleet, anchored in the river from Reedy Island to Newcastle, Delaware, and waited until General Howe could reduce the American fortifications and clear the channel. These were Fort Mercer at Red Bank on the New Jersey side and Fort Mifflin on Mud Island, near where the Schuylkill joins the Delaware. Down the river at Billingsport, New Jersey, *chevaux de frise* in the water blocked the ships. A similar osbtruction reached across the river between Forts Mercer and Mifflin.

These obstacles Washington sought to preserve by putting as strong a force as he could spare, about 450 men, into Fort Mifflin, and about 400 into Fort Mercer. Howe, intent on clearing the river and opening a water route for the supplies, detached a much stronger force and sent it down the New Jersey side to begin the operation by capturing Billingsport and dragging out the *chevaux de frise*. Washington was informed of the crossing promptly and judged that it brought Howe's army in Philadelphia and environs more nearly to the size of his own. All of this was a prelude to the hard-fought battle.

Moreover, Cornwallis, with some elite British regiments, was removed in Philadelphia while Howe, in order to interpose between the city and the Schuylkill fords, was strung out in Germantown four to six miles away, with pickets reaching still farther to the north.

If there is any valid criticism of Washington's generalship, which in the end proved so eminently sound, it is his frequent resort to councils of war, and they disclosed here, as elsewhere and in other wars, what is almost a truism, that "councils never fight." Generally, when he gave battle his decision was with the minority. Washington usually found most of his generals, and competent ones, in a "wait for further developments" attitude. Wayne, however, appears to have been almost war was to fight it. Wayne, and one or two others, favored shaping and invariably in favor of combat on the premise that the only way to win a not waiting for the future, and in this respect he was far in the forefront, even well ahead of the prudent Washington.

Washington at this juncture called a council of all of his general officers. Eleven attended: Greene, Stirling, Stephen, Armstrong, Knox, Wayne and several other brigadier generals, some relatively new in the Pennsylvania campaign. Among them were Alexander McDougall, the New York merchant from the Scotch lowlands who had fought with Washington at White Plains. He had come down from the New York highlands as a reinforcement from Putnam. Francis Nash of Orange County, North Carolina was there, and under him his intrepid English-born colonel, Edward Buncombe. Both would receive their mortal wounds in the impending battle.

Nash, for whom the capital of Tennessee was named, was cautious at the council, as were most of the leaders—Greene, Stirling, Stephen, Armstrong, Knox, Maxwell, McDougall, and the vaunting sol-

Henry Knox, brigadier general and chief of Washington's artillery during most of the war, major general in 1781, subsequently commander in chief of the Army and Washington's first secretary of war. He was confidant and friend of Wayne during the Fallen Timbers campaign.

dier of fortune Thomas Conway, a brigade commander who had arrived from France before Brandywine.[1]

What Washington proposed was that since Howe had divided his army and Cornwallis was in Philadelphia, the Americans should attack the residue at Germantown, consisting mainly of Grant's and Knyphausen's divisions. When the time came at the council for Wayne to speak, he announced what all expected of him, a vote in favor of an attack. He was sending to Washington from time to time his familiar letters recommending that the British be driven from Philadelphia before the winter arrived. Now that October was here, the opportunity for operations would not long remain. Smallwood and a few others stood with Wayne.

None of these votes was as consequential as the last, Washington's. He remained dissatisfied with the showing at Brandywine. Viewing the overall picture, he believed it incumbent on the army from the standpoint of world opinion to assail Howe before the British bedded down comfortably for the winter. He was, in truth, rather sanguine of success because conditions for surprising Howe while divided were never more inviting. He held another council of war and again reviewed the situation. Howe had sent an additional regiment across the Delaware. The second council finally gave Washington a unanimous vote in favor of attacking.

Washington now issued a rare detailed order of battle in writing, so that each command would know exactly how to proceed to Germantown and what to do when it got there. The distance was fifteen miles from the American camp at Metuchen Hill on Skippack Creek, an exacting march in darkness and one requiring strict conformity to orders if the different units were to converge on the British camp simultaneously, in accordance with Washington's intention.

Four roads, roughly parallel, offered connections between the American camp and Germantown. The most important was the Skippack Road, which led directly through the center of the village and there became the Germantown Road leading into Philadelphia. Wayne and Sullivan were ordered to advance on this road, with Conway's brigade providing an advance party and covering the flanks.

The second, the Ridge (or Manalawany) Road, farther west, hugged the Schuylkill River and missed Germantown village but intersected roads leading into it, then went on to Philadelphia. Along this road Armstrong was ordered to advance with the Pennsylvania militia. Washington accompanied this column so that he might have personal supervision of the army's right wing.

The left wing, commanded by Greene, advanced on the two eastern roads. Greene's own division, plus Stephen's Division and McDougall's Brigade, were ordered to march down the Limekiln Road, a route four miles longer than Wayne's and Sullivan's. On approaching Germantown this road curved to the right, or west, merged into Church Lane, an east-west thoroughfare that bisected Skippack Road, which had here become the main street of the village, and ran into Ridge or Manalawny Road near the Schuylkill. Where Church Lane crossed Skippack Road, at the main corner of Germantown, stood the Market House and diagonally across from it the German church.

The fourth road, on the extreme left, was the old York Road, down which Smallwood, supported by Colonel David Forman, was to move until opposite the British right rear. Then he was to turn and join in the attack that was expected to push Howe's army to the Schuykill and there capture or destroy it. Thus the plan of battle was a frontal attack by Wayne, Sullivan, and obliquely by Greene, with flank attacks by Smallwood and Forman on the enemy right and by Armstrong on the enemy left.

At the southern end of Germantown was an eminence called Logan Hill, and nearby Howe had his headquarters in the Perot house, in the rear center of his camp. Farther north, near the center of the straggling village, stood the spacious mansion of Benjamin Chew, Maryland physician and Quaker.

Washington's main reliance was on surprise, with Wayne and Sullivan the key factors. His camp on Skippack Creek was astir on the afternoon of October 3, 1777. As darkness wore on the divisions began their march. Wayne and Sullivan had to move for a time on the same road with Armstrong, until they could take their position on the right center. Then the entire Continental Army, tired but confident, was on its way over the rough roads and terrain in an effort to conform to its close time schedule. This would place the line of divisions within two miles of the enemy position at 2 a.m. Two hours were then allowed for rest in the near presence of the enemy. They were then to form and be in attack order at 5 a.m. The reserve would consist of Stirling's Division plus Maxwell's and Nash's brigades.[2]

The obvious weakness of the plan was that it was conditioned on the meeting of converging columns, always difficult even with veteran troops under driving leadership. An advance of fifteen miles minimum over four separate roads in darkness would severely test any army or plan. Still, Howe's army was grievously exposed and divided. Now of all times appeared to be Washington's chance. He would have to defeat Howe quickly. Cornwallis could march to his chief's aid from Philadelphia with infantry in an hour and a half, and with cavalry, of which he had a considerable body, much more speedily.

Such was the situation when Wayne and Sullivan pressed down the Skippack Road as dawn came on October 4, 1777, a murky dawn, heavy with one of the fogs that not infrequently attend the Philadelphia area in mid-autumn. Wayne, who but a few days before had sustained with good spirit the calamity of Paoli, had a portent of victory on the night before Germantown. A few minutes before his division began its march, he wrote to his wife Polly from Pennypacker's Mill, timing his letter at 7 p.m. He addressed her as "My Dear Girl" and exuded confidence: "I have often wrote to you on the eve of some expected and uncertain event but never on any equal to the present—before this reaches you the heads of many worthy fellows will be laid low." He told her it was not for any mortal to "Command Success nor length of day," but declared that before darkness he would be "entering Philadelphia at the head of Troops Covered with Laurels." He could become rhetorical: "My heart sits lightly in its mansion—every artery beats in unison—and I feel unusual ardor."[3]

The battle opened almost as Washington had planned it, delayed only a trifle. Wayne and Sullivan, with Conway's brigade on their flanks providing patrols through the woods, pressed down the Skippack Road. Instead of reaching the British pickets on Chestnut Hill in darkness, though, the dawn was advanced before they issued from the timber and suddenly pounced on the Redcoats guarding the eminence.

Though Washington had planned an earlier attack, perhaps it was well for the Americans that the day arrived before they felt the enemy. Rain had threatened all night and the march was made in deep, thick blackness. Daylight showed sullenly through the mists but there was at least some visibility when Wayne encountered the pickets and then the light infantry that guarded Howe's front. The attack was only a mild surprise. Howe had been alerted to the likelihood of it the day before, when an officer of his light infantry wrote that Washington, by accounts received that day, was not distant and "intends to move near us to try the event of another battle." Others heard that the Americans were coming. In such a war, with many observers always at hand, surprise was difficult.

The British pickets hastily retired and Wayne formed his line of attack on Mount Airy, a mile north of the Chew House near the center of Germantown. He drove forward and almost at once encountered the 52nd British Foot, which had heard the exchanges with the pickets and was already alerted when Wayne and Sullivan struck. By resisting Wayne's onslaught and courageously attempting two counter attacks, the regiment showed its sturdy character, especially when it perceived that Wayne's men were hungry for revenge for their bloody defeat at Paoli. One of the British lieutenants told how the pickets had scarcely come in when the regiment heard Continentals shout, "Have at the bloodhounds" and "Revenge Wayne's affair."[4]

Wayne now had his turn with the bayonet and showed that his drilling had not been wasted. His men were eager to display that they were fully as deft with steel as Grey's. They plunged recklessly ahead, cutting and hacking as they went, driving back the enemy when he made a spirited effort to gain the offensive. Wayne knew that since both

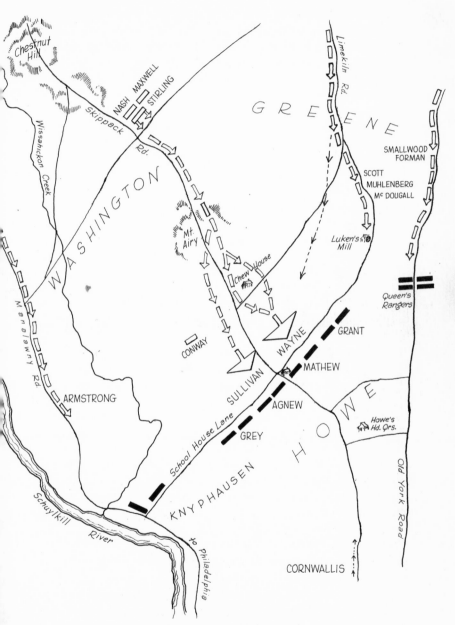

BATTLE OF GERMANTOWN
October 4, 1777

sides were half blinded by the fog, he must hold the impetus of his forward motion else the battle would lag far short of his objective. The key to Washington's success at this moment was held by this little division. Stirred by the frenzy of combat, Wayne relished in the thrusts and jabs of his men and havoc caused by his quick assault.

In a letter to Polly two days after the battle he described the fury of the advance. "Our officers exerted themselves to save many of the poor wretches who were Crying for Mercy, but to little purpose. The Rage'd fury of the Soldiers was not to be restrained for some time—at least until a great number of the enemy fell by our Bayonet."[5]

The 52nd British regiment stood until Wayne was reaching past its flanks. Sensing that Washington's entire army was being hurled against Germantown and having lost heavily from Wayne's impetuous attack, the regimental commander ordered retreat. Wayne pursued hotly, eager and inflamed, pressing them at each step. As the junior British officer explained, "Indeed had we not retreated at the very time we did, we should all have been taken or killed." He added: "This was the first time we had retreated from the Americans." That sentence could soon be applied to a considerable part of Howe's army. The distinguishing feature of this battle was that for the first time in a major pitched engagement the colonists routed and drove their veteran foes fleeing before them.[6]

Howe, anxious, was now coming forward with two brigades which took position at Beggarstown, down the slope from Mount Airy, where he met retreating pickets and remnants of the worsted British regiment. Highly chagrined, he "got into a passion," as one of his men described it. He cried out: "For shame, light infantry! I never saw you retreat before. Form! Form! It is only a scouting party."

The British soldiers understood the situation better than the newly arrived Howe, who moved with a group of aides and officers to the protective branches of a large chestnut tree and hurled out his demands for a rally. Quickly the head of Wayne's advance appeared, hauling three pieces of artillery at their front. These guns emitted a discharge of grape at the pretty target presented by the red-coated officers under the chestnut tree.

Wrote the young British lieutenant, Martin Hunter: "I think I never saw people enjoy a discharge of grape before; but we really all felt pleased to see the enemy make such an appearance, and to hear the grape rattle around the commander-in-chief's ears, after he had accused the battalion of having run from a scouting party."[7]

Howe mounted, whipped his horse into a gallop, and sought the rear, followed soon by the two succoring brigades that were unable to stand against Wayne's assault and the dull gray of his bayonets in the early morning fog.

Meantime Conway and Sullivan's main elements had inclined to their right across fields of buckwheat, leaving the attack down the left side of the Skippack Road to Wayne, and behind him the brigades of Maxwell and Nash, comprising Lord Stirling's reserve division.

When Howe retired from his chestnut tree and the two forward British brigades retreated precipitately to the main crossroads of Germantown, Colonel Musgrave, who had helped to hem in Wayne's division at Paoli, held his 40th Foot together in its retirement down the Skippack Road. He had advanced from his camp on the Chew House grounds and to it he returned. On Wayne's approach he threw six companies of his regiment into this stone citadel, the mansion and spacious grounds covering what would now amount to a large city block. The house was surrounded by shrubbery and trees through which were scattered marble statues, vases, and urns.

This was the strong point in the British alignment, though it was somewhat in advance of the main British line. The house was readily converted into a fortress protecting Howe's center. In the rear of the Chew House, Howe drew out his line of battle, Knyphausen on the left, reaching along School House Lane from the Market House to the Schuylkill, his corps composed of "Cold Steel" Grey's and James Agnew's brigades. The center was held by Brigadier General Edward Mathew with six British battalions and a squadron of horse. Major General Grant with the regiments of guards and dragoons was on the right, reaching to the woods around Luken's Mill. The Queen's Rangers held the York Road on the far right. The Rangers were hussars, all being provincial Loyalists.

Soon Wayne's forward drive reached the Chew House. Clearly it would require time before Musgrave could be blasted out of his stronghold. Meanwhile the American initiative would be lost. The routed foe farther on would be allowed a breathing spell to reflect and reform. Bravely, Wayne thrust ahead. He passed around both sides of the forbidding citadel, its lower and upper windows now emitting through apertures in the heavy shutters the sharp musketry of the British marksmen, the effectiveness of their firing, fortunately for his Pennsylvanians, being hampered by the fog. Finally he came against the main line of the British army, deployed along Church and School House Lanes and centered at the market place.

Sullivan had kept good pace on his right. What they now needed was instant support from Lord Stirling's division, the brigades of Nash and Maxwell, and the arrival of Greene and Stephen, then Smallwood and Forman, to roll up Grant's corps on the British right.

At this juncture two developments occurred to snatch victory whimsically from Washington's army. The first, during Musgrave's stubborn defense of the Chew House, was the unhappy arrival of General Henry Knox. He appeared in front of the Chew House at the time Maxwell's Brigade, following Wayne, was puzzled about how to deal with the stone fortress Musgrave had seized. Maxwell was just ahead of Woodford's Brigade of Stephen's Division, the first element of Greene's command to arrive at the combat area after its march down the Lime-kiln Road.

Maxwell's and Woodford's Brigades, brought to a halt at Chew's, awaited word from the gathering of officers. In this council Knox's opinion unhappily prevailed. It influenced Washington, who, at this stage of the war was impressed with the bearing and assurance of his portly artillery chief. Knox delivered his opinion out of the books instead of from a view of the circumstances of the battle. His stentorian voice and huge bulk made his words seem weighty. "Never," he stated didactically, "leave an enemy castle in the rear."[8]

Others demurred strongly. Adjutant General Timothy Pickering, later Secretary of State, remonstrated as vigorously as he could against higher rank. Joseph Reed, who had retired from the post of adjutant after serving Washington well from Boston to Trenton, challenged Knox abruptly. "What," he exclaimed, "call this a fort and lose the happy moment!"

The group then sought the counsel of Conway, but failed to find him. One report was that he was hiding in a barn. Reed and Cadwalader claimed to have discovered him there. When the question got across to Washington, Knox's judgment prevailed and Wayne waited. The artillery was brought up and the Chew place was invested.

Knox bombarded the house with solid roundshot. The heavy walls merely sent back their contempt with dull thuds. Pickering, who watched, reported that the well-directed fire of the British muskets was effective and felled a "great many" officers and men. Then a disappointing attempt was made to set the house on fire and scorch out the defenders.

The effort to reduce the Chew mansion was futile and time-consuming. The reserves Washington had dispatched to support Wayne and Sullivan facing the British line were deterred for fully half an hour in a trivial operation against six companies of British foot that might have been kept indoors by a company or two of marksmen. That half-

Attack on the Chew House in Battle of Germantown, from an old engraving showing attempt to break through front door. *(Photo from National Archives)*

hour was precious, the difference between victory and defeat. Up to that time the rout of the entire British army, already severely handled by the onrushing Americans, appeared inevitable. Washington, who had moved to the center from his position on the right, was elated with the progress of Wayne, Sullivan, and other units, and momentarily expected the arrival of Greene, Stephen, and Smallwood to crush Grant and drive Howe either into the Schuylkill River or into Philadelphia. Greene's guns already could be heard to the left, signalling his approach.

As Washington described the situation at this hour: "The tumult, disorder, and even despair, which, it seems, had taken place in the British army, were scarcely to be paralleled; and, it is said, so strongly did the idea of retreat prevail, that Chester was fixed as a place of rendezvous."

Greene, always diligent, was drawing close to the enemy's right, where he dislodged Howe's flank guard of Queen's Rangers and descended on Grant's corps strung out behind School House Lane. He assumed that he would soon be joined in the attack by Armstrong on the right and by Washington's main elements—Wayne, Sullivan, and Stirling—in the center. He could see little and determine less about how the army was faring. The heavy smoke of battle, held down by the moist air, lowered visibility on most parts of the field, so that Wayne in his advanced position was unable to know more than did Greene about what was occurring at the Chew House or elsewhere.

Now occurred a second development that wrested victory from Washington's grasp and nullified all of Wayne's gallant work of driving through the British center. Stephen, who was moving forward on Greene's right, and was presumed to be under Greene's command, strayed in the smoke and fog and became detached. While one of his brigades turned up near the Chew House, the bulk of the division passed or tarried in Wayne's rear, an event that proved the most disconcerting element in the final stage of the battle. On this cold, damp, October morning Stephen had been seeking the comforts of the bottle and was in a mental as well as climatic fog.

How portentous was this moment! Burgoyne was faltering in upstate New York and later in the month would surrender at Saratoga. A victory at Germantown, apparently easily won if Wayne and Sullivan were supported by the divisions of Stephen and Stirling, which were close at hand, would signal to the world the destruction of Howe, or would lead to his close investment in Philadelphia. The result of two such catastrophes to British arms nearly simultaneously would almost inevitably lead the home government to conclude that the colonies could not be subdued by any reasonable expenditure of men and money. If independence were not recognized, the war would trickle out. Already there was enough opposition to it in England. Such was the state of affairs at the instant when Stephen's division under its inebriated commander appeared through the fog marching obliquely across the left rear of Wayne's.

Well might Wayne and his men believe they were in danger of being pocketed in their exposed, front line position. Wayne was aroused—near maddened, some have said—by the frenzy of this combat. His beautiful mount had been shot from under him almost at the outset. A stray musket ball ripped across the back of his hand and a rolling cannon roundshot, such as always looked innocent as it bounced along, but carried the momentum that could tear off a leg, glanced off his foot. Already he had driven for three miles, as he calculated it, through the center of the British army.

Through the scudding fog, this large, unexpected body of men loomed up, not moving in battle line toward the British arranged along the Church and School House Lanes, but closing in rapidly on his own left rear. Then, to his further amazement, the newcomers fired a fusillade into his division. Obviously it was intentional. Part of it caught Sullivan's left. Wayne's men replied and for a moment Americans were fighting Americans.

Still another new element appeared in the British line. "Cold Steel" Grey on the British left had felt no pressure from Armstrong. Howe was free to shift him to the center and his elite brigade appeared at the critical juncture immediately in front of Sullivan and Wayne. Cornwallis, riding in haste from Philadelphia with 2,000 mounted troops, now reached the field. Like Armstrong's on the American right, the intended encircling movement of Smallwood and Forman on the far left had failed. These troops had not yet arrived at the combat area. Musgrave kept up his annoying fire against Maxwell from the Chew mansion windows.

Everything was in a jumble on the thick, blurred battlefield. The appearance and firing of Stephen's division on Wayne's rear, plus a canteen with too much whiskey in it, unsettled the entire army and cost Washington the success that seemed his for the reaching. The dénouement followed rapidly. Despite all that the officers could do to restrain it, the American army suddenly left the field, and Wayne's division went with it.

The departure was anything but rational. It was capricious, psychological, unreasonable. There are few other instances where an army on the verge of victory suddenly has decided to cast off the control of its officers, stop fighting, and walk away. There was little running at Germantown. The army simply marched away, taking all its cannon, suffering few casualties in its retirement. The steadfast troops were Wayne's and Greene's who covered the retreat.

Washington was humiliated. He reported three days afterward "with much chagrin and mortification, that every account confirms the opinion I at first entertained, that our troops retreated at the instant when victory was declaring herself in our favor." He attributed the defeat to "the extreme haziness of the weather." In another letter he said that not until the battle was over did the army know "how near we were to gaining a complete victory."

Wayne, his hand gushing blood, blackened and crimsoned by the fray, tried to stem the retreat. Like monstrous billows it engulfed and flowed past him. Farther back he was able to re-form most of his men and set up a rear guard that battled Cornwallis and Grey on the Skippack Road abreast of Greene, who retired on the Limekiln Road. The

British soon abandoned pursuit. Victory had fallen into their lap so unexpectedly that they were satisfied. For his enterprise with the whiskey, Stephen was tried by court–martial and cashiered.

The battle lasted two hours and forty minutes, during which time the American loss in killed and wounded was about 1,070, about 10 percent. The British loss was considerably lower, probably about 600.

Wayne summed up the action in which he had played such a commanding role: "Fortune smiled on us for full three hours, the enemy were broke, dispersed, and flying in all quarters—we were in possession of their whole equipment, together with their park, etc. A *wind-mill* attack was made upon a house into which six light companies had thrown themselves, to avoid our bayonets. Our troops were deceived by this attack, thinking it something formidable. They fell back to assist—the enemy believing it to be a retreat, followed,—confusion ensued, and we ran away from the arms of victory open to receive us."

Word of Germantown created surprise in Europe, extending to amazement in France. An age that looked upon warfare as an art lingered studiously over Washington's audacity and near success in grasping the offensive and assailing Howe, and driving the British and Hessian veterans more than two miles, then losing through freak circumstances and the weather.

Wayne expressed high optimism in his letter to Washington following the battle: ". . . you are now, in my humble opinion, in as good, if not better, situation than you were before the action this day. Your men are convinced that the enemy may be driven, and although we fell back, yet our people have gained confidence and have raised *some doubts* in the minds of the enemy, which will facilitate their total defeat in the next trial, which I shall be happy to see brought to issue so soon as expedient."

"Upon the whole," he wrote to Polly, "it was a glorious day. Our men are in high spirits, and I am confident we shall give them a total defeat the next action, which is at no great distance."[9]

Hardships and Capers at
Valley Forge

WAYNE ARGUED in a letter to Washington on November 25 that some loss was certain if he made an attempt to clear the British from Philadelphia before the winter, "yet it is my Opinion that you will not be in a [worse] Situation, nor your arms in less Credit if you should meet with a misfortune, than if you are to remain inactive. The eyes of the world are fixed on you." Here was Wayne, the brigadier general, still pushing. Anything was better for him than inaction; yet inaction, while it has never won a battle, has not infrequently won wars.[1]

Washington replied on December 3, 1777, and asked the advisability of a winter's campaign in the open field. He wanted to know the practicability of attacking Philadelphia with the aid of a considerable body of militia that might be assembled at the proper time. Wayne in reply the next day made the suggestion that was a factor in the selection of Valley Forge for the winter encampment. "I am not for a Winter's Campaign in the open field," he stated frankly, though a bit inconsistently. "The Distress and Naked Situation of your troops will not admit it."

Throughout November Washington mulled over the prospects of battling Howe again, although only a scattering of officers, Wayne included, favored an assault. The weighty majority opposed it. Washington reconnoitered and found Howe's defenses too secure, with trenches frowning above a deep ditch, and fraised or protected by abatis, for which the neighboring apple orchards had been felled. The apple trees with their spreading branches and tough-grained limbs proved excellent for the purpose.

Washington was not an eyewitness, as Howe was, of the carnage of Bunker Hill, but he could just as easily visualize the bodies that would be strewn in front of such embattlements as Howe had erected, even if he were successful in storming them, and of success there was of course no assurance.

The attack under study was another involving several columns converging on Howe in Philadelphia. Lord Stirling drafted it and Wayne urged it with all its complications. Anxious as the commanding general was to answer the public clamor for an attack, and eager as his men and junior officers were to share in the applause that was going to Gates and the northern army after Burgoyne's surrender, Washington had the stamina and good judgment to resist the annoying popular pressure. He would not subject his army to a Bunker Hill by assailing Howe's forbidding chain of redoubts. He returned to his White Marsh camp resigned again to the defensive. That was the prudent course, with winter at hand.

Even Wayne, after this urgency for action had failed, was at length satisfied that the near shoeless and coatless army could not undertake a campaign of active operations. He explained his feelings in his letter to Washington of December 4. He said that if taking a position at Wilmington or thereabouts, or "hutting at a distance of about twenty miles west of Philadelphia," which would support the honor of the army in the eyes of Europe and give confidence to the home people—if that should be deemed a winter campaign, then he was for it.[2]

Washington decided on "hutting." Various positions were recommended but Wayne's choice prevailed. Washington confirmed it and it was perhaps the strongest available in the area, the gentle elevation of Mount Joy, the location being known as Valley Forge. Howe was probably wise not to assail it.

While the army was there, during the winter of 1777–1778, some of the most notable events of the Revolutionary War occurred—the

Conway Cabal, which sought to oust Washington from his command and install the less competent Gates, showy at Saratoga by the fighting of Arnold, Morgan, Stark at Bennington, and other subordinates; another, the return and assignment of General Charles Lee to high command; the coming of Baron von Steuben; the gradual rise of Washington to heroic proportions and the dawning recognition of his stature by the people and army; the departure of Howe and transfer of the top British command to Sir Henry Clinton; and finally, the most significant of all, the arrival of news that France had recognized the independence of the colonies and would supply money and men.

The advantage of Valley Forge was that Howe could not bypass it in quest of supplies and leave the American army on his flank or in his rear, between him and Philadelphia. This restricted his foraging to a relatively small area, a radius of not more than a dozen miles around Philadelphia, and those disputed by Washington's vigilant patrols. Wayne recommended to Washington that militia units be employed to harass Howe's foraging parties and they played an important role.

When the defensive lines were laid out it was seen that the Valley Forge position was one of unusual strength. The camp was arranged in an orderly manner, in accordance with Washington's precise instructions. It consisted of two defensive lines. The outer, on Mount Joy, was occupied by ten brigades of the Continental Army, beginning with Muhlenberg's on the left, overlooking the Schuylkill River, and ending with William Woodford's on the right, commanding the low area, or valley between Mount Joy and Mount Misery. Wayne had a position in the right center, between the brigades of Charles Scott and Enoch Poor. To the north, as reserves in the rear, were the brigades of Maxwell, Huntington, Conway, Knox's artillery, and other units. The rear line was protected by abatis and strong redoubts on either flank, called the Star Fort and Fort Washington. Pickets were extended for several miles in front.

Valley Forge was six to seven miles up the Schuylkill from Swede's Ford, the present site of Norristown, on the opposite bank from that city. Midway was King of Prussia, then mainly a tavern, past which Washington marched in transferring his army from White Marsh to its winter encampment. Valley Forge derived its name from the forge set up there by Isaac Potts, a Quaker preacher, who developed the iron ore found in abundance in the area and built one of the typical Pennsylvania stone houses on Valley Creek. His house served Washington as headquarters. From its east window the commander in chief had a good view of a substantial part of his camp and army.

During the winter Wayne lived in the nearby house of Joseph and

Sarah Walker. Sarah, known as "grandmother" to all in the neighborhood, was his cousin. She was a strong but compassionate woman, still gracious and benign after the loss of three of her children in the devastating smallpox epidemic of 1764. Waynesborough was five miles distant from the camp. The fact that the British had looked for Wayne there at the time of the Paoli "Massacre" and might do so again made it unsuitable for regular occupancy even had he wished to live at home; so Walker's spacious stone house became his headquarters. A secret closet had been built into a bedroom and this he used for hiding his confidential papers. He stationed a guard to protect the property from foragers and scavengers.[3]

A Walker son, Lewis, born after the epidemic, was eleven years old when Wayne passed the winter there. He rememberd well when five deserters were captured, returned, and tried by court-martial held in the Walker house, Wayne presiding. Under the stern code of the day, devoid of sentiment when men around them were dying and suffering hunger and cold in their country's cause, the sentence was that they should be shot. Lewis Walker said of his mother, "Ah, that noble, that queenly woman!" When Sarah Walker learned of the sentence, she had General Wayne summoned to a side room: "Cousin Wayne," she said, "I hear five deserters have been taken and are sentenced to be shot. This must not be. Poor fellows, hungry, cold and almost naked. If I were a soldier, I would do so too." Anthony was moved and the five were pardoned.

Lewis, the son, remembered and his daughter recorded in the family's papers, how his mother at times countermanded the general's orders. The guard would not permit wandering soldiers to enter her farmlands. Yet almost as much as from the lack of clothing, the soldiers suffered from the want of green things and vegetables. The Walker meadows at the time abounded with docks and greens. Sarah was greatly disturbed that the craving of the soldiers was not being appeased. She violated orders and opened the fields to them. Then she collected greens herself, boiled them with salt pork, and distributed them as far as they would go.[4]

Large numbers of Wayne's soldiers were Irish, using the American Revolution as a means of fighting England. While most were from the lower counties, many were a part of the heavy Irish immigration that came to America before the war and brought families who produced army and political leaders. But at Valley Forge they had not yet undergone the melting pot process and though they hated England bitterly they "feuded" severely with each other.

Wayne's veterans enjoyed making sport of the recruits. Sometimes

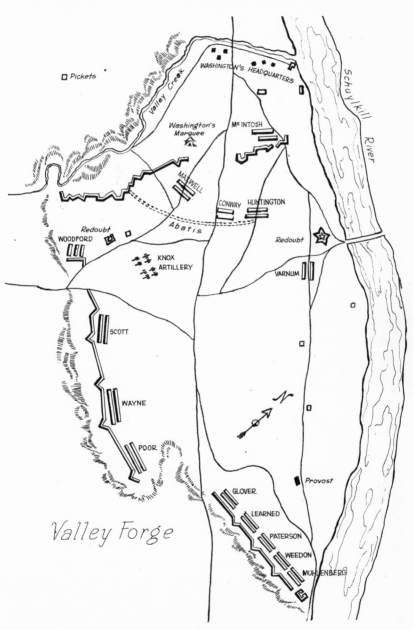

ENCAMPMENT AT VALLEY FORGE
Winter of 1777–1778

the jests were heavy-handed or downright mean, as when a captain of Proctor's artillery stealthily put the words "small pox" on the doors of cabins close by the huts of some newly arrived replacements. He came near to being court-martialed for what he looked on as a harmless prank. When not playing games or engaged in sports, such as racing or wrestling, some tried to stir up trouble. A group of the newly arrived Irish from Maryland were observing St. Patrick's Day when one or two of Wayne's Pennsylvanians fashioned a figure-four trap out of an old harrow having spiked teeth, then put some potatoes beneath it for bait. They hid and watched as curiosity overcame the Marylanders. Some one asked what it was for and a more wary soldier answered, "A trap to catch the Irish."[5]

This the Irish recruits regarded a grave insult and a battle began. Soldiers poured out of their huts with naked bayonets and hunting knives, took sides, and a bloody brawl that would have delighted the British got underway. Then a horseman raced toward them at a gallop—"a marvelous exhibition of horsemanship," someone called it. Down the slope of Mount Joy the rider came, dashing at full speed. As he rushed into the fray the battlers were at first amazed, then awestruck, and quelled to absolute silence. It was Washington. Imperiously he ordered the crowds to disperse. Such was his commanding presence, aided by the anger he could so readily show when his men were making fools of themselves, that the mob melted. All Valley Forge had something to talk about for days and veterans cherished memory of the incident thereafter.[6]

The Scotch-Irish made up the "bone and sinew" of Wayne's division at Valley Forge. They were descendants of the Scots who went to Northern Ireland after the defeat of the Old Pretender, or else children of the Scotch Covenanters who encountered the displeasure of merry Charles II in the heyday of the Restoration. Probably two-thirds of Wayne's division were these "independent, stubborn, hard drinking and fierce fighting sons of Ulster . . . officered by men of the same breed." Almost to a man, they belonged to a secret society called Orangemen, the first lodge of which in America was formed at Valley Forge. A lodge of Free Masons flourished also in Wayne's division and met in the Beaver House.

Wayne kept up his drill during the winter, still obsessed that his command should be the best disciplined of the army. Bayonet practice and maneuvers occupied the men's time. The marvel of Valley Forge and perhaps the greatest testimonial during the war to the faithfulness of Washington's army was that the troops did not mutiny under the hardships. One factor was the mildness of the weather. Happily for the

American cause, the winter of early 1778 was the least severe anyone recalled in the neighborhood.

Still, "for some days," Washington wrote, "there has been little less than famine in the camp. A part of the army has been a week without any kind of flesh, and the rest three or four days. Naked and starving as they are, we cannot enough admire the incomparable patience and fidelity of the soldiery, that they have not been, ere this, exciting by their suffering to a general munity and desertion."[7]

Wayne was one of Washington's main reliances at Valley Forge. The commander in chief, in referring to the reassignment of Major General Benjamin Lincoln, added that "the whole charge of his division is now upon General Wayne, there being no other brigadier in it than himself." Thus Wayne was required to perform the duties normally discharged by a major general and two brigadier generals.

At the beginning, on December 30, 1777, while his men were about to complete their new huts, Wayne wrote to this friend Richard Peters, who had been Secretary of the Board of War for the Continental government from its inception. Making the best of it, he said his men would be covered with huts in a few days but "naked as to clothing—in which respect they are in a worse condition than Falstaff's recruits, for they have not one whole shirt in a brigade—he had that to a company. . . ." He expressed regret that Pennsylvania had not followed the pattern of the states farther east and clothed its own troops, and urged the adoption of that plan.

He told Peters of his own efforts: "If I had not sent out some of my officers to purchase shoes, stockings, breeches, and blankets, (for which our clother-general refuses payment) the Pennsylvania troops must either have perished, or deserted before this time." He thought he would be able to procure the necessities to make them comfortable, but as to recovering his own health, he felt a respite of three or four weeks from camp would be needed. He had been struggling with a cold that hung on stubbornly for weeks, attended by a pain in the chest which he attributed to the fall when his roan mount was shot from beneath him at Germantown. "This caitiff complaint," he explained, "had taken post in my lungs and throat. . . . Unless I am permitted to change my ground, I dread the consequences." How faithful he had been to the cause may be seen from his next sentence: "I have now been on constant duty for twenty-three months, sixteen of which I served in Canada and Ticonderoga, the remainder with his excellency, during which I have never had one single moment's respite."

He finally obtained a leave but instead of resting at Waynesborough he went to Lancaster, which shared with York as the seat of

government, and was the temporary capital of Pennsylvania, his purpose being to fulfill a parting promise to his men that he would see to
their comforts. This he did, by importuners to Congress and his patriotic friends. The result could be seen in the added robustness and more
soldierly appearance of the Pennsylvania Line later in the winter.

After the battle of Germantown, Congress adopted a resolution to
prevent barter with the enemy, providing that anyone captured within
thirty miles of Philadelphia, or any place the British army occupied,
who was transporting supplies to the enemy would be dealt with by
martial law. Wayne encountered some personal embarrassment because
of it, and it causes one to wonder about just what kind of person his
wife Polly was. Anthony was compelled to write her a letter which
discloses that she had no compunction about dealing with the British
when they came as buyers. He had to instruct her as though she were a
child, unconscious of the deadly earnestness of the struggle her husband was helping to lead with all his heart and soul. Apparently he
received intelligence about her commerce with Philadelphia from Light
Horse Harry Lee, who patrolled the roads efficiently.

Though Wayne's home was within the American picket lines he
rarely visited it. How many times it is impossible to tell but it has been
mentioned that he went there "once or twice." The reason why he went
so infrequently is ordinarily attributed to the diligent, full-time attention he gave to his men in camp and his efforts to find clothing, food,
and comforts for them when away. Martha Washington came in February and remained with the commanding general during the worst period
of the winter. Mrs. Henry Knox came to live with the chief of artillery.
The wives of other officers came, but apparently not Polly Wayne. She
and Anthony seemed immersed in their own affairs, steadily growing
apart from each other.

In mid-February Washington detached Wayne for an incursion
into New Jersey to collect supplies. Only dire want induced the commanding general to risk an important element of his army on a venture
so far removed behind the enemy's lines that he could not give succor if
it encountered unusual danger. Danger it did encounter, but Wayne
skillfully extricated it in a series of affairs, usually against superior
numbers, and returned to Valley Forge driving a herd of cattle, some
excellent cavalry mounts, heavy horses with loaded wagons, and quantities of badly needed forage. So depleted had the stocks of forage
become around Philadelphia that Howe was compelled to bring his in
by water, but Wayne was able to find hay and fodder in places the
British had overlooked. More than that, he brought with him some
New Jersey militia who became attached to his command.

Wayne was skillful in throwing off his pursuers. When Howe learned of his activities in southern New Jersey and knew he was compelled to move slowly with his several hundred head of cattle, he sent Lieutenant Colonel Robert Abercrombie down the Delaware River to intercept him, then ordered Colonel Thomas Stirling to take the 42nd Regiment and the Queen's Rangers directly across the river and block him at Haddonfield. Another regiment held Cooper's Ferry and the American general with his slow-moving convoy appeared to be well hemmed in.

Wayne was intent not so much on eluding as on fighting his pursuers. He advanced boldly from Mount Holly toward the most dangerous adversary, Stirling. That colonel, seeing that he was menaced by the combative American, retreated. Wayne followed him closely but the Englishman avoided a meeting.

Wayne's foraging expedition was a delayed response to the "great hay raid" made by a large part of Howe's army under Cornwallis over the Christmas period of 1777 in which Cornwallis kept his troops in such compact order while his party scoured the Pennsylvania countryside that they offered no opportunity for the Americans to attack. Because New Jersey was closer to the British than to the Americans, everything Wayne brought into camp would otherwise have been seized by Howe's foragers, had they looked as closely as Wayne did. The British tried to show their contempt by dubbing him "Drover Wayne."

The army found conditions improved when Nathanael Greene shouldered the load of quartermaster general, in addition to commanding his division. He replaced Thomas Mifflin, who had handled the demanding task badly. Almost at once Wayne's division noticed that supplies arrived in a more orderly fashion. Gone were the days when Wayne told his friend Peters that some of his aides had given a party "to which no one who had a whole pair of breeches was admitted."

TEN

Named for Gallantry at
Disappointing Monmouth

SPRING CAME AT LAST to Valley Forge, invigorating Washington's army that as winter ended had been solidly reinforced. As
violets bloomed along Valley Creek and the maples were coming into
full leaf, an event of profound bearing on the future course of the war
was being enacted at far off Falmouth Harbor (now Portland, Maine).
There the French frigate *La Sensible* stole into port through British
North Atlantic patrols, bearing a messenger from the government of
King Louis XVI of France.

On May 7, under the usually salubrious sun of the Pennsylvania
springtime, Washington paraded his entire army on the drill grounds in
front of Mount Joy. Some were still in tatters and some clothed with
grotesque uniforms made of last winter's blankets; but it was observed
that they appeared fairly robust after one of the most severe ordeals of
privation an army had ever experienced. Through these hardships, now
happily being relieved, the private soldiers were sustained in no small

114

measure by an ever increasing confidence in and affection for their commander in chief.

The parade was given religious implication by Washington's order that the brigade chaplains should preside. They read copies of a paper that had been carried at top speed from Falmouth by the royal French messenger. The words proclaimed that France had recognized the independence of the American colonies and would join them in their war against England.

Thereupon the drums rolled, fifes piped, and the guns roared out a salute such as had followed no victory on the battlefield; the ranks pealed forth cheer after cheer, and the rest of the day was given over to jubilee and celebration. Dawn was beginning to show through the darkness that had clouded the American cause during the winter of near despair, a mild winter as seasons went but ghastly still—a winter that had showed few beams of promise while the army anguished and Washington labored and prayed.

As if to offer a rough sort of ominous compensation for the heartwarming intelligence from France, the depressing Major General Charles Lee, self-centered to the point of rudeness, wordy to the point of boredom, returned on May 20 to the army from his captivity as a prisoner of war, bringing with him the pack of hounds whose ears he liked to stroke, and assuming by right of seniority the place of second in command of the Continental Army, inferior in rank only to Washington. Few catastrophes could have been greater than the return of Lee, though none at the time was fully aware of it. A few days later Wayne, the zealous combat leader, was assigned to serve under this lethargic veteran who had been absent from the army during its most stirring engagements—Trenton, Brandywine, Germantown—and while it had been toughened spiritually to the cause through winters at Morristown and Valley Forge.

Wayne's new commander requires some attention. The circumstances of Lee's capture had been so singular as to stir wonder, but in the end it was attributed to fell coincidence or bad luck. Yet there remained doubters. Lee on the occasion certainly allowed bad luck full play to operate against him. A skinny, vain man, with shoulders thin as a greyhound's, Lee was not only a wisp physically but also one of the mental scarecrows seniority not infrequently tosses up in military as well as political affairs. Any warmth that may have existed for Lee among officers and soldiers was chilled in camp when he threatened whimsically to cane a junior officer, and when he denounced profanely and contemptuously the resolution of Congress setting aside a day for thanksgiving and prayer to gain Heaven's favor. He knew little of discipline, though he was supposed to have observed and practiced it in the best armies of Europe, even in the army of the great Frederick. Personally indolent, he was either haphazard or inscrutably designing in his military methods.

After he had been captured in New Jersey there lingered suspicions of collusion on Lee's part, which was probably a softer charge than another that he was merely stupid. He appeared to have been dealt with severely by the British as something of a deserter, having held a commission in the British army, but that, too, might well have been a subterfuge.[1]

Meantime the British in Philadelphia felt the impact of the French-American alliance even more acutely than had Washington's army at Valley Forge. The first apprehension there and in London was that the new commander Clinton would be bottled up by the French fleet. That fleet, under French Admiral Comte Charles d'Estaing (a cavalryman, no less!) was known to be under sail for America. Clinton, ordinarily rated a superior general to Howe, had the advantage of the fairly well united country behind him due to the fact that the war had assumed an entirely new complexion. No longer was it a civil strife between two parts of the British Empire, but a challenge to Britain's survival by her ages-old antagonist whose fleet would soon be sailing impudently off Plymouth. The minister's orders to Clinton were to evacuate Philadelphia by water and return to New York.

Clinton found that the transport tonnage was insufficient for his army, the stores accumulated in Philadelphia, and the hosts of loyalists who elected to accompany him. He decided to march overland across New Jersey. At 3 a.m. June 18, he began his evacuation with about 10,000 troops and twelve miles of baggage train.

Washington had expected a more deliberate withdrawal. By 10 a.m. on the 18th the entire British army was on the New Jersey side of the Delaware and by nightfall, after a brief skirmish, was concentrated at Haddonfield. Maxwell's light infantry brigade of the American army was by that time harassing its flanks and front.

Washington had left his old campground on June 10, moving to the neighborhood of Radnor and Bryn Mawr, for the purpose of getting "a touch of fresh air." He remained in his advance position of observation for ten days. Clinton had made a threatening move in his direction but it was merely to cloak his purpose of crossing the Delaware River. Ashington followed him, crossing at Coryell's Ferry, about forty miles north of Philadelphia.

Behind, he left the desolation of his old Valley Forge huts and drill grounds, replete with memories of hope and suffering, of high confidence and utter despair; memories that must have been regarded in some instances with amusement, now that early summer was at hand: old carpets used in place of shoeleather; the fare of salt pork, bacon, and salt pork again, dragged up from the Carolinas and Virginia, the regular issue meat familiar to most armies of that day; and finally, the grotesque profanity of Steuben, swearing in three languages when angered over the stubborn ineptness of the recruits at drill.[2]

On the hillside where Wayne's men had camped, phantom sentries kept silent vigil. Each winter wind seemed to carry the low moans of the dying. The whir of rustling leaves became a death rattle. Neighbors would not cross the gruesome fields alone at night, where the ghosts of spies that had been freed from their nooses lurked and darted amid the spirits of the patriot dead. Later the ground came to be not haunted, but hallowed.

On the day before he departed from Valley Forge Washington, probably because of a letter from General Lee, called one of his familiar councils of war. Lee on June 15 had condescendingly written to the commanding general suggesting the plans Clinton might be expected to follow. Lee had been conversing around the camp in his customary cynical attitude. His burden at the council, however, where he was the most articulate, was opposition to any kind of an attack. That remained his recommendation, even his urgency, throughout the ensuing campaign. John Marshall characterized his opposition as "vehement." Still he had influence. His impressive arguments of British superiority in discipline, together with references to the satisfactory condition of the American cause now that an alliance with France had been formed, led most of the officers to concur in his wait-awhile entreaty. Not Greene, nor Wayne, nor Lafayette, nor Cadwalader was impressed. Wayne was where he might always be found, on the side of waging aggressive warfare. He and Cadwalader favored attacking the enemy; Lafayette leaned that way, while Greene opposed the mere watching the others favored.

Washington was at heart aggressive and enterprising and instinctively on the side usually taken by Wayne, Greene, and Lafayette. Such was the weight of the opposition, though, that he broke off the council and found refuge in requesting the generals to give written opinions. These were of no consequence because the next day, June 18, Clinton evacuated Philadelphia and the American army was confronted with an entirely new set of circumstances.

When Washington crossed the Delaware into New Jersey, he had no certainty of Clinton's retreat route but he quickly began the formation of reconnaissance and pursuit parties. On the morning of June 24,

1778, when Washington was in the Hopewell area, during an eclipse of the sun that became total at 10 a.m., another council of war was held an hour before as the sun darkened. Again the question was whether to attack. Here again Lee had the answers. Though his breath reeked with liquor, he proved so dominating in his contention that the most absurd thing the army could do was to fight a battle, that once more he persuaded the other generals. Cadwalader was absent. The lone dissenter was Wayne. This was the occasion on which, when Washington had polled the others, he came at length to the brigadier commanding the Pennsylvania Line, and inquired "What would you do, General Wayne?" Wayne turned from the book he was reading. His simple and characteristic answer was: "Fight, Sir!"[3]

Lafayette was strongly for action but thought the proper course was to employ a strong advance party to pounce on the British baggage train when it was moving or off guard. Greene took a similar view. When the council registered its minutes favoring the employment of the army as circumstances might warrant, but specifying that a harassing force should be sent out, Wayne was the only officer who refused to sign. He was wholeheartedly in favor of bringing the enemy into a general engagement. That, in truth, proved to be Washington's desire, but he felt again the restraint imposed by the council.

When he reached Kingston on June 26 and learned the next day that Clinton was marching toward Monmouth Court House (now Freehold, New Jersey), he detached Wayne to accelerate the pursuit. The division Wayne still commanded, formerly Mifflin's, consisted of the 1st and 2nd Pennsylvania brigades, to which had been added Conway's brigade after that general left the service. Wayne had drilled the troops all winter and had the assistance of Steuben in the spring. Washington appointed Lafayette to take command of the advance party after Lee declined it. Lafayette's resourcefulness during the Valley Forge spring and his aggressive demeanor, second only to Wayne's, at the councils reassured Washington on the score of his competence. On June 27 Washington decided to cast aside the verdicts of the recent councils of war and to act on his own good judgment. He felt superior to his antagonist in numbers and could see no great hazard in an engagement on even terms. His advance party now consisted of Scott's brigade of 1,500 men, Maxwell's and Morgan's light troops, and Wayne's division which, though consisting of three brigades, numbered only about 1,200. Altogether the advance party of Washington's army became a respectable force, aggregating 5,000 men. Washington ordered Lafayette to attack the rear of the enemy at "the first fair opportunity."

At this juncture Lee changed his mind. Possibly he had not anticipated that the advance party would be so sizeable or would contain
such fighting units as Wayne's, Scott's, Morgan's, and Maxwell's. It
seemed strange that he suddenly wanted to fight the British when he
had maintained so vehemently that they could not be vanquished in any
manner by Continental troops. Possibly he saw a clear opportunity to
demonstrate what he had been contending all along, that a battle was
inadvisable and should be avoided. With such an unfathomable man
the motives are not readily discernible. In any event, just after Lafayette had put Wayne's, Maxwell's, and Scott's commands, plus some
militia units, into motion toward where the British might be caught on
the move, Lee intervened.

Lee first directed his appeal for the command to the marquis
instead of to Washington. Lafayette, addressed on the basis of his
honor, stepped aside. When Washington learned that Lee had asserted
his seniority he felt he had no other course than to recognize it. Lafayette, in turning over his command to Lee, recommended that two more
brigades be added to the advance party and this Washington ordered
done.[4]

So the loquacious general who had declared at the time Lafayette
first took charge that he was "well pleased to be freed from all responsibility for a plan he was sure would fail," was now in command of that
movement. His mission was a familiar task for advance parties in land
or sea battles. The qualities required were the audacity to attack vigorously and the tenacity to hold faithfully against superior odds until
relief arrived. Charles Lee had neither quality. Either he was timid to
the point of cowardliness, or treacherous, and in its relation to victory
one quality is about as bad as the other. It appears to be a fair conclusion that Lee possessed about an equal quantity of each.

Clinton's route showed that he was marching toward Sandy Hook,
where he would be transported by the fleet to Staten Island. Obviously
he did not intend to move overland to New York by way of Brunswick
and Elizabethtown. Monmouth consequently would be the last likely
place where Washington might give him battle. Beyond that he would
enter the more easily defended country around Middletown and then
gain the security of the fleet's guns. On reaching the vicinity of Freehold, or Monmouth, he decided to halt for a day, rest, and look about
for possible favorable developments. His account refers to his main
army as his "gross" and his forward elements as his "avant garde," in
keeping with the European custom. From his reconnoitering around
Monmouth on June 27, the day before the battle, he concluded that the

defiles, boggy ground, and streams between his and Washington's armies were too forbidding for open action. He discarded any thought of a decisive battle.[5]

Washington decided to attack the British with his advance guard the moment they marched from their resting place at Monmouth. He had word at 5 a.m., June 28, 1778, that the enemy was in motion and immediately sent orders for Lee to attack the British rear. The battle that ensued at Monmouth was a comparatively simple affair, with Wayne doing most of the fighting and Lee the retreating. There were distinct phases: The attack by the American advance guard under Wayne and its defeat of the British; Clinton's turnabout with some of his best troops followed by the unnecessary and amazing American retirement; the arrival of Washington with his main army and his inconclusive battle with Cornwallis' "gross"; and finally, the British retirement at night, their abandonment of the field, and retreat to Middletown.

The Monmouth area was bisected by three ravines, or bogs, which Clinton described as morasses. They influenced operations on the field but in no measure affected the outcome. Since Clinton was on the defensive most of the time they were of greater assistance to him than to Washington. The most important of these bogs made Clinton's initial position strong when Wayne moved in to attack it, since it could be crossed only by a causeway.

Clinton's primary concern was to protect his long baggage train and keep it removed as far as possible from the zone of combat. He entrusted it to Knyphausen and sent it off toward the highlands around Middletown, a distance of twelve miles. To Cornwallis he assigned what he termed his "elite," or "the flower of his army," and gave him the task of beating off the American pursuers if they pressed too closely before Knyphausen had the baggage safely removed. Although Knyphausen's convoy struck out at 5 a.m., Cornwallis held his position of high ground near Freehold Meeting House for three hours, then began to follow. Clinton remained with Cornwallis.

Washington had visited the forward elements of the army on the day before the battle, talked with Lee, then called Wayne, Scott, and Maxwell into conference. Though addressing Lee, he told the group to work out a proper mode of falling on the enemy the instant he marched. He asked that there be no dispute about rank in the conduct of the battle. He felt that while Maxwell was the senior brigadier general in the advance party, the troops he commanded were the greenest of the lot, and he therefore wanted the attack begun by a "picked corps," which, as Wayne quoted him, "would probably have a very happy impression." He wanted the battle to open with spirit and enterprise and, if possible, with a success, and for that he preferred veterans. Whether he was thinking of Wayne's command was uncertain, but it came to pass that Wayne's troops were the ones selected.

The stakes were high. Well within the realm of hope was the possibility that Clinton, laden with his long supply train, might be hemmed in and captured. Washington had ample troops. On the whole they were better disciplined and drilled after the spring months with Steuben at Valley Forge than at any previous time in the war. Burgoyne had been captured when away from his base, why not Clinton?

Most of the forward elements had bivouacked on the night of the 17th in front of Penelopen, now the town of Manalapan, about five miles from Monmouth Court House. There Washington visited them for the second time during the night or early evening. In the night he awoke and became so concerned that the British might make a night march and elude him that he sent another message to Lee directing him to send out a corps of observation to approach close to the British position at Monmouth Court House and give warning if they moved under cover of darkness.

Cornwallis at the court house had about 8,000 soldiers. Lee's assignment was to locate the flank of the British wing under Cornwallis, on which Dickinson with his militia was already hovering, turn it, and cut in between it and the convoy guard under Knyphausen.

The main road over which Lee advanced ran east and met almost at right angles the road from Monmouth Court House running north to Amboy, the juncture being little more than a mile north of the court house. Moving along it, Lee crossed two valleys, or morasses, the "west ravine" and the "center ravine." To Wayne he assigned the center of his line and told the Pennsylvanian that his was the post of honor in the attack—the forward element of the battle, which Washington in his instructions had wanted entrusted to battle-tested soldiers. On Wayne's right were Lieutenant Colonel Eleazer Oswald's four pieces of artillery and beyond that battery, one of Wayne's regiments, detached from his main body, under one of his favorite colonels, Richard Butler. Scott's Brigade was on Wayne's left. At the outset there was a gap between Wayne and Scott, filled a little later by Maxwell and Colonel William Grayson's Virginia regiment detached from Scott's brigade. Lafayette had no command on the field but assigned to himself the supervision of the left. As the action began he saw instinctively that the army had no leadership and wrote urgently to Washington imploring him to hasten forward as rapidly as possible and assume command.

Colonel Butler led Wayne's advance. A body of British soldiers could soon be sighted through the trees. This British rear guard was supposed by Lee to consist of about 1,800 men. Against them he sent Wayne with 700 infantry and two pieces of artillery, then ordered Scott with his 1,400 men to move on Wayne's left, while he with the balance of his troops would take a short cut to the left, as he explained it, and sever their covering force from their main body. From Wayne's position it could be seen that he moved slowly. Wayne skirted a woods, passed over a ravine, crossed the rivulet, and came up against a sizeable detachment of the British covering party, supported by a body of British horse, the Queen's Rangers. He opened fire, upon which Clinton, thus notified of his advance, ordered his dragoons to charge, supported by an infantry detachment. Wayne, with the stalwart assistance of Butler in front, met them with a volley, then promptly drove them back with a bayonet charge.

This marked the first phase of the battle, and it was a highly spirited phase. Wayne assumed that the two armies had clashed for the purpose of fighting to the finish. The memory of Germantown was heavy on his mind. Here was a chance to redeem the failure of that field. As Wayne told the story of this initial action, he had marched about a mile when the command halted for half an hour. He received a message through one of Lee's aides to go forward and take command of all of the troops at the front, as it was "the post of honor," to use Lee's own words. His command was now coming up and he ordered Butler's and Colonel Henry Jackson's regiments to move to the front. They had to cross the morass by a causeway to get into position and form a line of battle. Just then Wayne received a disconcerting order from Lee that he was not to deliver a full-scale attack against the British in his front but was merely to feel them out and detain them, while he, Lee, would make a circuit to their right and cut them off from their main body.

Wayne surveyed the enemy position through his field glass and noticed the horse drawn up in order some distance ahead of the infantry, which he could see with difficulty through the woods. Because the body of the horse seemed exposed, he ordered Colonel Butler to attack it and drive it back. Butler performed admirably. He drove the heavy cavalry into the village beyond the court house in considerable disorder. Wayne looked through his glass and his spirits lifted because, as he later reported, he saw the enemy retiring "in very great disorder and confusion." The horse halted on the British infantry and there restored their formations.

Wayne dispatched a messenger hurriedly to Lee—the first of

Charles Lee, British-born major general next in rank to Washington, an agitator and marplot who by either treachery or timidity, or both, turned an almost certain triumph at Monmouth into a drawn battle, at best. Wayne, the front-line hero of the engagement, testified against him when the court-martial found him guilty of disobedience. *(Courtesy the Historical Society of Pennsylvania)*

many he sent during this phase of the battle—requesting that Lee's troops be pressed forward, but he was told to advance with his own detachments, consisting mainly of Butler's and Jackson's regiments. This he did at once. He crossed the east morass, the last of the three boggy ravines that gave protection to Clinton's front, and found the enemy yielding. He moved ahead until he was about three-quarters of a mile east of Monmouth Court House, and came up to the road between Monmouth village and Middletown, the road over which Knyphausen and then Cornwallis had retired earlier in the morning. East of Monmouth the road debouched into a plain, about a mile wide and three miles long, rimmed by forests.

All Wayne needed at this instant was support from Lee and the disorder that had occurred in Cornwallis' rearguard might have been communicated to his main body, which had up to this stage been moving off toward Middletown. But when Wayne's second messenger reached Lee, that general said he would see Wayne himself and then did nothing further about it. Wayne, having fighting contact with the British on their direct line of retreat, had a finger-nail hold on their army.

This was the juncture of the battle when Clinton reversed the march of Cornwallis. Clinton's rear guard became his "avant garde," and with it he prepared to attack the Americans as they issued from the court house area into the plain. Wayne, already on the plain, had advanced about 200 yards when the British opened on him with three pieces of artillery; then a body of Redcoats moved off to get some high ground to his right, nearly in front of the court house. Wayne sent Major Bliss, his third messenger, to ask help from the American troops he could see behind him, on his side of the morass.

Major Bliss returned with intelligence that the troops he saw had been ordered by Lee to retire and were already filing across the morass to the rear. Wayne found Lafayette, who said he too had been ordered to retire across the morass and form between the court house and woods. Though Wayne was supposed to be in command of the front line elements, his supports were being yanked out from behind him, leaving him isolated, without the commander, Lee, giving him any information about it. The nearest unit in supporting distance was Scott's brigade and it, too, now began to withdraw across the causeway.

In desperation Wayne sent two officers, Bliss and Major Fishbourne of his staff, to find Lee. They returned with the information that the troops had indeed been ordered to retire from the area of the court house and were now in the process of retiring. Had Wayne's attack been too strenuous and too successful for General Lee? As he was witnessing the retreat of the troops in his rear, Wayne received a message by one of Lee's aides, apparently repeated, saying "it was not General Lee's intention to attack them in front, but he intended to *take them*, and was preparing a detachment to throw on their left." Wayne went back to General Scott; he again viewed the ground around the court house, and again sent a messenger to Lee requesting that the troops that were retreating be restored to their former positions.

He could see about 2,000 British soldiers, Cornwallis' advance element, coming up in his front, about a mile across the plain. They were moving to gain the high ground on his right. As he stated it: "Major Fishbourne returned and informed me that the troops were still retreating, and that General Lee would see me himself. Afterwards I perceived the enemy begin to move rapidly in a column toward the Court House. I again sent Major Lenox and Major Fishbourne to General Lee, requesting him at least to halt the troops to cover General Scott, and that the enemy were advancing, and also sent to order Colonel Butler to fall back, as he was in danger of being surrounded and taken." What Lee meant when he said he would see Wayne himself was not further explained. He made no effort to go forward to Wayne's position but fell back abreast of the retreating troops who had now retired a mile behind Wayne's regiments.

Lee had been growing irascible on the field. When Colonel Forman observed the repulse of the enemy's horse by Butler's regiment, he went to Lee and offered to take a detachment by a road on the left and double the enemy's right flank. This was the very maneuver Lee had been talking about when he told Wayne not to be too aggressive in front. Forman quoted Lee's answer, "I know my business." No answer could have been further from the fact. Similarly, Lafayette was taking two regiments, Colonel Henry B. Livingston's and Stewart's, the latter being one of Wayne's Pennsylvania Line regiments, to undertake to turn the British left flank, but before he could get the operation under way he was checked by Lee's order for a general retirement.

These developments occurred while Cornwallis was reversing his march and returning to the court house and while Washington, hearing the cannon ahead, was marching his main body from Englishtown to the battlefield. Wayne had performed splendidly in his front line assignment. Nothing could have irked him more than that the fruits of his enterprise, the rapid march to the field, the labors of his men across three morasses, and their steadfastness under the charge of the heavy dragoons and infantry supports and under the British artillery fire, should be thrown into the discard—as all his efforts had been at Germantown—by the pusillanimous conduct of a boasting general who had insisted on his right to lead, then had demonstrated that he had no leadership quality in his soul.

Wayne's command was grievously exposed. On the left, Scott's Brigade, responding to Lee's retreat order, recrossed the ravine and retired. Wayne, menaced by the return of Cornwallis, who now loomed on the heights above him, had to extricate himself. He pulled back in good order. Much of Lee's retirement, as such matters usually go, became precipitate and disorderly, but the Americans formed on rising ground in the rear. There, on an elevation, the retreating Lee ran directly into Washington, who was advancing at the head of his main army.

Washington had been riding to the battlefield with confidence that all was going well with his plans. The firing had signaled the beginning of the fray and though there were lulls, he had received a message from Lee—the only one Lee sent during the morning—stating that he was turning the British right and expected to cut off the British advance corps from the main.

Dumbfounded when he saw his retreating forces, Washington rode forward with his anger mounting. Whatever doubts remained with Washington were soon removed. Colonel Israel Shreve of the 2nd New Jersey, far from being frightened by the British, showed some amusement when Washington asked why he was retiring. His simple answer was that he did not know the reason, he had been ordered to fall back and such he was doing. Others had much the same story. Colonel Aaron Ogden of the New Jersey Line uttered what was described as a "strong expletive" and said, "By God, they are flying from a shadow."

Lee came back with the last retreating unit. Washington rode toward him and jerked him up abruptly: "What is the meaning of this, sir?" he demanded. Lee, who was usually willing to do most of the talking, was rendered speechless. He hesitated uncertainly, even sheepishly. Washington was surcharged with passion—he was "terrible," said Lafayette, who was nearby and observed it. Some heard him unloosen an oath, some a torrent of oaths, that would have done credit to Steuben. As is not unusual at a moment of high passions, those who heard had different versions. What Washington actually said to Lee became one of the controverted points of the battle, but there is little doubt, despite the disclaimers, that the language was richly ornamented. At the subsequent court-martial of Lee none of the witnesses quoted profane words from the commander in chief; still, profanity in that era was regarded in bad taste when put into cold type, and the absence of the words from the accounts does not mean that General

Charles Scott was wrong when he said Washington's oaths made the leaves shake.

Never was there a period of more intense activity in Washington's army, though never had the humidity been so depressing or the heat so intense. He laid out a new line of defense, part of which happily ran behind a hedgerow: Lieutenant Colonel Nathaniel Ramsay and Stewart on the left, and following down the line, Brigadier General James M. Varnum, Wayne, Livingston, and Oswald with four guns on the left. Stirling and Greene soon occupied strong positions. Steuben was assigned to collect fugitives in the rear. None paid any further heed to Lee, though when Washington accosted him a second time he declared grandiloquently that he would be the last to leave the field. Nobody cared.

When Lieutenant Colonel Robert H. Harrison, one of the aides accompanying Washington, met Wayne, whose troops had been among the last of the retreating units, he was standing with General Scott and Colonel Stewart of his own command. Wayne knew no more about why the army had retreated behind him than did the others. As they talked some light British troops appeared from a woods in front of Clinton's position and pressed ahead until within 400 yards of the group. On observing them, Wayne told Harrison the enemy advance could be halted and seemed unconcerned about the show of strength in his front. He requested that the aide inform Washington of the existence of a road to their right, which passed a hostelry, Taylor's Tavern, on which a body of troops would have to be stationed to prevent a British turning movement of the American right flank. Harrison rode back to Washington and gave him the first information of the proximity of the enemy, who would be on him, the aide calculated, in fifteen minutes. By that time the last of the retreating American troops had been halted.

Wayne, who had found himself well near deserted on the field, had had considerable difficulty in extricating his command and leading it intact across the swamp to the position where a sort of informal rally of the advance guard was occurring and where Harrison encountered him. He kept a good formation and caught Washington's eye with it. He had reached a hedgerow at about the time Washington arrived. One glance was sufficient to inform the commanding general that here was a body of troops on which he could place reliance. Washington ordered Wayne to hold where he was, and on the Pennsylvania troops, stationed behind the hedgerow and through an orchard, the rest of the army was formed.

Cornwallis now occupied the ground that had been held by Lee at the beginning of the battle and from which Wayne had launched his attack on the Queens Rangers. All through the scorching afternoon the two armies exchanged musketry and artillery fire. Cornwallis tested both flanks of the Americans and was repulsed in each attempt, on the left by Stirling, who had a strong position on a commanding hill, and by Greene, with well-posted artillery. But the main action of the afternoon was in front of the orchard that extended toward an eminence called Comb's Hill, where Knox had posted four guns under the able artillery-man, Lieutenant Colonel Eleazer Oswald. Washington kept personal command of the center.

Washington had given Wayne a second "post of honor," the position on the orchard hillside nearby a parsonage and large barn, partly protected by a small stream and a bog on its left front. Here the main battle of the afternoon was fought. Wayne, although devoted to the bayonet, understood equally well the importance of fire superiority, even in the day when the musket lacked the precision and reliability of the later rifle. Cornwallis' line was now well within range, and Wayne kept up a near constant fire against it, some of his troops shielded by the barn. Cornwallis perceived that he could make no progress against either the American center or right until he had cleared Wayne from the orchard and checked his destructive fire. He ordered a frontal assault by some of his best troops.

He selected Lieutenant Colonel Henry Monckton and his celebrated grenadiers, the Sherwood Regiment. This was among the top-ranking units of Clinton's "flower," composed of sons of many leading British families seeking military distinction, and led by one of their most intrepid officers. Recognizing that this was a crucial moment, Monckton aligned his men promptly. A regiment of grenadiers joined as a support. He exhorted them in words that could be heard even to Wayne's position, urging them to charge home with the bayonet. He told them of the pride they might feel in being selected for this attack, and appealed to their stanchness as British soldiers. His words were held to have done as much to inspire Wayne's men as his own.

As the formidable British line approached in beautiful order, Wayne held his fire. The action that ensued was a small scale Bunker Hill, perhaps not less consequential to the American cause than the affair near Boston. Wayne, like Colonel William Prescott, went down the line to exhibit his coolness. He told his men to wait until he signalled. He instructed them to take notice of the officers as they neared the orchard, make sure of their aim, and bring them down first.

There were minutes of tense waiting and silence as Cornwallis and Clinton made this bold effort. In their resplendent uniforms, the regiments marched across the depression and swampland, passed the rec-tory, and charged into the center of the regiments Wayne had trained assiduously for this sort of a trial. There was not a waver in his confident line as his men watched these beautiful, brave soldiers come forward. Most of them knew that here the battle of Monmouth was to be won or lost.

They rushed on Wayne in a furious frontal assault that exhibited high courage. Coming up to battle hand to hand with Wayne's men, they were greeted by a deadly, devastating fire, a volley that seemed almost a sheet of flame. It brought down the brave Lieutenant Colonel Monckton, killed a number of his officers, and shattered the red line of guards and grenadiers. Though the courageous British made a number of valiant efforts to rally and return, they were never able to penetrate Wayne's fire sufficiently to recover their colonel's body, and in the end the regiments of which any army might be proud were driven back in confusion.

Monckton fell at the end of the causeway across the morass and was buried by the Americans the day after the battle in the graveyard of the Freehold Meeting House. He had marched his grenadiers in such a solid column that the story was told of how a single cannon ball fired from Comb's Hill on Wayne's right enfiladed an entire British platoon and knocked the muskets from the hands of every man in it.[6]

Monckton's defeat ended the fury of Cornwallis' assaults. He made no further effort. By now it was late afternoon. As 5 p.m. approached Washington noticed a letting up of the British musketry and artillery fire. Still, the red line remained strongly posted on the elevation behind the low swamp. Wayne's men and the other front line troops had slogged through this bog hopefully in the early morning and now again it was a barrier protecting a much stronger enemy force. Cornwallis had found he could not carry the American lines, either on the flanks or by direct approach, and he, in turn, was not easily assailable.

Clinton reasoned that he had accomplished his purpose of getting his supply train away safely and that the heat made further operations virtually impossible. So intolerable had the heat become that, as he put it, neither army could endure it longer. He said that if he had had four more regiments and less torrid weather he might have expected an advantageous turn in the battle.

That night Washington, exhausted, slept on the ground beneath a large oak tree, with Lafayette stretched out nearby, and his staff scattered under the wide spreading branches, while farther out, the tree was ringed by the bodies of the dead. As darkness came and the British remained in his front, he grew confident of victory on the morrow. But at midnight Clinton withdrew his army. He moved his men so stealthily that General Enoch Poor's corps of observation Washington had stationed near the British bivouac was not aware of their departure. General Poor's scouts went out at dawn and found the British gone.

Clinton refuted all American claims of victory. He made a strong case that the British army was by no means defeated but accomplished its mission of crossing New Jersey with its baggage intact despite being vigorously assailed by the Americans en route.[7] From Washington's standpoint, a victory was wrested from the defeat into which Lee had nearly plunged the army. The Americans remained in possession of the battlefield. They beat off Clinton's best troops when he turned to the offensive. The Americans lost probably 6 officers and 61 men killed, 24 officers and 136 men wounded, and 130 missing, total casualties of 357. Some of the missing, prostrated by the heat, rejoined the ranks. The Americans took exception to Clinton's own casualty figures of 124 dead and 170 wounded. American burial parties reported they had interred 4 officers and 242 enlisted men. Clinton's losses were indeed heavy. The greatest carnage, it was found, occurred in front of Wayne's position in the apple orchard.

Inconclusive as it might seem—a drawn battle, as a neutral analysis would inevitably class it—it became one of the most important of the Revolutionary War. That was because it was the last test of arms between the two main armies, here under Washington and Clinton, prior to the meeting of Washington and Cornwallis at Yorktown. It relegated Clinton to defensive warfare. In the three years of fighting that remained, much of it sanguinary, most of it desperate, only one major military event occurred in the territory north of the Potomac River, and that, at last, as he had long wished, was under the independent command of Anthony Wayne.

In his report to Congress Washington mentioned but one name. It was Wayne's: "Were I to close my account of this day's transactions without expressing my obligations to the officers of the army in general, I should do injustice to their merit and violence to my own fellings. They seemed to vie with each other in manifesting their zeal and bravery. The catalogue of those who distinguished themselves is too long to admit of particularizing individuals. I cannot, however, forbear mentioning Brigadier-General Wayne, whose good conduct and bravery throughout the whole action, deserved particular commendation."[8]

Charles Lee, at his own request, was court-martialed, and his conduct at Monmouth was more in question than his past arrogance. Stirling presided. Wayne was a leading witness and told a straightforward story of all he knew and saw of the morning battle and retreat.

Lee was found guilty of disobedience to orders, improper behavior before the enemy, and disrespect for the commander in chief. Any one of these was grave enough to cause his dismissal, but the generous court merely suspended him from his command for twelve months. That proved insufficient to halt his penmanship. He chose to write an impertinent letter to Congress and that caused him to be struck from the army rolls.[9]

At length he confronted Wayne and young John Laurens of South Carolina, one of Washington's secretaries and aides. Lee turned on Wayne because that general had testified too pointedly against him, as Lee interpreted it. Lee published in a Philadelphia newspaper a sharp rebuttal of some of the points of Wayne's testimony, which caused Wayne, when in Elizabeth, New Jersey, in early January of 1779, to demand an accounting from him. Wayne addressed him: "Sir—The very severe strictures which you were pleased to make on my evidence in the course of your trial on account of the action at Monmouth, and the ungenerous, though free manner, in which you affect to treat my opinion and military character in that, and a late publication in Mr. Dunlap's paper, give a sensation which I can more readily feel than express.

"If it was your intention by these strictures to injure my military character in the eyes of the world, I know that you will have the candor to acknowledge it, as well as courage to accept my demand for honorable redress."[10]

Lee replied with a much longer letter saying Wayne had been mentioned "as the author of my wicked persecution," but he had exculpated the Pennsylvanian of that charge and done justice to his courage. What he had condemned was Wayne's position respecting moves in the battle. He though the step Wayne proposed, the duel, would do Wayne more damage than him but if Wayne persisted he would accommodate him after he had taken his final leave from Congress, published his side of his case to the world, and recovered his vigor from an accident.

Wayne heard from Lee no more. This was the only time in his life he had felt called on to avenge an insult on his character, nor was he ever challenged. John Laurens, resenting Lee's strictures on Washington, whom Laurens felt could not act for himself, challenged Lee and in the duel injured him severely but not critically. Lee went to Virginia to live with his hounds until, on a visit to Philadelphia, he sickened and died. He is an example in American history of a general who fought too little and talked too much. He might have learned much from Wayne.

E L E V E N

Demotion-and a New Challenge

GERMANTOWN GAVE Anthony Wayne a name in the American army; Monmouth made him famous. As Charles Lee emerged from the battle stripped of his prestige, Wayne found his deeds everywhere on the lips of soldiers and civilians alike. He had shown at Germantown that he could plunge through the British army and into its heart; at Monmouth he demonstrated again that his bold, impetuous attacks could disconcert British veterans who had long been contemptuous of Americans and drive them back. The battle had disclosed likewise the tenacity with which his troops, after a winter's drill at Valley Forge, could stand against the close-order assaults of the best soldiers the British generals could hurl against him. The statement of the British colonel after Wayne's attack at Germantown, that "never before had we retreated from the Americans" marked a significant turn in the war. Then came Monmouth, where Wayne confirmed that the day when the Americans gave ground instinctively before the red line of guards and grenadiers had passed into history. The opposing armies would henceforth fight on more equal terms.

Wayne could not yet know the admiration and affection that was being poured out in Philadelphia whenever his name was mentioned. Meanwhile, his home town friends discerned readily that his achievements were ahead of his rank. But just as the public was effusive and at times excessive in its praise, so the governmental establishment was niggardly with rank and money. Some Philadelphians, weak in the details of ancient history but familiar with heroic names, spoke of the orchard at Monmouth in terms of Thermopylae, and of Wayne as an eighteenth-century Leonidas. Wayne had to remain with the army and let the city buzz.

Congress returned to Philadelphia after the British evacuation and the people, after celebrating what appeared a stinging rebuff to Clinton at Monmouth, entered into one of those inexplicable orgies of public misbehavior with which revolutionary wars seem to abound. The two principal reasons were, first, that the city had learned a lack of restraint and a familiarity with easy morals such as in wartime ordinarily arises from occupation by an enemy army; and second, the belief spreading over the country that since France was now engaged with her ancient enemy, the main actions would be fought in Europe and on the seas, with the war in America dwindling off into a subordinate position. Legislative bodies grew reluctant to appropriate American money when, with a little waiting, the war might be won by the presumably vast resources of France.

Wayne advanced with the army to the Hudson River highlands. Both he and Washington were quickly aware of this cooling of the popular ardor. Wayne sent two of his faithful Pennsylvanian colonels, Walter Stewart and William Irvine, to Philadelphia to discern the cause of the apathy and to tell the Pennsylvania Assembly that the province's troops were entering the winter in wretched condition, with their pay grievously in arrears and their clothing again in tatters. Had the Assembly given serious heed to Wayne's entreaties at this time, voiced by his colonels, and later by himself, the critical difficulty with soldiers of the Pennsylvania Line, which for a time menaced the entire cause, no doubt would have been averted.

Washington meantime grew alarmed at the slackening of the public's interest in the war. He detected that the common concern of the people was making money. He had passed through many gloomy days but felt that the liberties of the country were never in greater danger and that nothing could save them except a reformation of the country's own conduct or some decisive turn of affairs in Europe. "It is a fact too notorious to be concealed," he continued, "that Congress is rent by party, that much business of a trifling nature and personal concernment withdraws their attention from matters of great national moment, at this critical period—when it is also known that idleness and dissipation take the place of close attention and application."

Dinner and supper parties were held costing 200-300 pounds while the army in which the hope and future of the country reposed was wearing rags and eating scant rations in the cold. Walter Stewart's letter to Wayne reporting on his mission contained some illuminating paragraphs. First, the stalwart leaders who had nurtured the revolutionary movement were missing from the assembly halls. "How much are we disappointed," he wrote, "in respect to the representation in Congress; the pleasing ideas we had formed of it are now no more. We unfortunately find a real set of Caitiffs have supplied their places. . . . Nothing but party reigns in different bodies."

Colonel Stewart attributed the unhappy state of affairs to the long presence of the British in the country. "Permit me to say," he continued, "a little of the dress, manners, & customs of the town's people. In regard to the first, great alterations have taken place since I was here. It is all gaiety, and from what I can observe, every lady and gentleman endeavors to outdo the other in splendor & show. The manners of the ladies are likewise much changed. They have really in a great measure lost that native innocence which was their former characteristic & supplied its place with what they call an Easy behavior, &c."[1]

Wayne did not get a chance to reply until later in the winter, after he had visited the city and seen for himself what Stewart was describing, experiencing the prevailing atmosphere of indifference. "I need not attempt to give you," he wrote, "a description of the manners, customs, fashions and extravagance of this place, as you had a sample of them on your way through; all the difference is, that the whole rather increase than diminish; and party runs so high, that all public business is at a stand, and all public bodies lulled into an unworthy torpidity, from which nothing will rouse them but the approach of the enemy."[2]

Washington concentrated his army in Westchester County, New York, after Clinton occupied Staten and Manhattan islands. D'Estaing's French fleet arrived while the British fleet under Admiral Howe was inside Sandy Hook but the shallow water prevented him from closing with his larger French ships and he sailed away to cooperate abortively with Sullivan in the siege of Newport. Severe weather and the reluctance of some of the French captains to give him their full confidence because, after all, he was not a seaman sent d'Estaing to Boston to refit and then to the West Indies. Admiral Lord Howe in the late summer of 1778 followed his brother, Sir William, and returned to

England.

When Clinton began withdrawing troops from New England, with the exception of the Rhode Island garrison, and raiding into New Jersey, Washington shifted his main body to the west side of the Hudson, with headquarters at Middlebrook, New Jersey, on the Raritan River, his forces being concentrated there and at nearby Bound Brook. During the winter the army occupied quarters sprawled around New York City from Danbury, Connecticut, through Middlebrook, and on to the Delaware River, with nine brigades west of the Hudson and six east, and a separate garrison at West Point.

While hutted for the winter on a wooded hillside near Middlebrook, Wayne's division was stirred from the top command to the greenest recruit, first, with rumors and then with official intelligence. The Pennsylvania Line was to be reorganized. The procedure was called the "New Arrangement," which the state assembly argued and discussed, then passed into law in February, 1779. Ordinarily a reorganization would have been sensible under such circumstances because the regiments had suffered heavily through three battle campaigns and the winter at Valley Forge, from combat casualties, deaths from illness, desertions, transfers, and other causes. Some of the companies and battalions were so thinly manned that they existed more in name and tradition than in any reasonable strength on the drill ground.

With the Pennsylvania Line, no casualty had occurred at the top. Wayne was there, a brigadier general commanding the division. At times it had dwindled to brigade strength, but for close to three years he had watched over it, drilled it, led it in combat. Between the men and the general there grew an exchange of mutual confidence such as probably did not exist in any other command in the army.

Whatever consternation, then, was occasioned by news of the Pennsylvania Line's "New Arragement," it was mild indeed compared with the upheaval that followed. Official information came that Anthony Wayne, the firm, hard-fighting, confident, much-admired commanding general of the division, was to be degraded to the command of a brigade and that his place would be assigned to Major General Arthur St. Clair.

Few of the men knew St. Clair. Perhaps none knew him favorably. One reason was because on the field at Monmouth, as a volunteer aide to Washington, he had performed but one action of consequence as far as anyone in the division was aware, and that of countermanding Wayne's order for three brigades to come up when he was battling on the front line and sorely needed assistance. With a lack of generosity and with no comprehension of what was occurring in the battle, St.

Clair allowed only three regiments, a mere dribble, to go forward to support his fellow Pennsylvanian. Wayne had never admired the jealous St. Clair but on the Monmouth battlefield his distrust was turned into contempt. Was St. Clair so motivated by petty spite that he would thwart a fellow officer who was carrying the main load of the battle? It seemed so.[3]

St. Clair had been an officer in the British army in colonial days, which, in Wayne's opinion, was so constantly on his mind that he could never view the Continentals with anything but amusement, regarding them as amateurs. He has been described as "a man of mere rules and forms, without a spark of genius," and again, "Possessed of no quick invention, and unable to take advantage of circumstances—adhering to his rules. . . . he failed miserably." On the other hand, "though St. Clair failed in energy and great genius, he was a noble man in his feelings and sympathies, and was not unsuccessful for want of patriotism, or willingness to sacrifice himself. Washington knew this, and hence never withdrew his confidence."[4]

Others have not been so generous in their appraisal of St. Clair, but have regarded slyness and jealousy as his chief traits. Certainly his attitude toward Wayne seems to justify the contention that he was morbid with jealousy. The truth appears to be that he was intolerant of rivalry and looked with envy on those who were winning greater acclaim than he.

Washington, an excellent judge of character, made few mistakes, but his most inexplicable blunder in this respect was his nursing St. Clair along through the war and even after he became President, when the calamitous nature of the man's generalship was at length brought into full view. But Washington did not place him over Wayne. The change was the work of the Pennsylvania government in its reorganizing frenzy. St. Clair had never achieved a victory with Pennsylvania troops nor shown any special brilliance with troops from any quarter, but the strategists in Philadelphia were, in effect, jumping him ahead of some of the best combat officers in the army.

Wayne's reaction on learning that he was to be superseded was at first incredulity, then anger, and at length resignation. These were his men to whom he felt warm personal attachment, who had stood with him at Chadd's Ford, formed the rear guard and held the enemy after Germantown, advanced the farthest and withstood the most spirited attacks at Monmouth. They were linked to him by memories of their lost comrades buried under the snow on the hillside at Valley Forge. The officers were his closest friends—Irvine, who now again led his old brigade; Butler, his peer as a hard fighter and a personal comrade he did not want to lose; Walter Stewart, whom he warmly admired, and many more. St. Clair might command them officially but Wayne would always hold their hearts.

By accepting demotion he would, in turn, be abetting the demotion of some of his worthy colonels. If he returned to a brigade, then some brigade commander would have to be downgraded to the command of a regiment. The squeezing process would demote others. Irvine would become a regimental commander again; so might Butler, and Stewart. Wayne vowed that he would never allow himself to be the cause of degrading his subordinates, which meant very clearly that if he were returned to the brigade level, he would have to leave the service.

Writing from Millstone, New Jersey, to Joseph Reed, now the chief executive of Pennsylvania, Wayne concluded his request for tents, blankets, hats and other urgent requirements, with this suggestive paragraph: "I neither ask nor desire any thing on my own account. I wish for nothing more than an opportunity of returning to my *Sabine field*, with safety to my country and honor to myself."[5]

Reed was astute enough to understand, if he chose, that the state might lose the outstanding officer of the Pennsylvania Line unless it made better provision for its troops and came to a recognition that the war was still far from won.

The "New Arrangement" put the field officers in a disturbed frame of mind. When they heard of it their first impulse was to resign in a body. The rumors began to arrive in mid-October, 1778, only four months after Wayne's superb conduct at Monmouth. With St. Clair's offense against him at Monmouth close in his mind, Wayne wrote a letter bristling with resentment, and though it never was sent, it gives a clear understanding of his sudden rage. He cited St. Clair's scornful remarks about the court-martial that acquitted him of blame at Paoli, then related the incident of that general's failure to support him at Monmouth. Since the letter must have been intended for President Reed or Richard Peters, secretary of the Board of War—apparently being a rough first draft—it probably would have done little good. Of St. Clair's denigrating him throughout the army for Paoli, Wayne impulsively wrote: "Could I but once fix the Caitiff, this world would want a place to hold us both." He was unable, quite clearly, to pin the gossip irrefutably on St. Clair.

After time for reflection, he did write, but to Washington requesting a leave of absence. That would give him a chance to determine his future course. What would be the condition of the army if he should resign at the moment when all the field officers of the division were threatening and might resort to the same action? His affection for the cause and for Washington personally would not allow him to take part in destroying the truly elite command of the army, even though the civil authorities seemed intent on dulling its cutting edge. In the end patriotism triumphed. His letter to Washington was couched in the most reasonable and respectful phraseology.

Wayne wrote to Washington on January 10, 1779, giving as the reason for requesting a leave that he had been summoned to wait on the Pennsylvania legislature, which was in the throes not only of making provisions for the war, but was considering a new constitution to replace what nearly everyone considered a grotesque document no longer suited for the new order. Washington was in Philadelphia and could not influence or participate in the events of Wayne's leave-taking. The Pennsylvania Line was paraded in its glory and strength, even if in appearance most of the men represented sorry spectacles as soldiers of an oncoming and already powerful nation. Wayne restrained himself from any display of mawkishness. There was a legend in the Line that once his heart had been so touched by the miserable appearance of his men that he had broken down in tears at the very front of his division. That was not in character. As he stood before them now, though, there were few dry eyes in the ranks. Their old chief of combat and glory was on the way out. Many of them had been with him at the stand at Three Rivers, on the grueling retreat through the Canadian forest, and in the long winter at "Old Ti." The band played. There stood the adored general, handsome in his white and blue uniform and long, blue capecoat. He made the round of his officers. Even Humpton had been forgiven for failing at Paoli, then instituting the court-martial charges against his commander, and was firm and fresh in the general's confidence. The hills shimmered and the blue Raritan rippled on toward Brunswick and the tides. The carriage door closed and Anthony Wayne was gone, to command the Pennsylvania Line no more.

In a day and half he was in Philadelphia, expecting to meet Washington. But the general had departed before his arrival, going up one bank of the Delaware River while Wayne was traveling down the other. Wayne wrote to him again, mentioning his previous letter and the necessity that he attend the meeting of the Pennsylvania Assembly. He had wanted to wait on the commanding general for a leave of absence, and regretted missing him when they traveled on opposite banks of the river. He told how he had undertaken to make his men comfortable before leaving. Now that his anger had cooled, he accepted the inevitable, especially since Richard Peters had told him that nothing could be done. St. Clair was his senior and therefore entitled to command. Wayne graciously added that the men would be happy under "a gentleman of distinguished merit," and that he "cheerfully" gave place to him. He was positive in his statement that he could not command a brigade in the Line. Then, unaccustomed to closing a letter to the commander in chief without a suggestion, he brought up one of rather novel nature:

"It is known to your excellency that, although a brigadier, I have commanded a division nearly the whole of the last two campaigns, whilst the colonels of the Pennsylvania Line have, for the greater part of that time, alternately conducted brigades, on account of the deficiency of general officers; I have so much sympathy for the feelings of those officers that I cannot think of resuming the command of a brigade.

"I, therefore, wish to be indulged with a situation in the Light Corps, if it can take place without prejudice to the service, or the exclusion of an officer of more worth and experience; but if it cannot be done—I beg your excellency not to spend another thought, or give yourself a single moment's uneasiness on the occasion—but permit me to hope for the continuance of that friendship with which you have heretofore honored me, and, in case of an active campaign, the pleasure of serving near your person as a volunteer."

As the letter sped to Washington, Wayne was surprised to find that all Philadelphia greeted him with marked fondness and honored him above any other officer except Washington. While Mifflin and St. Clair held major general's rank, Anthony Wayne was Pennsylvania's true combat soldier. Greetings of admiration and warmth accompanied him wherever he went, wreaths of boys surrounded him, groups waited at his carriage, toasts were delivered at the taverns in his honor.

One of the noticeable aspects of Wayne's homecoming was that he went, not to his wife Polly, but to Sharp Delaney's house on South Second Street, which he converted into the headquarters of a general without a command. But he adored his children and as soon as his business allowed he rode out to see them. There had been no outward rupture with Polly. They simply ceased to be essential to each other. Meanwhile, Anthony must have seen Mary Vining—how often none can know. Certainly, he was on her mind, because a little later she presented him with a plume for his cap, which suggests that their friendship had been freshened.

He did go to Waynesborough for a short period early in his leave. On his return to the city he found the friendliest note from Washington, dated February 16, 1779; "My opinion of your merits will lead me cheerfully to comply with your request as soon as the arrangements of the army and other circumstances permit the formation of that corps."

Nothing could have elated Wayne more. "When the arrangements of the army," he replied, "and other circumstances will afford an opportunity for the formation of the light corps, or upon any movement of the enemy, I shall expect to be happy to receive your excellency's commands. In the interim, I have an affair of some delicacy [apparently the hangover of the challenge to General Charles Lee], as well as matters relating to my private fortune, which claim some attention; but these shall never prevent me from doing my duty in the field, when my general or country requires my attendance." He told Washington that if his presence could facilitate the formation of the light corps, the commanding general had but to ask.

Wayne did not forget his men for a moment—the men who once were his. He addressed the Pennsylvania Assembly eloquently on their behalf; he had been a member of that body during the uncertainty and turmoil when war with the mother country loomed and when strong men had to decide whether their first loyalty was to home or king. Many of the Assembly members he knew; all were acquainted with him; most of them had followed his actions through each campaign and appreciated the great services and sacrifices he had made to the commonwealth and nation. He gave a full accounting of the Pennsylvania Line, described the scarcities, the wants of the officers, the fortitude of the men whose pay was almost always in arrears, and worth little when it came. The Assembly was not unresponsive. Shortly it passed a pension act that would reward the veteran for life after the war ended; his land taxes were cancelled as long as he served; the men and the miserably clad officers were to be provided with new uniforms suited to their ranks. He helped with the drafting of a new state constitution. The relaxation he had anticipated proved elusive, but a change in the nature of his labors was his reward for the hard army years. They had won him fame, not leisure.

His address to the assembly had repercussions. The field officers of the Pennsylvania Line learned of it and sent him a testimonial letter of their sense of loss by his departure. It disclosed as well as any document in the war the feeling entertained for Wayne by those who had served under him. They expressed "The highest opinion of your integrity and worth" and said they esteemed him as "a Friend, a Brother, & Commander." They mentioned "the open goodness of your heart" and the proof they had of his attachment to them.

Wayne appreciated this and the testimonials of affection that came to him from civilians on all sides. To Colonel Stewart, he said he had enjoyed every minute since arriving in Philadelphia, and participated in the pleasures the city offered "without the least contamination." "I must do the citizens justice to say," he wrote, "that they have honored me with every attention, and treated me with every possible politeness. You know that I have a fondness for ladies' society, yet, excepting the few days which I spent with my family in Chester county, I have not been at a single tea-party since my leaving the army. I have many cards of invitation, and I mean to avail myself of them; this is an indulgence I have some right to claim, having been sequestered nearly four years from the society of the fair, and perhaps the next bullet may make my *quietus*; but a truce of this."

Wayne probably did not expect the developments that followed the leaking of intelligence that a light corps was being formed and he would command it. The reaction was letters from old officers in the Pennsylvania Line and from some officers in other commands, asking to serve under him. The letters reflected the esteem in which he had come to be held throughout the service. He had at first desired to come to the army while the corps was being formed but the letters dissuaded him. He wrote to Washington on May 10 that he preferred to be absent lest it be thought his personal partiality to certain friends was giving them places.

Washington's order came on June 21, 1779, directing Wayne to join the army as rapidly as he could. He left at once, writing a letter of farewell to his family instead of going out to Waynesborough for leave-taking. Delay was unthinkable. He and his orderly rode straight through without sleep from Philadelphia to Smiths in the Clove, New York, whence Washington had marched the army from Middlebrook. Wayne was intensely eager, ardently yearning for combat again.

"Now for the field of Mars," he wrote. "I believe that sanguine god is rather thirsty for human gore. The horrid depredations of the enemy, to the southward, indicate an inundation of it. For my own part, I have never ceased, since the commencement of this war, sincerely to wish that it could be conducted with more liberality; but if that is not the choice of Britain, let us, however reluctantly, adopt the alternative, by neither giving nor receiving quarter; the sooner we close with them on their own ground, the better—as then we shall know what we have to depend on, and our lives be no longer the sport of premeditated and cool villany, but become the price of much blood, and at too great a hazard for Britons to make many purchases."[6]

While Wayne had been involved in affairs in Philadelphia, Steuben, under Washington's direction, had been busy with the formation of a unit that would contain some of the select officers and troops of the army. Washington, who conceived and fathered the Light Corps, was forming an affection for Steuben and a recognition of the benefits of his firm and informed methods. He consequently entrusted to the German disciplinarian the organizational details. Steuben was aided by Colonel François Louis de Fleury, one of the best of the French soldiers drawn to Washington's army and a collaborator with Steuben in the preparation of a manual of infantry drill regulations for the discipline of the army informally entitled, because of its cover, the "Blue Book." This concise manual endured long in the army and was the guide of officers up to the War of 1812. Fleury had been awarded a horse by Congress for his gallantry at Brandywine and would gain later honors, and come to be esteemed by Wayne and Washington.

Fleury commanded a battalion under Wayne after the light corps was organized. Both Steuben and Fleury were familiar with the light troops of Europe, the chasseurs of France and jägers of Germany, and conversant with their methods and their value for rapid movements. When the corps was finally ready for the field, it had among its colonels the officer who was closest to Wayne in all his long service with the Pennsylvania Line, the fearless, intelligent, hard-hitting Colonel Richard Butler—always "Dickie" to Wayne and those who knew him well. He commanded the 2nd Regiment. The Danish Lieutenant Colonel Christian Febiger, an immigrant to Virginia, led the 1st Regiment, which had Fleury as one of its battalion commanders. Febiger had performed ably at Bunker Hill and survived Arnold's march through the Maine wilderness and the attack in the blizzard on Quebec.

The 3rd Regiment, drawn from Connecticut, was commanded by a colonel whose unusual name, Return Jonathan Meigs, would become familiar in later years as governor of Ohio, cabinet member, legislator. The fourth regiment consisted of the North Carolina battalion under Major Hardy Murfree of the North State, and a Massachusetts battalion under the Bay Stater Major William Hull. Hull, an intrepid soldier under Wayne, would be one of the few subordinates not acutated by Wayne's precepts on reaching high command in later years. His pusillanimity in surrendering Detroit at the beginning of the War of 1812 to an inferior force of British, Canadians, and Indians, led by Major General Isaac Brock and the Shawnee chief Tecumseh, caused a court–martial to find him guilty of cowardice and sentence him to be shot. President Madison spared him because of his advanced years and earlier gallant service under Wayne. He had reached the ripe age of fifty-nine! He was twenty-four when he joined the light corps. The artillery complement—two guns—was small, which doubtless pleased Wayne, who knew the use of cannon but still preferred the bayonet.[7]

And now, once the corps was organized and turned over to its new commander, Washington had an immediate task for it.

TWELVE

Stony Point– The Capture that Turned the Tide

WASHINGTON'S ASSIGNMENT for Wayne was one of the most difficult of the war, the capture of the forbidding citadel of Stony Point on the Hudson River at the upper neck of the Tappan Zee. The Hudson upward from its great expanse near Tarrytown narrows where the rock-strewn eminence that naturally would win the descriptive name of "stony" juts into the stream from the right, or west short, reaching toward a companion promontory, Verplanck's Point, on the eastern shore. These two points, less than 1,000 yards apart, commanded the passage of vessels up and down the Hudson. Stony Point had an additional significance in that the western landing of the King's Ferry, the main crossing of the Hudson for military units or civilian travelers between New England, the mid-Atlantic and southern provinces, was immediately to the north, in range of either artillery or small arms from the rocky height.

Stony and Verplanck's points were stepping-stones toward West

Point, around which Washington had collected his army. There he made his headquarters from time to time, regarding it as the main fortress of the highlands. West Point was twelve miles up the river by direct line from Stony Point. For a period when the light corps was being organized, headquarters were at Smith's in the Clove, as Washington named it in his correspondence, but often termed Smith's Clove, a mountain pass not far from Haverstraw, New York.

Above Stony Point and on the west side of the Hudson the Americans had Forts Montgomery and Clinton, both roughly opposite the high east-bank ridge called Anthony's Nose. Above Stony Point, the highlands, one of the outstanding scenic charms of eastern America, extend for about twenty miles past Donderberg, or Thunder Mountain; past Bear Mountain and on past West Point and the Storm King. The river above Stony and Verplanck's points widens again into what the Dutch knew as the Zuider Zee, or Little Sea, near the top of which, eight miles above Verplanck's, is Peekskill. There Fort Independence had been built. Stony Point and Verplanck's separate the Tappan from the Zuider Zee.[1]

When Sir Henry Clinton sailed up the Hudson in October 1777 in a gesture of cooperation with Burgoyne, he captured Forts Clinton (named for Governor George Clinton of New York) and Montgomery, which the Americans had built in early 1776 of stone and earth. At Fort Montgomery the river had been blocked by a huge chain, chevaux de frise, and a boom extending from Poplopen's Kill on the west bank to Anthony's Nose on the east. After capturing the forts the British cleared these obstructions and opened the Hudson to their ships and transports. The Americans evacuated Fort Constitution across the river from West Point. All of this was while Howe was on his campaign against Philadelphia and Burgoyne was gradually being hemmed in and pressed toward Saratoga.

More than a year and a half later, in the summer of 1779, Washington had nullified these British advantages by shifting his main army to the highlands. Clinton had been content with organizing raiding parties in Chesapeake Bay, New Jersey, and Connecticut, on which there was a deal of incendiarism and looting that gained no military advantages but merely angered and incited the Americans to more stubborn resistance.

While the British were thus engaged, and before Washington transferred his army from New Jersey, he began to fortify West Point. He reactivated Forts Clinton and Montgomery, built Fort Lafayette on Verplanck's and began the construction of a fort on Stony Point. In late May, 1779, learning that Sir Henry Clinton, whose headquarters were in Phillipsburg, (now Yonkers) had moved up to White Plains, he accelerated the shift of his army and reached the highlands in early June. Meantime Clinton, informed of American activities in fortifying the highlands, assembled a flotilla of ships and barges under Commodore George Collier and with about 5,000 men again sailed up the Hudson. He landed downstream, on the east bank, as though to threaten Peekskill, but in the morning fog of May 31 crossed and easily captured Verplanck's and Stony Point. The latter's fortifications had not been completed and the thirty soldiers who comprised the garrison escaped. Washington, being short of men, had garrisoned Stony and Verplanck's lightly, merely to protect King's Ferry from marauders.

Clinton began at once to strengthen the two natural citadels, giving preference to Stony Point, which he garrisoned with 600 men under Lieutenant Colonel Henry Johnson, of the 17th Regiment of British foot, who had, attached to that regiment, a company of the 71st grenadiers, a company of American Loyalists, and a detachment of the Royal Artillery. About the only weakness in the British resolution to hold Stony Point was that the works now constructed were ample to accommodate a garrison of more than twice the size. Johnson therefore had to man his ramparts thinly.

As a natural bastion Stony Point was formidable. It comprised about 100 acres of almost solid granite, washed on three sides by the river and at high tide on four, but in those days connected with the mainland at low tide by a swampy isthmus difficult to traverse. The approach up the incline from the swamp side was gradual until an elevation of about 150 feet above the river was reached. On all three of the water sides, north, east, and south, the descent to the river was sharp from the summit.

The defenders built in June and early July well-conceived and carefully constructed fortifications. At the summit they erected a stone and earth fortress consisting of a series of redoubts, with artillery placed to the best advantage. About fifty feet down the slope they stretched a heavy abatis. This, a conventional defense of the day, consisted of felled trees with the branches pointed toward the enemy. The branches were then sharpened into points at the ends and the loppings were thrown among them, thus making a barrier nearly impenetrable for foot soldiers. The readiest method of entry was to cut through the branches and brush with axes, a hazardous task when the abatis was well defended. Artillery sometimes was employed. The first row of abatis, moving down from the summit, was given added strength by the construction behind it of three redoubts frowning with brass 12-

pounders and manned by grenadiers. Farther down lay another row of abatis.

Little likelihood existed that the fort could be carried by surprise. Pickets were posted on the mainland at four strategic points on the promontory itself. The artillery complement had the strong armament of four brass field pieces, four iron cannon, five mortars, and a howitzer. Added to all this, Clinton designed to have the garrison protected from the water by the armed British vessels in the river, conspicuously the sloop-of-war *Vulture* anchored nearby.

As General Nathanael Greene described it after an inspection: "the place is as difficult of access as any you ever saw, strongly fortified with lines and secured with a double row of abatis. The post actually looks more formidable on the ground than it can be made by description. . . ."

Wayne took command of the Light Corps on July 1, 1779 at Sandy Beach near Fort Montgomery, though it had not yet been fully assembled. Colonel Butler's battalions were there. Washington gave Wayne a letter of general instructions telling him his chief purpose was to oppose any movement of the enemy against the American forts, to examine the possible landing places and approaches, gain all possible information about the designs of the enemy, engage trusty persons as spies, and to take advantage of any opportunity that appeared for an advantageous stroke. Washington sent an additional private and confidential letter calling his particular attention to the need of repossessing Verplanck's and Stony Point, telling him to gain exact knowledge about the garrisons, the terrain, enemy vessels in the river, and the precautions being taken by the enemy for security. Then he disclosed the reason why he had summoned Wayne: "It is a matter I have much at heart to make some attempt upon these Posts (in the present weak state of the garrisons and before the enemy commence any other operations) if warranted by the probability of success." He told Wayne to acquire the necessary information, then report on the feasibility of surprising one or both of the posts, "especially that on the West side of the River."

There is a tradition of long standing, perhaps historical, first related by Washington Irving, that when Washington divulged to Wayne that the purpose of summoning him was to have him storm Stony Point, and looked at him questioningly, Wayne impulsively replied: "General, if you will only plan it, I'll storm Hell!" To this a comment from Washington has sometimes been added: "Perhaps, General Wayne, we had better try Stony Point first."[2]

Wayne could have felt complimented had he known that when

Wayne Wounded at Stony Point. Personally leading his men in the night attack, Wayne carried the citadel with the bayonet and gave fresh inspiration to Washington's victory-starved army at one of the low periods of the war. A musket ball hit him in the forehead as he neared the top abatis. Blood gushed and the wound appeared fatal but he insisted that the men carry him into the British works so that if he died, he could die at the head of the column. *(Courtesy the Historical Society of Pennsylvania)*

Washington organized the Light Corps and decided to take Stony Point, the first and only general he considered for leading the attack was Wayne. Morgan had wanted the assignment and resigned temporarily when he did not get it.

Though it was the intention that the corps be composed of the elite of the army, the companies, drawn from a number of states, were all in the conventional army tatters and lacked equipment, these being the first matters to which Wayne gave attention. Another of his requisitions was for enough copies of Steuben's new "Blue Book" on tactics that every officer in the corps could be supplied. He found that there were but two copies in the entire corps. He ordered a supply of espontoons (spontoons), a type of short pike or halberd used by subordinate infantry officers of the eighteenth century. Wayne carried one of these in the action. To the infantry soldiers he gave his favorite assignment, bayonet drill.[3]

While the preparations were under way, Wayne complied with his instructions to examine the country. He took Colonel Butler and Major John Stewart of Maryland (not to be confused with Walter Stewart, his colonel and friend of the Pennsylvania Line days) to reconnoiter the enemy positions at Stony Point. They went to the top of the Donderberg, looked down through the summer foliage on the fort and its approaches, studied it long and returned late at night.

Wayne from the mountain top prepared a sketch of the territory which he submitted to Washington. It differed little from a map Butler had made earlier, but as he told Washington, it would give a general idea of the strength of the enemy works on the west side of the promontory. They were too formidable, in his opinion, to be taken by storming, while much time would be required to reduce them by regular approaches, since there was no ground within half a mile that the guns of the fort did not command. He also described the works on Verplanck's Point, then suggested as a possible plan sending a reconnoitering party to approach the fort as a bait, after letting its whereabouts be known beforehand to one suspected of being a spy. The garrison thereupon might prepare an ambush, upon which the main body of the Americans, which would be nearby, would enter the fort with them as they retired. He toyed with the notion and planned the venture, but did not carry it through; on further examination it did not offer much promise.

He invited Washington to reconnoiter the works with him and agreed to cover the commander's movements with an adequate force. Washington accepted and two days later they went out early. So easily did intelligence spread that the *New York Gazette and Weekly* published on July 12 a letter from Stony Point dated July 7, saying: "Yesterday Mr. Washington, with several other Rebel Officers were reconnoitering our Post, attended with about 500 men, 13 of which Number chose to come to us in the Course of the Day, by whom we learn, That the Report among them is, That an Attack on the Post is intended. I have no doubt that it will prove a serious Affair to them."

Since the letter was published in New York three days before Wayne made his movement, there is little question but that the garrison had been put on the alert. Still, Captain Allan McLane, one of Washington's best scouts, who had gone back and forth into Philadelphia at will during the Valley Forge winter, was keeping his chief informed in the highlands. Disguised as a farmer, he went into Stony Point, gained a good impression of the defenses, and inspired the chief with the confidence that by a properly executed plan the place could be carried by *coup de main.*

Washington was growing restive for some kind of successful action, well aware that the country fretted over the raiding parties Clinton was sending out from New York. He felt the reputation of the army was at stake, and hoped that a fuller examination might show that the works were vulnerable. A deserter had told him of a sandy beach on the south side of the promontory running along the flank of the works, which might offer a safe approach: "I wish you to take every step in your power to ascertain this point, and to gain a more accurate knowledge of the position in general, and particularly on the flanks and in the rear," he told Wayne.

Washington followed this on the next day, July 10, with a long letter setting forth a detailed plan of operations for a surprise by a party of 1,000-2,000, preceded by a vanguard of "prudent and determined men," who would secure the sentries and remove the obstructions, then advance with fixed bayonets and unloaded muskets. Each officer was to know exactly what part of the enemy line he was to possess so there would be no last minute confusion and indecision. The main body was to follow to make good the advantages gained or to bring off the advance party in case of a repulse. He suggested that a white feather or cockade or other visible badge be worn by Wayne's troops and that a watchword should be established to distinguish friends from foes. Secrecy was essential; a single deserter might destroy the entire project. Because the usual time for such exploits was just before dawn, he suggested that the defenders might be most vigilant then, and recommended the attack be made at midnight.

"These are my general ideas of the plan for a surprise," he wrote, "but you are at liberty to depart from them in every instance where you think they may be improved or changed for the better.—A dark night and even a rainy one if you can find the way will contribute to your success."

There were additional details. The letter, in Washington's own hand, shows the amount of thought he had given to the attack and how important he believed it was to lift the country's morale and its confidence in the army. After studying the letter, Wayne, on the next day, July 11, made another reconnaissance, accompanied by Colonels Butler and Febiger, after which Wayne drew up his own plan of attack. He followed in most respects Washington's suggestions. This plan he submitted to Washington on July 15, the day he began his movement. The day before, Washington had received a report from one of his competent engineers, Colonel Rufus Putnam, whom he had sent to make an independent reconnaissance. Putnam had devoted three days to his survey of the works and the countryside and reported favorably on the prospects of an attack. A recommendation had been made for a post-ponement but Wayne was impatient and brushed it aside. So did Washington. Finally, on July 14, Washington authorized Wayne to make the attack on the night of the following day. Wide latitude was given to the corps commander as to the time and mode of the attack, irrespective of former plans or orders. At 11 a.m., July 15 Wayne delivered to Washington his "Order of Battle" which he had worked out after his last reconnaissance. It altered Washington's plan by providing for two attacks, in place of one main attack, and for one feint. This feint proved one of the important features of the assault.

Wayne also ordered Colonel Ball's Virginia regiment to follow in the rear of the light corps on its march and said he would give it out that the entire Virginia Line was in support. That might add to the confidence of the soldiers—"it can have no bad effect—but it may have a very happy one." In the end, he did order Muhlenberg's brigade, mainly Virginians, to stand by.

On the morning of the 15th, before beginning his march, Wayne sent three parties of picked and reliable men under trusted officers to go to the neighborhood of the fort and hold the passes employed by the countryfolk for taking in provisions, so there would be no remote chance of word getting through. Washington directed that the storming party be accompanied by two artillery platoons that could man the heavy ordnance of the fort and play on Verplanck's across the river and on the British shipping, once Stony Point had been won. General Robert H. Howe was under orders to storm Verplanck's as soon as he got Wayne's message of success at Stony Point. About twenty artillerists marched with Wayne, leaving behind their two field pieces.

Secrecy remained paramount. No soldier would be allowed to stray from the ranks. If under any circumstances a soldier had to drop out, an officer would remain with him until he returned. Strict silence was ordered. None of the soldiers knew beforehand the purpose of a movement that obviously was imminent but some could make good guesses. Not until July 14, the day before the march would begin, was Meigs' detachment brought over from the east side of the Hudson and concentrated with those of Butler and Febiger. Though there were four regiments, or demi-regiments, the force was indeed small for such a venture, numbering about 1,400 officers and men. But they were selected men, the best Washington and Steuben could assemble. Rufus Putnam kept his regiment on the east side, occupying Fort Constitution. In some accounts he is mistakenly placed in the assault party. Hull's battalion was brought down from West Point. Technically it was not a part of the Light Corps but was merely attached to it.

A significant point in Wayne's preparations was that there would be no unusual assembly of troops at or near Stony Point. He astutely guarded against any tell-tale concentration that would warn of an impending movement, well knowing that farmers were continually entering Stony Point with fresh provisions and might purposely or innocently divulge what was happening.[4]

July 15 began as any other day with the light corps except that its strength was augmented by the acquisition of Meigs and Hull. There was no drill. Wayne was busy reviewing his final "Order of Battle" and sending it to Washington while the soldiers, by his command, shaved and powdered their hair. As he had told Washington, he was "prejudiced in favor of a soldierly appearance." Some of the soldiers noticed packs of dogs being brought in by Light Horse Harry Lee's scouts. Wayne had given orders that every dog within three miles of Stony Point should be brought in or destroyed. A single bark might defeat the entire enterprise. The men expected they would be dismissed for the noon meal. Instead, the officers made the closest inspection and then Wayne passed down the ranks, frowning and correcting any dereliction, his eyes dancing with delight when he passed an exemplary platoon. The espontoons had arrived. The corporals and sergeants had been familiarizing themselves with the weapons that were already becoming novel in warfare and carried them now instead of their muskets. Then, still with no break in the ranks for dinner, the adjutant at noon bellowed the command of forward and the Light Corps of Washington's army was off on a venture that would become one of the high points of American military history.

At Sandy Beach they were fourteen miles by the winding trails and roads from Stony Point. They worked over the rough, rocky ground and through midsummer thickets, much of the time in Indian file. They looped back from the river to pass around Bear Mountain and then skirted the western base of old Donderberg looming above them, wrapped in its own silence. Wayne himself gave a graphic description of the march: "The roads being exceedingly bad and narrow, and having to pass over high mountains, through deep morasses, and difficult defiles, we were obliged to move in single files the greatest part of the way."

Their timing had been perfect. They had rested and refreshed themselves once at a farm house and finally, at 8 p.m., when the sun had sunk behind the tossed and rounded hills, they reached the cleared land of David Springsteel's farm south of Donderberg Mountain. Stony Point was only a mile and a half away. So carefully had the march been patroled that Wayne could be confident they were still undetected. As

an added precaution he had seized and sent back every civilian encountered or passed on his route. While the tail of the light corps was
coming up and being formed, Wayne went ahead to get a final view of
the Stony Point approaches. Four hours remained before attack time.

In front of him rose the lowering, craggy citadel Washington coveted so earnestly. There at length was a worthy test for his bayonets;
before him fame and glory—victory that would fire the people with
fresh confidence. There, too, was possible failure—death. Still, he
would lead the attack on foot, picking his way through those great piles
of brush and over the jutting shelfs of stone to the summit. Those were
the thoughts that apparently passed through his mind as his eyes swept
over the hills and across the river, and made one last close study of the
thin strip of beach along the south shore of the jutting crag, and the
meager causeway of slush and sand, lapped by the wavelets of the river.
All seemed normal and calm at the fort.

He returned to Springsteel's. Standing in front of his men, he gave
them their first positive information that they were to capture Stony
Point at midnight. The little army was divided into two parties, as it
came up—Febiger's on the right with his own regiment in front, followed by the regiments of Meigs and Hull. Wayne would move with
this column. Butler commanded the left column, his own regiment
being followed by Hardy Murfree's North Carolinians with their special
mission. The attack party made a sort of "rainbow division," being
composed of troops or officers from Massachusetts, Connecticut, Pennsylvania, Maryland, Virginia and North Carolina. All of the orders
were delivered in low voices. Unusual sounds, shouted commands,
might travel a mile and a half on the night air.

Ahead of each attacking column would go an advance party of
150 men. Wayne's officers called for volunteers and they stepped forward eagerly, the question being who would be left behind. The officers
already had instructions about the routes they would follow in approaching the fort at the summit. They took their places at the heads of
the columns. The advance party on the right was commanded by the
scion of the famous French house, Lieutenant Colonel François Louis
de Fleury. The vanguard of the left column, Butler's, was commanded
by the Marylander, Major John Stewart.

Then came the selection of two "forlorn hopes." Each had twenty
hardy men and each was as quickly filled with volunteers as were the
two vanguards. So many volunteered that the acceptances had to be
made by lot, and according to a current newspaper account one soldier
who was excluded "spoke of himself as a child of misfortune from the
cradle." That on the right was led by Lieutenant George Knox, on the

left by Lieutenant James Gibbons, both Pennsylvanians. Each man in the "forlorn hopes" was provided with an axe. The duties were to cut passage ways through the two rows of abatis so the advance parties might enter.

Each man of the Light Corps was given a square piece of white paper with instructions to fix it prominently on the front of his cap. Washington had foreseen the need of this but paper was more readily procurable than cockades. Then came the admonitions and finally the announcement of the awards. Among the first, silence. No soldier (with the exception of Major Hardy Murfree's regiment) was to carry a loaded musket. All soldiers were to advance with fixed bayonets, the noncommissioned officers with their espontoons. None in the assault columns was to fire a shot, on pain of death. Anyone who disobeyed orders would be shot by an officer on the spot. If there were a skulker, if any man retreated, an officer would shoot him down. There would be no panic in Wayne's command; for him a soldier faced in only one direction.

As Wayne stated it in his address to the men: "The distinguished honor conferred upon every officer and soldier who has been drafted into this corps, by his Excellency General Washington, the credit of the States they respectively belong to, and their own reputations, will be such powerful motives for each man to distinguish himself, that the General cannot have the least doubt of a glorious victory."

Finally, the adjutant doing the suppressed announcing stated that on the word of General Washington the first man to enter the enemy works at the summit would be given a reward of five hundred dollars. The second man inside would receive four hundred, the third three hundred, the fourth two hundred, and the fifth one hundred. Then it was made known that Wayne would lead the attack personally.

More so than at any other time in his fighting career, Wayne had a premonition of death as he waited before moving forward. In the tense half-hour after all had been made ready, he went into the Springsteel's parlor and wrote a letter to his friend of long standing, Sharp Delaney, whose house he had but recently left in Philadelphia.

Some wonder has been expressed that he did not write his last letter to his wife, Polly, but Wayne lived in a man's world, as far as his affairs were concerned. He wanted the papers he carried with him, mostly his orders and correspondence relating to this campaign, in competent hands. The letter showed no lack of concern about Polly. It made the most affectionate references to her, asking that she be comforted. It was not to be sent unless he fell in the attack, but it was preserved by him carefully, as were most of his letters. It is a revelation of Wayne's deep respect for his commander, Washington, and his bitterness, grown almost to an obsession, over what he regarded the neglect of the army by Congress. Two paragraphs:

> you have often hear'd me default the Supiness & unworthy torpidity into which Congress were lulled—& that it was my decided Opinion this would be a Sanguinary Campaign in which many of the Choicest Spirits, & much of the best blood in America would be lost, owing to the parsimony & neglect of Congress.
>
> if ever any prediction was true it is this—& if ever a great & a good man was Surrounded with a Choice of Difficulties it is Gen Washington—I fear the Consequences—I see clearly that he will be Impelled to make *other* attempts & Efforts in order to save his Country—that his numbers will not be adequeat to—& that he may also fall a Sacrifice to the folly & parsimony of our *Worthy rulers*

One of the engaging, human interest stories about the march from Springsteel's to the river was obtained by Benson J. Lossing, who visited the Stony Point country in 1848. According to the story, Wayne was guided on his approach by a Negro slave named Pompey, who belonged to a Captain Lamb in the neighborhood. The story was accepted and used by Washington Irving in his *Life of George Washington*, and subsequently by others. If true, it is a conspicuous example of Negro contributions to the cause of American independence.

Lossing found that an old Stony Point ferryman was well acquainted with the slave Pompey, whom he described as astute and observant. When the British occupied Stony Point in early June he went there to sell strawberries. Being of a friendly disposition, he found that the British officers received him pleasantly and asked him to return. He brought more strawberries and when cherries ripened brought them too, and developed a regular business, but all the while he was observing their work on the defenses and reporting what he saw to Captain Lamb, his master. Lamb, in turn, a stanch supporter of independence, forwarded all the intelligence to Washington. Then, as the story went, Pompey told the British he could come no more in daytime because corn hoeing season was at hand. The British wanted his fresh fruit and vegetables and regularly gave him the password so that he could come at night. The British countersign on the night of the attack was, according to the old ferryman's account, "The fort is our own," which Wayne, when he learned it from Pompey, adopted.[5] While Wayne was before the soldiers at Springsteel's, the adjutant gave them the countersign, or watchword. It was to be shouted when they entered the enemy works and not before that—"with a Repeated & Loud voice." It was "The Fort's Our Own!"

Surprising the first of the British pickets, on the mainland west of the marsh and causeway, Wayne's men were able to overcome and gag them before they sounded an alarm. This throws some credence on the story that they were guided by the Negro Pompey and were able to approach by using the British password. Pompey was accompanied by two stout soldiers disguised as countryfolk, according to the ferryman.

When they came to the riverbank they found that the tide was in and the marsh and causeway were flooded. The flood tide was a risk they had to take in order to deliver their attack at midnight. Probably the garrison would not expect an attack with the tide in. The high water slowed them for twenty minutes and threw them that much behind their schedule, which had been adhered to scrupulously. Febiger's column, with Wayne at its head, preceded by one of the "forlorn hopes," and the advance party under Fleury, went to the right, or south, where it was able to pick its way along the ribbon of the shoreline. The tiny creek that ran across Stony Point imposed no obstacle. They did not have to wait for the axemen to clear the first abatis, but moved around its end, for the most part, where it reached the water.

Apace with Wayne and Febiger, Butler's regiment, followed by Murfree and preceded by the advance party under Stewart and the "forlorn hope" under Gibbons, kept to the left, crossed the little brook at what had once been a bridge, and came to the foot of the sharp rise reaching toward the citadel. There they captured another British picket, but by this time the approach had been discovered, the picket fired, and an alarm, "To arms! To arms!" was being shouted from the ramparts of the fort. There was firing also by the picket that had detected Febiger's approach on the other bank.

At this point came a most important phase, the dénouement of Wayne's attack plan. By prearrangement, Major Hardy Murfree's two North Carolina companies moved to the right of Butler, took a position in the center abreast the main road to the fort, outside the lower abatis, and opened a fusilade directly on the enemy works. These were the only men privileged to have charges for their muskets. Their orders were to keep up a galling fire. They fired at will and so rapidly that, as Wayne had hoped, Lieutenant Colonel Johnson believed they constituted the main American attack and that it was being delivered against his center. With what under normal circumstances would have been commendable enterprise, Johnson took a sizeable portion of his garrison, upwards of 200 men, left his enclosure, and charged down the hill to drive the impertinent attackers back through the morass and away from the point. The night was dark—altogether starless, some said. That was mainly because the cannon and musket smoke quickly spread a heavy cloud over defenders and assailants. The stars had been out when Wayne's men moved from Springsteel's. Murfree's two companies, like the Americans on the flanks as they clambered toward the summit, were aided immensely by the white paper tags on their hats. Even in the murky blackness there was no instance where, as at Germantown, Americans fought each other.

Meantime Johnson's artillery had opened with grape and bomb shells, and some in afterthoughts held this fire to have been highly effective. In fact, it did little if any slaughter. The guns were posted primarily for protection against hostile vessels or landing boats coming from the river. They could not be depressed readily to sweep the land approaches immediately beneath them, and most of the grape and shells passed over the heads of the attackers and fell in the water. Wayne mentioned only grape in his report. Through the incessant roar of the guns and the sharper clatter of the musketry, Johnson and his men fighting Murfree suddenly heard shouting above them—the shout of the American watchword, "The fort's our own!" Hastening back up the hill, they found that indeed it was true. The British inside the fort were laying down their arms and asking for quarter. Johnson's only course was immediate surrender. It was all over in the brief span of twenty minutes.

The right column, with Wayne, Febiger, Meigs, and Hull, was first. It floundered across the morass, the water coming to the shoetops of some of the men, to the waists of others. The splashing and miring in the water alerted a sergeant with a picket and the fire aroused the garrison of the fort at about the time another picket opened on Butler's column. After skirting the end of the lower abatis, they started up the incline. Wayne, carrying a spontoon, was at the head, with his two aides, Henry W. Archer and Benjamin Fishbourne, closely behind him. The musketry ahead was incessant. The axemen of Knox's "forlorn hope" cut the second abatis apart and the gallant Fleury pushed ahead of the advance party as the Americans poured through. The fort was fifty feet above them, so close they could hear the British soldiers shout tauntingly through the clatter of the firearms, "Come on, you damned rebels!" On they came, the Frenchman Fleury still in their front, the others close behind.

At this top abatis, Wayne suddenly spun and fell. A musket ball had hit him at the center of his forehead. Anyone at first glance would have pronounced the wound surely fatal. Stunned by the impact of the heavy ball, he was on the ground an instant, then rose and rested on

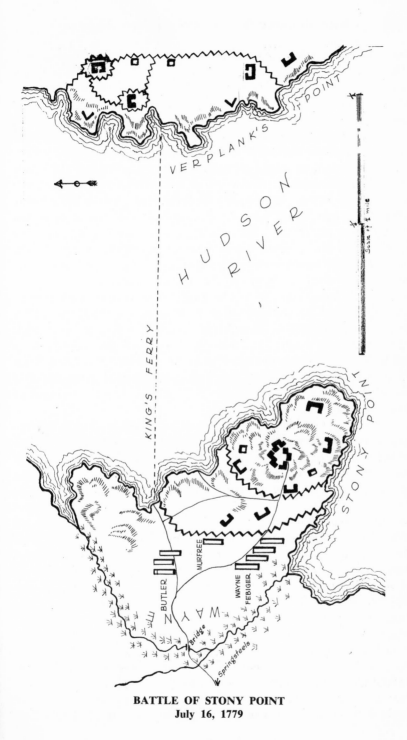

BATTLE OF STONY POINT
July 16, 1779

one knee. He assumed that his premonition of death had been correct, for the blood poured down his face. His first remark was "Forward, my brave fellows, forward!" His aides, Fishbourne and Archer were quickly with him. "Carry me into the fort," he told them. "If I am to die I want to die at the head of the column!"[6]

Soon it was apparent that the ball had not shattered his skull but had merely grazed across it for two inches, leaving an annoying wound and later a scar that would carry Stony Point with him until his death. Again he took the lead, wielding his spear to point at the objective, and directed the remaining men through the hole in the abatis. Writing about it later to Major Thomas Posey, who was among the protesters for more credit after the battle, he said it was "too well known that I myself continued to direct it (the battle) even after I had Rec'd my wound—& that at the point of my Spear—I at least helpt to direct the greater part of the Column over the Abatis and into the Works, & to take measures to Secure them and the prisoners after (which perhaps may not be so well known to you Sir as to other Gentlemen)." The last caustic remark indicated Major Posey may not have been there, though his contention was that he was the first in the works. Helped by his aides, Wayne went into the fort with Febiger's main body. Later Major Hull claimed he and other officers had carried him up. No doubt a group assembled around him after he fell and helped or accompanied him into the fort.

Those of the right column, alarmed and angered by their leader's fall, many believing the report that he had been mortally wounded, charged desperately with the bayonet, hurling themselves furiously over the rocks. Reaching the ramparts, Lieutenant Colonel Fleury jumped ahead and over them and let out the shout, heard clearly by those below in strong French accents, "The Fort's Our Own!" Later there were other claimants but Fleury's was the name Congress put on the silver medal it struck for him, the words being, "A memorial and reward of valor and daring. The American Republic has bestowed [this medal] on Colonel D. de Fleury, a native of France, the first over the walls." The reverse side showed the fort and batteries and stated: "Mountains, morasses, foes, overcome," and, below the fort, "Stony Point stormed, 15th of July, 1779." The date should have been July 16, as it was after midnight.

Fleury probably never saw the token of appreciation. He returned to France soon after the storming. Seventy-one years later a lad digging aimlessly at Princeton, New Jersey, turned up the medal. The supposition was that Congress received it when in session at Princeton, or when some of its officers were there, and lost it. During his brief stay in

America, Fleury left an enviable record, his part in the sanguinary repulse of the Hessians at Fort Mercer, and now his performance at Stony Point. The award of five hundred dollars he distributed to those of his advance party who went in just behind him.[7]

Fleury, on reaching the fort, seized the British flag flying above it and hauled it down. Following close behind him came Leiutenant Knox, commander of the right "forlorn hope," the second man inside the fort. After that, pressing, came Sergeants Baker and Spencer, both of the Virginia Line. Baker, who was third, had four wounds, Spencer two. The fifth to enter was Sergeant Dunlop of the Pennsylvania Line, who bore two wounds.

Fleury beat Major Stewart's advance party on the left by no more than an instant. The left column had had more difficulty at the abatis, where seventeen of the twenty men of Gibbons' "forlorn hope" were either killed or wounded. Despite this, they breached the two barriers and Stewart, followed by Butler's regiment, mounted the ramparts. The American artillerists quickly turned the fort's guns against the ships off Verplanck's Point. When dawn came they bombarded also Fort Lafayette on Verplanck's, but ineffectually.

As Wayne explained his own part: "I placed myself at the head of Febiger's regt. or right Column, and gave the troops the most pointed orders not to fire on any account, but place their whole dependance on the Bayonet; which order was literally & faithfully obeyed. Neither the deep morass, the formidable, and double rows of abatis, or the strong works in front and flank could damp the ardour of the troops, who in the face of a most tremendous and incessant fire of musquetry, and from Cannon loaded with grape shot forced their way at the point of the bayonet through every obstacle; both columns meeting in the center of the enemies works nearly at the same instant."

As soon as he had the prisoners under guard he wrote at 2 a.m. a dispatch to Washington: "Dear Genl The fort & Garrison with Colonel Johnston are ours. Our officers & men behaved like men who are determined to be free. Yours most Sincerely Anty Wayne." The British lost sixty-three killed, 543 prisoners in the action; the Americans, fifteen killed, eighty-three wounded.

On the next day, July 17, Wayne wrote a detailed report of the engagement for Washington. While of all the accounts of the battle it is one of the best, it nevertheless, in the hurried preparation, left some embarrassing omissions. Mention was made of Meigs, but he remonstrated, feeling it too little. Wayne, entirely by an oversight in the excitement of making his first report to Washington, also failed to applaud Murfree's performance, a factor in his quick victory, about which he was most contrite when the omission was called to his notice. He had a chance to rectify the errors in later letters to Washington and the Congress.

Wayne had no doubt about the noble work of the two advance parties. He told Washington: "Too much praise cannot be given to Lieut. Col. Fleury (who struck the enemies standard with his own hand) and to Major Stewart, who commanded the advance parties, for their brave and prudent conduct." Apparently after looking over his report Wayne felt he should add another paragraph: "I am not satisfied with the manner in which I have mentioned the conduct of Lieutenants Gibbons, and Knox, the two Gentlemen who led the advance parties of twenty men each; their distinguished bravery deserves the highest commendation. The first belongs to the 6th Penns. regt and lost 17 men killed, and wounded in the attack; the last belongs to the ninth d^0 who was more fortunate in saving his men, tho' not less exposed."

One of the happy features was that none of the enemy was slaughtered after the surrender, though such had often been the custom in night attacks in the practice of the strange "art of war." There was unusual restraint under Wayne's firm grip, but high anger when it was discovered that among the prisoners were the sons of prominent New York Loyalists whom Wayne's soldiers looked on as traitors to their homeland.

Washington, warm in his felicitations, came down on the second day after the capture, his austere face radiant, and shook hands with every man who had participated in the attack. Steuben, who was with them, looked them over with fatherly pride. They were his lads, as well as Wayne's. Wayne, who liked to entertain, capped it all with a dinner party with plenty of Madeira. After all, Stony Points were captured only once in a lifetime!

The men likewise were remembered. Congress divided among them money equal to the value of the military stores and ordnance captured. The estimate was $158,640, which went to the officers and men in proportions judged proper.

Under the plans Major General Howe was to have attacked Verplanck's as soon as Stony Point fell. But the messenger from Wayne failed to get through to him promptly and Clinton quickly sent help from New York to the Verplanck's garrison. Washington stripped Stony Point of its armaments and stores, destroyed the fort, and abandoned it. He did not have the men to garrison it adequately and would not risk the sacrifice of an insufficient force, as the British had done. The heavy guns were put on a lighter to be transported up the river to West Point but the sloop of war *Vulture* sank it with a direct hit.

Sir Henry Clinton was chagrined: "The success attending this bold and well-combined attempt of the enemy procured very deservedly no small share of reputation to the spirited officer (General Wayne) who conducted it, and was, I must confess, a very great affront to us, the more mortifying since it was unexpected and possibly avoidable." But Clinton absolved his post commander from any negligence: "I do not, however, mean by this to impute blame to the garrison or the officer who commanded it, who has unquestionable merit and was honorably acquitted by a court-martial." He explained the reverse as due to the fact that the fort's defenders depended on the armed vessels in the Hudson to cover their flanks, and that the one vessel left on guard happened that night to be removed. In this he appeared to be misinformed, because the sloop of war *Vulture* had to cut her cables after daybreak and drop down the river to avoid the guns directed on her from Stony Point. The *Vulture* was surely there because the only British soldier who escaped swam out to her.[8]

Most English comments accepted defeat graciously. The most serious complaint from British sources was that Wayne had slaughtered all of the farm dogs of the countryside. Commodore George Collier, who temporarily commanded the British fleet and naval stations of North America, wrote a bit condescendingly in his journal that "a young man of the name of Johnson, who was Lieut.-Colonel of the 17th Regiment, was left with the charge of this important post; he was reckoned a brave and good officer for his years, but the force was certainly inadequate for its defense." Collier told how "on the first alarm from the piquets he ran down with the main guard to defend his abattis and support them." The rebel column was stopped but to the colonel's "grief and surprise, he heard the cry of 'Victory' on the heights above him and the 'Fort's our own' which was the rebel watchword." He soon learned the Americans were in full possession of the works.

Wayne's main column, the commodore explained, took a short detour and climbed up the perpendicular height above the river: ". . . nobody expected an enemy on that side; and the surprise of the King's troops at seeing them in possession of the works was extreme." But Collier conceded: "The enterprise was really a gallant one, and as bravely executed."[9]

If Monmouth had made Wayne famous, Stony Point made him, for a time, the hero of the war. Congratulations poured in—Greene, Lafayette, his old Philadelphia friends, countless others lifted to new confidence by his exploit. One of the most pleasant messages was from his warm-hearted friend Dr. Benjamin Rush: "My dear sir, there was but one thing wanting in your late successful attack upon Stony Point to complete your happiness: and that is, the wound you received should have affected your *hearing*; for I fear you will be stunned through those organs with your own praises. Our streets, for many days, rang with nothing but the name of General Wayne. You are remembered constantly next to our good and great Washington, over our claret and Madeira. You have established the national character of our country; you have taught our enemies that bravery, humanity, and magnaminity, are the national virtues of the Americans."

General Greene wrote the day following in unstinted praise: "The attack was made about midnight and conducted with great spirit and enterprise, the troops marching up in the face of an exceeding heavy fire with cannon and musketry, without discharging a gun. This is thought to be the perfection of discipline and will forever immortalize Gen. Wayne, as it would do honor to the first general in Europe."

Well might the New Hampshire *Gazette* ask: "What action has Clinton to boast of, that may be compared with this master-piece of soldiership by General Wayne?"

Even General Charles Lee, with whom Wayne's affair of honor was still pending, wrote, but perhaps as much to show his familiarity with warfare as in any heartfelt appreciation issuing from his singular character: "What I am going to say, you will not, I hope, consider as paying any court in this hour of your glory; for, as it is at least my present intention to leave this continent, I can have no interest in paying my court to any individual. What I shall say, therefore, is dictated by the genuine feelings of my heart. I do most sincerely declare, that your assault of Stony Point is not only the most brilliant, in my opinion, throughout the whole course of the war on either side, but that it is the most brilliant I am acquainted with in history; the assault of Schweidnitz by Marshal Landon, I think inferior to it. I wish you, therefore, most sincerely, joy of the laurels you have deservedly acquired, and that you may long live to wear them."

Congress awarded a gold medal to Wayne. One side showed the Hudson River with six British ships in the offing, a different count from Clinton's. The other has an Indian queen, for some reason, holding toward Wayne a wreath in one hand and a mural crown in the other, with an alligator and the American shield at her feet. The symbolism is not apparent unless to show that even in those days the ways of Congress were obscure. A mural crown was one of gold usually awarded to the first man to mount an enemy battlement and put a flag on it. Wayne did not do that, but he seems to be taking the wreath instead of the crown. Major Stewart was awarded a silver medal companion to

Fleury's. It likewise has an Indian queen with an alligator at her feet but she is presenting a palm leaf. The reverse shows an officer, presumably Stewart, leading a bayonet charge, and it, too, has ships in the offing.

Stony Point and King's Mountain, the latter fought in South Carolina a mile and a half from the North Carolina line, October 14, 1780, were combat pinnacles in the closing years of the fighting. They kept alive the patriotic ardor that was abating despite the French assistance. Though they came more than a year apart, they were alike in showing the country it need no longer doubt the fighting qualities of American soldiers—high points on the road to independence. Wayne had served his cause well.

THIRTEEN

Bull's Ferry and Succor
for West Point

ANTHONY WAYNE, like most other enterprising officers of Washington's army, and especially the commander himself, endured unhappily another of the dull periods of the Revolutionary War, from mid-1779 until mid-1780. Whether the spirit of discontent that permeated the army was sifted down from the top or rose to it from the enlisted personnel is of little consequence and perhaps each group had about an equal share in it, but both officers and men found a ready scapegoat in Congress, which, far from being the alert body that had entered zestfully into the war, had become almost supine.

Washington was among the first to discern that thirteen separate little governments could not wage any sort of aggressive warfare. The line that stands out in his letter from Morristown that bitter winter was: "I have almost ceased to hope." Again, in a letter to a Congressman, he dwelt on the "unwarrantable jealousies" that confronted him. Perhaps no general in modern history had to operate under as many different jurisdictions.

Wayne had at Fort Montgomery what many have felt was the finest body of fighting troops brought together by Washington during the war—a selected brigade responding to no state but to the comman-

164

der in chief as the representative of the central authority, carefully drilled by one of the best drillmasters of his day, Steuben, fired by the high esprit de corps that comes only from success in battle, and commanded by one of the most spirited, confident and resourceful combat generals of the service.

But within half a year after Stony Point the Light Corps had been gradually eroded. Febiger's splendid Virginia regiment was urgently needed at home when the war began to touch the Southern provinces. Murfree's Tarheels departed for service in North Carolina. Hull's demi-regiment was detached and eventually Butler's veteran Pennsylvanians, who with their colonel were cemented in strong affection to their brigadier, went back to St. Clair and the Pennsylvania Line. What was left went into winter quarters at Morristown with Washington. Wayne, no longer having a command, went back to Philadelphia and Waynes-borough.

Lethargy settled over the Pennsylvania Line under the administration of St. Clair. He did not possess the soldiers' confidence, nor did he have Wayne's eager spirit and fertile imagination to make suggestions for his own division or for the army's employment. He was often absent. His generalship in 1779-1780 appeared to have dwindled away almost to a cypher.

Wayne dallied in Philadelphia and Chester County through the winter and spring months, recognizing all the while that he needed the army and the army needed him. Though rankled deeply by the injustice done to him, he held his peace and advanced no protest. All the while he must have known that if Washington called him he would respond. Even Washington could not utilize him during this most hopeless of all winters and generously allowed him the comforts of the city and his home. Meanwhile the cause of independence lay dormant.

When the land dried and the fresh blood of springtime coursed once more through the arteries of the chief, and alike, those of the lowest privates whose devotion had held them steadfast through the hardships, Washington wrote a note to Wayne. Dated May 18, 1780, it said simply: "I shall be very happy to see you at camp again, and hope you will, without hesitation, resume your command of the Pennsylvania line."

Wayne was no Achilles sulking in his tent. Whatever he might think at the time of the legislative bodies to whom he had paid his bristling respects on different occasions, he was, in this desperate fray, still actuated by patriotism and an insatiable love of glory, quests he had found always merging. One marvels at Wayne, who liked wealth and could approach being lavish with it; who enjoyed large parties, choice vintages, splendid horses, dapper clothes, but who could serve so perseveringly while he knew his estate was going downhill because of his long absences. During them Polly showed a complete lack of managerial ability, and the help he could acquire in wartime was unreliable in the extreme. His opinion of Robert Shannon, his plantation manager, was low.

The story of what was happening at Waynesborough while he was serving the country was summed up in a letter he wrote after the war: "Mr. Shannon has sunk for me since the beginning of January, 1776, until he went away, upwards of two thousand four hundred pounds in livestock, exclusive of the interest for near eight years. Nor do I believe he has made much for himself, although he has certainly injured me to the full amount of three thousand six hundred pounds, counting only the principal and interest; had he managed my stock, horses, cattle, sheep, in trade to that advantage which others have done in the course of the late war, I ought to have, at a moderate computation, *seven thousand pound*s in stock, in place of nothing."[1]

Wayne would have been much better off had he closed his business affairs entirely during the war years. The receipts from his tannery shrunk continually due mainly to lack of good management. Still, Wayne was not yet stripped, nor did the financial loss of which he was constantly aware diminish his ardor for military service, in which he bought his meticulously tailored uniforms and entertained with a freedom that ranged from liberality to prodigality. Washington was more frugal by comparison. Wayne continued to refuse compensation for his services, though any amounts being paid to officers or enlisted men were meager indeed due to the near worthless currency.

But the point was that when Washington called, Wayne came. Clinton, who had been in the South, was back in New York, threatening with Knyphausen to advance on Morristown, where Washington had accumulated some military stores that could not have included much food. Wayne's assignment was to follow and molest the enemy's right flank. Clinton made a feint toward the North River, and Washington, fearing West Point was again endangered, moved in that direction. He left Greene at Springfield, New Jersey, while Wayne, with a part of the Pennsylvania Line, was ordered to keep contact with Clinton's main army and report on its movements and apparent intentions.

Though he did not supplant St. Clair as the ranking officer and commander of the Line, the pleasant development in Wayne's return was that he was not serving under St. Clair either, though he was on paper a part of the division his fellow Pennsylvanian commanded. St. Clair was such a shadowless figure that he could be with the army though not be a vital part of it; he was, in fact, coming and going and appeared to be away when important events were in the making. Perhaps Washington—though there seems to be no certainty of it— arranged that Wayne should be spared the burden of taking orders on combat matters directly from one he disliked so heartily. When Wayne went on ventures, the orders came directly from the commanding general or Greene and not from or through the chief of the division.

Wayne's assignment was to cooperate with Greene in New Jersey. When Washington moved his small army to the highlands in answer to Clinton's threat in that direction, he left Greene with 800 men to cover Morristown and its storehouses. The militia was assembling and the net result of the Clinton-Knyphausen effort was the burning of Springfield. This pleasant little town southwest of Newark had only four houses left standing when the enemy retired to Elizabethtown, harried by militia and Light Horse Harry Lee's cavalry. Clinton had mistakenly thought, on the basis of rumors reaching him, that the New Jersey troops were so disaffected they would refuse to fight if he appeared in force. He merely aroused them to stronger efforts. The very army alleged to be so unsteady in its loyalty checked Knyphausen at the Rahway River, and when the Hessian commander saw Greene coming up from Morristown, he turned back.

Wayne, close by, wrote a report of it to Washington: "You no doubt have heard that the enemy, after burning Springfield, are retired to their former post on Elizabethtown Point. Their number, from the best observation, did not exceed 4,000. They brought out three days' provisions, which probably is to serve them until they reach the vicinity of West Point."

He went on to report Clinton's feint toward West Point, made immediately on his return from the capture of Charleston in May. If a favorable opening occurred, he would attack Washington's main army while Greene and Wayne were detached facing Knyphausen.

"I have not yet seen Gen. Greene," Wayne told Washington, "but from good intelligence, the grenadiers and light infantry, composing two battalions, together with all the other troops lately arrived from Charleston, except the legion, embarked last evening, but had not sailed this morning. May they not wait the return of those who marched from the point (Elizabethtown) this morning, and proceed in conjunction up the river, in full confidence that this manoeuvre has drawn your excellency's attention to this quarter?"

Washington replied that same evening saying he was informed the enemy had retired from Elizabethtown Point and asking Wayne to return to the main army, explaining that it was difficult at the moment to discern the enemy's intentions. Clinton termed the excursion of his forces into New Jersey fruitless. He took the army back to Phillipsburg to rest it. Thus the unproductive summer campaigning of 1780 in the north was ended for the armies as a whole.

Washington, on July 20, 1780, detached Wayne with the 1st and 2nd Pennsylvania Brigades, four pieces of field artillery under Colonel Thomas Proctor, and Colonel Stephen Moyland's dragoons, to undertake the destruction of the blockhouse at Bull's Ferry, at times termed the Bergen Blockhouse, on the New Jersey side of the Hudson River below Fort Lee. Washington said the blockhouse was for the purpose of covering the enemy's woodcutters and giving security to the refugees who garrisoned it and conducted raids on the farmsteads of citizens loyal to the American cause. The commanding general's description was moderate compared with another that termed the occupants "refugees, tories, and all the bandetti, robbers, and horse thieves of that country."[2]

Wayne brought up his little army and reconnoitered the fort. While some of his men were rounding up beef badly needed by Washington's army, then concentrated around Suffern, he, with Humpton's brigade and some supports, bombarded the blockhouse with field pieces hauled up to within sixty yards of it. Meantime it was noticed that the British were in motion across the river with a relief party. Irvine's brigade was detached to meet this thrust from Manhattan Island. The blockhouse timbers proved so sound that the round shot and grape bounded off its walls as harmlessly as the roar of guns echoed back and forth along the nearby Hudson River Palisades. The fort had only seventy defenders, who kept up a galling fire despite Wayne's concentration of his musketry on the portholes.

Wayne continued his artillery bombardment from 11 a.m. until 12:15 p.m., by which time he was assured that his guns were too light for the job. Their metal made little impression on the solid logs. Several vessels loaded with troops were seen moving up the Hudson from the Manhattan side. Since his dragoons had rounded up a large herd of cattle that were on pasture for eventual use by the British garrison in New York, he called off the attack. Something of Wayne's aggressive spirit had become a part of the attitude of his men, however. When the 1st Pennsylvania Regiment learned that they were to retire without further effort, they threw off the restraint of their officers, who tried to check them, and impetuously charged over and through the abatis, rushed up to the walls and tried to storm the blockhouse. The excitement of the assault was communicated to the 2nd Pennsylvania, which followed the 1st to the bottom of the fort's palisades. There the two regiments stood, without ability to force their way inside, and with the prospect of heavy loss if they retired. When the futility of their charge became apparent, they listened to their officers and withdrew, but not until they had suffered sixty-four casualties, among them fifteen killed.[3]

Washington imputed no blame to Wayne in reporting on the affair to Congress. He summarized it thusly: ". . . those of the First and Second Regiments, notwithstanding the utmost efforts of the officers to restrain them, rushed through the abatis to the foot of the stockade with a view of forcing an entrance, which was found impracticable. This act of intemperate valor was the cause of the loss we sustained. . . . I have been thus particular lest the account of this affair should have reached Philadelphia much exaggerated." In spite of Washington's effort, Wayne was sharply criticized for a hairbrained adventure.

As he withdrew he sent an infantry detachment to the waterfront, where it destroyed a large number of sloops and flatboats being used to carry the fuel across the Hudson. Meanwhile, Moyland's dragoons brought in a sizeable drove of cattle and many horses, the number not specified in Wayne's report, but enough that they choked the road back to Suffern. The British did not follow except in rhetoric. André's ballad, "Cow Chase," finished at Elizabethtown August 1, 1780, was supposedly modeled after the ballad of unknown date, "Chevy Chase," though the meter is not the same. It is more a testimonial to his extraordinary industry than his poetic ability, but it does contain some well-turned couplets. The thought in it is that Wayne and the elite of the army were beaten off by seventy refugees and had to content themselves with driving cattle down the roadway—the celebrated combat general, a tanner by trade, turned drover!

In one of the theatrical skits by which the British officers amused themselves during the dull winter of 1779-1780, the principal hit seemed to be "The Interlude," a portrayal of the American officers arrayed as they would have been, in British eyes, for their pursuits of peace. Washington was depicted as a surveyor carrying a Jacob's staff of tremendous size, followed by a Negro slave groaning under the load of a great compass and dragging a huge chain. Greene was a gunsmith with hammer and old gun with broken lock; Wayne was a tanner wearing a leather apron with a buckle fastening it around his neck. The apron reached to the ground and must have looked ludicrous. In his hand he was carrying a large currying knife. The *Casket*, which told the story of it, related an incident. Just as the curtain fell one night an American sailor in the gallery shouted: "Honor to thy country, disgrace to old England for suffering their hides to be *dressed*, and their heads broken, by American tanners and gunsmiths." There was no account of what happened to the sailor except that the *Casket* averred: "This piece of well-timed humor bore off the palm of applause." There were some unexpected Yankees in the audience.[4]

Lafayette had been absent from Washington's army for more than a year, having with the consent of the Commander been granted an extended leave by Congress. He had created jealousies because of his high rank and some hoped he had gone forever, but the main reason for the leave was the good he might do America in France. He returned to Boston May 10, 1780. No doubt his reports were a factor in the decision by France to send a land army to America, even though he had stressed that the Americans did not desire an army as much as money and matériel. He conducted an energetic campaign to obtain command of the expedition when it was decided on, but he was only twenty-two years old and wrote long and frequent letters, which appeared to disturb nearly everyone on both continents except Washington, who developed for him a genuine and lasting fondness that reciprocated his own. The command went to Rochambeau, the Jesuit-educated lieutenant general in his mid-fifties, a reliable veteran who enjoyed the confidence of both Vergennes and the King. He reached Newport on July 7, 1780.

The events of Washington's journey from West Point to Hartford, Connecticut, to meet Rochambeau, and his return, shook the country and gave Wayne another chance to distinguish himself. Washington, attended by Lafayette and staff, met Rochambeau on September 21, 1780, but owing to the lateness of the season and the plight of the French fleet, blockaded in Narragansett Bay by a superior British force, the council made no definite plans for military operations. They would have to wait until the next year.

Before departing for Hartford, Washington had offered Benedict Arnold command of the left wing of the army, which seemed a suitable place for a general who had distinguished himself much more in combat than amid the temptations into which he had fallen during his command at Philadelphia. But Arnold, to the commanding general's surprise, was displeased with the tender and induced Washington to give him the command of West Point. This Washington did by an order of August 3, 1780. The army, which had been east of the Hudson seeking an encounter with Clinton or an opportunity to attack New York while the British general was reconnoitering Rochambeau's position at Newport, returned to the west side and took position around Tappan, almost directly across the Hudson from Tarrytown. Greene and Stirling commanded the two wings and Lafayette, though now absent with Washington, held command of the light infantry in front of the main body.

Wayne was at Tappan when Washington and his entourage, on their return from Hartford, reached West Point September 25 and discovered Arnold's treason. Knox and Lafayette were with Washington when the revelation came. He turned to them with his well-remembered question: "Arnold is a traitor. Whom now can we trust?"[5]

Never was a general more unexpectedly betrayed than was Washington by Arnold, whom he had shielded through controversies and attacks and dealt with gently when a court-martial decreed that he should be reprimanded. While Lafayette's first concern was with the apparently uncontrolled but feigned grief of the beautiful Peggy Shippen Arnold, Washington's was with the West Point defenses and defenders. The ramparts were still strong enough but he found from his inspection that the garrison was weakened and the supporting troops scattered to ease the projected British takeover. Washington could not but expect that, with Arnold having fled to the British, the post was immediately endangered. Enemy detachments might be awaiting a signal to pounce on the meagerly defended post.

Of all forts, this was dearest to Washington's heart. It was the key citadel of the highland defenses, the anchor to the American line when it swung west into New Jersey or east to menace New York City. It was a threat to Clinton's flank whichever way he might march, whether into Connecticut or New Jersey or if ever again to the north, trying to meet a British force coming down from Canada. Clinton, in explaining his negotiations with Arnold, made it clear that he, as well as Washington, recognized the importance of the forts around West Point:

Considerable time was spent by Washington, Knox, and others investigating the condition in which Arnold had left West Point and every minute and every revelation was disheartening. Washington's question, "Whom now can we trust?" was answered for him by Nathanael Greene, who commanded the main army at Tappan during his absence. A mounted courier sped southward through the evening to Greene, and moments later, to Anthony Wayne. Washington wanted the best disciplined troops available. Whose then but Wayne's? The situation was striking—Arnold, promoted but dissatisfied by what he regarded as neglect; Wayne, neglected, but satisfied to serve Washington and the American cause in any capacity, whether as cow catcher and drover or leader of a spirited assault like Stony Point.

Wayne was the general Greene and Washington relied on to hold the fort which Arnold tried to place in enemy hands. The courier reached Tappan at midnight September 26, 1780 and Greene reached Wayne by 1 a.m. Washington had divulged the reason for his urgency.

Wayne read the message. Already as he dressed the drums were rolling for the assembly. Irvine's brigade was roused to follow. Wayne confided with his men. He told them where they were going and why. Rations were issued, though there would be no halt for eating them. Out from the camp and up the winding mountainous roads they marched through the night, along by the Tappan and Zuider Zee, past Donderberg and over part of it; past Bear Mountain frowning down against the night sky, until as the day broke they reached the Haverstraw landing for West Point, the outpost requiring first protection. They had covered sixteen miles in four hours. Washington looked on Wayne in amazement, as though he might be a spectre. Then, visibly stirred, the chief exclaimed, "Now all is safe, and I again am happy."

When Clinton learned that the Arnold treason plot had been detected he called off his plans for a descent on West Point. Arnold had turned over nothing except his own body. It had been gallant in blue, but would be near worthless in a red uniform.

Wayne, like Washington, was ordinarily a good judge of character. He had at first admired Arnold for the perseverance and fighting resourcefulness so evident in the Canadian and Saratoga campaigns. But Arnold's conduct while in command in Philadelphia had caused Wayne to turn against him so violently that he could not even do the man justice. The treason seemed to emphasize the evil qualities Wayne had been detecting.

An astute military man, Wayne had sensed that all was not well around West Point under Arnold's command, but he had nothing on which to base his feeling except intuition and conjecture. After the treason he wrote to his legislator friend, Hugh Sheel, a letter bristling with invective. Wayne wrote of Arnold that "honor and true virtue were strangers to his soul" and, "he never possessed either genuine fortitude or personal bravery," and "rarely went in the way of danger, but when stimulated by liquor, even to intoxication."

Wayne, with Lafayette nearby, experienced the last agony of the plot, the execution of Major John André, caught out of uniform while carrying the plans of West Point from Arnold to Clinton. Lafayette wept, while Washington remained in his headquarters, his blinds drawn. Wayne could not have escaped thoughts of the Cow Chase ballad, which had precluded him from service on the court-martial that condemned André to death by hanging. The sentence was carried out on October 2, 1780, and before the end of the month, Greene took command at West Point and Wayne accompanied Washington to Morristown, where the army went into winter quarters. It had been a sad year.

FOURTEEN

The Mutiny—Wayne's Supreme Trial

THE CLIMACTIC YEAR of the American Revolution, 1781, opened with disorder and anguish. The calamity threatened for a time to nullify all of the efforts over the years by Washington, his generals, the people, and a harassed Congress, and end the war in a frenzy of fraternal bloodletting.

The Pennsylvania Line of six regiments aggregating about 2,000 men, was encamped on January 1, 1781, on familiar Mount Kemble, west of Morristown, New Jersey while Washington had the main body of the army in winter quarters at New Windsor, New York, fifty-five miles up the Hudson from New York City and six miles north of West Point.

The Pennsylvania soldiers at Mount Kemble had an extra ration of rum on New Year's Day and some of them obtained more. Wayne went through the camp at four in the afternoon and noticed that the men were milling about ill at ease. January 1 was his thirty-sixth birthday. While the fare of the winter encampment was not sufficiently plenteous for feasting, he asked his two favorite colonels, Richard Butler and Walter Stewart, to have dinner at his quarters that evening. He had fortunately declined an invitation to take dinner with a local family near Morristown, the Lucas Beverholts, using as an excuse the pressure of army business. He was usually able to produce a choice wine for special occasions, but happily neither he nor the colonels imbibed strongly that night. Instead of drink and prattle, they were playing cards when at 9 p.m. they began to hear the low rustle and undertones of many feet stomping across the parade ground, and muffled voices broken now and then by louder shouts. At first it seemed merely a temporary reaction from the drinking. Then someone fired a musket.[1]

Wayne dropped his cards and rushed to the parade ground in front of the huts where the men were quartered. Some were standing in groups. Parts of three regiments were slinging themselves together loosely under the command of sergeants, and the whole were forming under a quartermaster sergeant, as if for a muster.

Soon all was in a melée in the company and regimental streets. Officers, rushing out, told the men to get back into their huts. The men at first obeyed, but as quickly as the officer went on to the next hut, the occupants of the last were out on the drill ground again, claiming they thought a muster had been called because of an enemy advance. These pretenses were at length cast aside and the whole of the three regiments joined into the formation being drawn up by the sergeants.

The 2nd Regiment, Stewart's, appeared at first to be holding aloof but soon taunts and threats of retaliation forced it to join the revolters. The 4th Regiment under one of its captains, Thomas Campbell, seemed to respond to orders and the captain tried to lead it in a bayonet charge against the unruly regiments. The men of the 4th did advance a short distance, then began to drop off into the darkness until there was none charging except one or two officers.

One glance showed Wayne when he rushed out that the men were out of hand. Instinctively he drew his two pistols and pulled back the hammers. Immediately he was surrounded by three companies of determined, desperate men, their bayonets fixed, and half a dozen blades touching or pointed close at his breast. Then one of the sergeants, probably William Bowzer, though the accounts are vague, spoke to him firmly but courteously and not in anger: "General Wayne, we love you and respect you. You have led us often on the field of battle, but you do not command us any longer. We warn you to be on your guard. If you fire a pistol you are a dead man. If you attempt to enforce any commands, we will put you to death."[2]

That was the substance and probably close to the exact words of the ultimatum that broke the seal of relationship of soldier to officer, that made of the milling, frenzied mass of perhaps the most resolute and trusted division of the Continental Army, a full-blown mutiny. This was no little affair like that he had quelled at Old Ti, or a grumbling such as Aaron Burr had silenced when he cut off a soldier's arm at Valley Forge.

Wayne exhorted them but they gave him no heed. Here and there the firing of muskets sounded. Someone sent up a rocket. A few of the officers tried to resist. In the various little side affrays one captain, Adam Bettin, was killed by a musket ball in his stomach. Colonel Butler tried to admonish the men but in one of his efforts had to take refuge in his hut else he likely would have been killed. When Wayne continued his exhortation, half demanding, half reasoning and entreating, part of a company fired a volley over his head, which caused him to pull back his coat and exclaimed: "If you mean to kill me, shoot me at once. Here, at my breast."[3]

Probably he did have a few silent enemies in the ranks. What successful general did not? The control of the sergeants over the mutineers was not rigid, but for the large majority Wayne's life was almost as dear as their own, and of this they again informed him. They revered him, would fight for him, but they had more pressing business elsewhere. One of their own number was killed, mistakenly, by another mutineer. Several were wounded. Captain Samuel Tolbert of the Line was wounded severely in the thigh by a bayonet stab.

In the course of half an hour the mutiny became general; within two hours, despite all of the demands and supplications from Wayne, Butler, Stewart, and others, the men were in formation with their packs, muskets, and some hastily distributed rations, and, under the command of their "major general," a designation apparently settled on before the mutiny took shape, they were hitting the highroad toward Philadelphia. Behind them rolled six field pieces they had commandeered. They were a formidable array, 1,300 strong and perhaps more. Later a count showed 1,500 with the hangers-on they attracted. They were drawing 2,000 rations two days hence. This was a sizeable force to have wandering at will, under the command of a few sergeants, some of them unable to read or write. Some of the newly recruited companies that had no grievances were not involved. They stayed behind rattling around in a nearly empty camp. Those who marched were formidable enough to overpower the sages of the state and Continental legislative bodies, or wreck and sack Philadelphia, or if challenged with too much severity, or fired on, they could just as readily go over to the British army. None at this stage could know what their leaders intended or what the privates could be led to do.

Wayne's first fear when they began their march was that they might defect to the enemy in New York. His horse had been taken but he procured another, darted around their flank and took a position at the road fork, the right leading toward Princeton and the left toward Elizabethtown and Staten Island. With Butler, Stewart, and a few supports, he placed himself astride the Staten Island road. Perhaps it was their predetermined intention to take the right fork, though it was remotely possible his show of resolution caused them to take the Princeton road. At this division of the roads Wayne was determined to make his stand. If they came his way it would have to be over his body. They were not going to the British as long as he had an ounce of life to prevent it. Instead of attempting to brush him aside, the leaders parleyed briefly with him to reassure him that they had no intention of deserting to the enemy. Again they asserted that what they wanted, and all they wanted, was a settlement with their own governing authorities. Should the British and Hessians appear at that minute, they would align themselves behind their commander and fight as resolutely as they always had done.

His confidence somewhat restored, Wayne turned back to the camp, and again, his concern was for his soldiers. He knew that in their impetuous departure they had thought only of the food needed for the hour and day. He got some quartermaster wagons, filled them with provisions, and sent them lumbering along after the men. He wrote a full account of the events for Washington, called his aide, Major Fishbourne, and sped him off on the road to New Windsor. Then, recognizing that he was of no value in a nearly empty camp, he went after the men.

Knowing that Butler and Stewart had the confidence of the men, as officers who had always held the soldiers' interest uppermost and stood in the front with them, he took these two close friends with him. After a sleepless night, they rode down the Princeton highway until they came up to the mutineers halted for rest at Vealtown (now Bernardsville), where, almost in the dim past now, General Charles Lee had been captured by the British. There Wayne was told that he might accompany them but could not give orders. The mutineers by this time were under the command of a committee of sergeants headed by a sergeant of two armies, the ex-British soldier, William Bowzar. The committee of sergeants was made up of one sergeant from each of the ten infantry regiments and the one artillery detachment involved in the mutiny, and these eleven, a day later, elected as their president a sergeant named Williams. There were so many of that name in the Pennsylvania Line that there is no certainty which Williams it was, though it may have been John Williams, a British deserter. One of the sergeants had the nickname of "Macaroni Jack," which smacks of the British navy. For the most part they left no records because they appear to have been cautious about putting their names on paper, but they held regular meetings and did a creditable job of keeping an orderly camp and discipline that even Wayne was compelled to admire.

Considering the strong ex-British element in the leadership of the mutineers, Wayne was justified in fearing that the whole uprising might have resulted from British instigation, that Williams might be bargaining to have his desertion forgiven, and that the revolt would be directed in the end toward assisting Clinton. The main reason he went along was to provide a little insurance against any turn of the column toward New York. In that case, if argument failed, he intended to fight. Before leaving Mount Kemble he had alerted the New Jersey militia and had ordered a brigade to occupy Chatham, where it would be disposable in an emergency.

When Williams was selected to be president of the board of sergeants, Bowzar became secretary. The two were installed as the operating heads of the mutiny, though, as with most such formless movements, there was always much disagreement in the ranks. The private soldiers wanted to go to Philadelphia and get the business of their pay arrears transacted at once; the sergeants feared that if they crossed the Delaware each man, free of restraints, would want to go to his nearby home first, and see Congress later, in which case they would be shorn of their power, the mutiny would be dissipated, and they, the leaders, would be left dangling from the tree branch nearest to a quick court-martial. They moved the next day, January 4, through Middlebrook, preserving good military order, refraining from looting or robbing the inhabitants, and on January 5, in rather salubrious weather for January, reached Princeton, where they set up headquarters in Nassau Hall.

Why had the relations between such a stalwart body of troops as the Pennsylvania Line and the governments of Pennsylvania and the associated states been allowed to deteriorate? Though he was not the commander of the division, Wayne had been keenly alert to the approaching crisis. He had stormed at the Pennsylvania authorities in an effort to avert it. The record is ample and clear. So much has been written about the deplorable condition of the Continental soldiers during the winters at Valley Forge and Morristown that the words have lost some of their impact. No war offers pleasant living conditions but there is nothing in modern warfare to parallel the hardships endured by

Washington's army; they touched every phase of living comfort—food, garments, shoes, housing, and money. Had the men been paid regularly they might have shifted for themselves to some extent, and bought food from the surrounding farmers. As it was, pilfering and foraging were so strictly forbidden that when a neighborhood farmer complained usually someone was punished. The cruel practice of that day was to ply the knotted lash across the offender's back. In the matter of housing, Wayne's men in the harsh winter of 1779–1780 did not get hutted down until February 14, 1780, so constant was their activity and so slow the construction work on the log cabins. Thus they endured the worst winter of the war mainly in flimsy, worn tents that were a poor shield against the bitter cold.

The approach of the winter of 1780–1781 had caused Wayne much concern. He was close to his men, understood their thinking, tried to impress upon the Pennsylvania government the fact that their basic requirements would have to be satisfied. He was well aware of the discussion in the ranks about the terms of enlistment. The Pennsylvania Line enlistments were for "three years or during the continuance of the war." The statement was ambiguous. Did it mean the limit of enlistment was three years, as the men contended, or that the enlistment was for the duration, even if the war went on indefinitely, as the state and some of the officers maintained. The ambiguity had occurred in elistments in 1775 and was preserved in the reorganization of 1777, when Washington's main army came to be composed of Continentals serving under him and Congress, though recruited by the states. As Continental soldiers the state still paid them, or was supposed to do so. Some of the states had one-year enlistments and impressive bounties for reenlistments. Pennsylvania offered three half joes, or about twenty-five dollars. Some of the other states paid more. The pay for Pennsylvanians already in the service was not raised when the bounty for new enlistments was established, but the amount of pay had become altogether academic because the Pennsylvania Line had due to them pay arrears of one year. The plain truth was that the state authorities were either woefully indifferent or woefully incompetent in the matter of looking after the simple comforts of their soldiers.

The officer left with this difficult situation was Anthony Wayne. He had had no part in creating or in remaining indifferent to the abrasive relationship between the state government and its soldiers. One of his most laborious tasks over the years had been to get bare sustenance for them. As the situation late in the war now worsened, he importuned with increasing urgency. In his anticipation of difficulty as the year of 1780 drew toward an end, at a time when most of the men would have been in the Continental service for three years, he wrote courteously to President Reed: "When I look to a period fast approaching, I discover the most gloomy prospects and distressing objects presenting themselves; and when I consider the mass of people who now compose this army will dissolve by the 1st of January, (except a little corps enlisted for the war, badly paid and worse fed). I dread the consequence, as these melancholy facts may have a most unhappy influence on their minds, when opposed to a well appointed, puissant, and desolating army."[4]

A month later, on October 17, he wrote insistently to Reed about the need for blankets and winter clothing. The uniforms were worn out. The men tried to save them by repairing the elbows and other rent places but would require needles and thread. Easy as needles should have been to acquire, inexpensive as they usually were, close as was Philadelphia, Wayne did not get them. He wrote to Robert Morris, on November 9, 1780, and others of the Executive Committee. Some extracts of his letter are illuminating. They clearly forecast the revolt:

"Whatever gentlemen may think of matters, for my own part I very much dread the ides of January. It will be a crisis in which we shall be most vulnerable, and, as I have already observed, in which the minds of the troops will be most susceptible of impressions injurious to this service; and I have ground to believe that will be the season in which the enemy are instructed to operate. Should they then advance, and find our troops wretchedly appointed and pinchingly fed, the prospect will not be very flattering on our side. . . . No, gentlemen, it is impossible. The first and keenest feelings of nature (hunger and cold,) are not to be reasoned down by sophistry; especially if your adversaries make use of a more effectual argument, by holding out an immediate relief in one hand, and an invitation to partake of their friendship and plenty in the other.

"Believe me, gentlemen, that this is not a picture drawn by fancy's pencil. It is taken from the life, and it has stamped too indelible an impression upon my mind to be removed. Permit me to assure you, that it is not the prowess of our enemy I dread, but their taking advantage of our necessitous situation and internal disunion. . . . Exert every power for the immediate completion of your quotas of troops; establish magazines of provisions; adopt some efficacious measures to procure a quantity of specie; and, at all events, find means to clothe the soldiers who belong to this state by the first of January."

Nothing could have been clearer than this statement of the urgent nature of the requirements.

Once more he wrote to Reed, on November 19, holding a horseman at the door while he wrote, saying, "I take the liberty again to mention the absolute necessity of forwarding a quantity of hard cash and state stores with all possible dispatch, in order to keep our people in temper. . . . Our honor and credit are now plighted for near 200 half joes, to the soldiers who enlisted on trust."

Sullenness and discontent were apparent in the ranks as he took up his new position on Mount Kemble. Quickly headquarters became flooded with complaints from farm owners of marauding and depredations, offenses which under Wayne's strict code of discipline had to be punished. More onerous regulations were adopted but they only added to the disquiet. Anyone leaving camp was halted by the guard who examined his pass; anyone entering was subjected to strict scrutiny. The names of the occupants were put up on each hut and a check was made by officers and military police at tattoo to determine if every man was present or accounted for.

The height of indiscretion occurred when representatives of the state paid some green troops who had enlisted for six months bounties in gold for reenlisting, when the veterans did not even receive a paper scrap on their arrearages. At this stage, when there appears to have been as much if not more public apathy than there was in the North midstream in the Civil War, Washington's resolution and that of a few of his sturdy generals including Greene, Wayne, and Stirling, were almost all that cemented the cause and held the army together.

Wayne gave another account of conditions that showed his heart-felt sympathy for his suffering men: "Poorly clothed, badly fed, and worse paid, some of them not having received a paper dollar for near twelve months; exposed to winter's piercing cold, to drifting snows and chilling blasts, with no protection but old worn-out clothes, tattered linen overalls, and but one blanket between three men." He told how the officers, including himself, would stand for hours in the cold wind "among the poor naked fellows" helping them make their huts and redoubts, "often assisting with our own hands, in order to produce a conviction to their minds that we share, and more than share, every vicissitude in common with them: sometimes asking to participate their bread and water." He thought that while this prevented them from complaining in public it did not check their grumbling in private.

Wayne on December 10 and again December 25 reported to Washington on the security measures he had taken and received approval of them from his chief, but Washington's letter, written on December 28 did not reach him until after the events of New Year's Day. The main intelligence was that patriotic women working to help the army had made up between 2,000 and 2,500 shirts, of which he

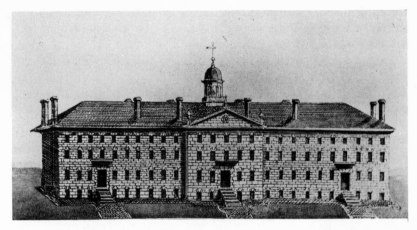

Nassau Hall, of the College of New Jersey (Princeton) as it appeared before the Revolutionary War. Completed in 1756, it became the meeting place of the Continental Congress in 1783. Here the veterans of the Pennsylvania Line, mutinous because of mounting pay arrearages and neglect by the legislature in supplying winter clothing, blankets, and other provisions, halted on their march toward Philadelphia. Through Wayne's tact and negotiations one of the best fighting elements of the army was saved for the service, instead of being allowed to take Philadelphia by storm. *(Courtesy the Historical Society of Pennsylvania)*

had directed that 800 be sent for the most needy of the Pennsylvania Line. Washington's fear of desertions to the British appeared in the statement: "I very much approve of what I hear is your determination, to hold all of your amusements within the line of your camp."

The 800 shirts would not likely have been sufficient to hold back the lowering storm; still, they would have shown good will by the authorities and in a season of high emotions might have caused the soldiers to reflect for another day or so. When they protested against rules more stringent than those obtaining in previous winter encampments, Wayne told them in effect that he would rather "be charged with strictness than relaxation of discipline or inattention."

Under these circumstances, the mutineers had marched to Princeton. The headquarters of two armies were stirred into quick action. Wayne reported the mutiny to Washington, writing at 4 a.m., January 2, after the mutineers had moved toward Vealtown: "It is with great pain I now inform your excellency of the general mutiny and defection, which suddenly took place in the Pennsylvania line between the hours of 9 and 10 o'clock last evening. Every possible exertion was used by the officers to suppress it in its rise; but the torrent was too potent to be stemmed. Captain Bitting [Adam Bettin] has fallen a victim to his zeal and duty. Captain Tolbert and Lieutenant White are reported mortally wounded—a very considerable number of the field and other officers are much injured by strokes from muskets, bayonets and stones; nor have the revolters escaped with impunity. Many of their bodies lay under our horses' feet, and others will retain with existence the traces of our swords and espontoons. They finally moved from the ground about eleven o'clock at night, scouring the grand parade with round and grape shot from four field pieces; the troops advancing in a solid column, with fixed bayonets, producing a diffuse fire of musketry in front, flank, and rear.

"During this horrid scene, a few officers, with myself, were carried by the tide to the fork of the roads at Mount Kemble; but placing ourselves on that leading to Elizabethtown, and producing a conviction to the soldiery that they could not advance upon that route, but over our dead bodies, they fortunately turned towards Princeton.

"Colonels Butler and Stewart, (to whose spirited exertions I am much indebted) will accompany me to Vealtown, where the troops now are. We had our escapes last night. Should we not be equally fortunate to-day, our friends will have this consolation, that we did not commit the honor of the United States, or our own, on this unfortunate occasion."

Washington's first impulse was to go to the scene of the action. He put his affairs in order, notified attendants to accompany him, and prepared for departure the following morning. Reflection during the evening brought the conclusion that his first duty was with the main army, to which the disaffection might spread. Clinton in New York would be alert to any weakening of the force at West Point and New Windsor, and the Hudson was still free of ice and open to his fleet. In addition, the issue was in the competent hands of Wayne, who had the personal affection of his troops as much as any leader in the army. Washington did not know what he could accomplish personally with the mass of revolters. If he failed to bring them into line his authority over the whole army would be weakened.[5]

He ended by writing a letter to Wayne that reveals his prudence and moderation in an hour of extreme trial, and his understanding of human reactions: "Opposition, as it did not succeed in the first instance, cannot be effectual while the men remain together, but will keep alive resentment, and may tempt them to turn about and go in a body to the enemy; who, by their emissaries, will use every argument and means in their power to persuade them that it is their only asylum; which if they find their passage stopped at the Delaware, and hear that the Jersey militia are collecting in their rear, they may think but too probable. I would, therefore, recommend it to you to cross the Delaware with them, draw from them what they conceive to be their principal grievances, and promise faithfully to represent to Congress and to the State the substance of them, and endeavor to obtain a redress. If they can be stopped at Bristol or Germantown, the better. I look upon it, that if you can bring them to a negotiation, matters may be afterwards accommodated; but that an attempt to reduce them by force will either drive them to the enemy, or dissipate them in such a manner that they will never be recovered."[6]

Washington called in some of his generals and asked them to report on the temper of the troops in the highlands. Information about the mutiny had not yet become general, but it reached Washington and Clinton on the same day, January 3, 1781. Washington's council felt that Wayne had acted prudently, then recommended that Washington prepare a corps of 1,000 men taken from different regiments judged to be sound, and hold the corps in readiness to march at once and employ force against the mutineers if that became necessary.

Wayne appears to have made only one unwise suggestion, which Washington immediately corrected. This was his recommendation to Congress that, at a time when it appeared the revolters would move speedily on Philadelphia, it vacate the capital city. Washington told it to remain, fearing that if the men arrived and found Congress fled they might in their anger loot the city. He may have had in mind also that since Congress had so often failed to come to grips with the realities of the war, it could stand a bit of jerking up by the appearance of 1,300 soldiers at its doorstep demanding the modest requirements of army life that ought to have been extended to them long since without any questioning.

To prevent the spread of mutiny, Washington sent General Knox on a quick tour of the northeast to call on the governors, warn them that the failure to forward supplies on a regular schedule was endangering the very existence of the army, and urgently requesting them to send at once money, food, clothing, and other supplies. That was about all Washington could do except wait. Of all the many emergencies he faced during the long struggle, this, the rebellion of his own soldiers, and the uncertainty of their intentions and the possibility that they might go over to the enemy, was undoubtedly the most tense; yet he rode through it unshaken. His correspondence shows a magnanimous concern for the men, but an unyielding determination that they should not be permitted to wreck the cause by putting their personal grievances, valid as they were, above the country's welfare.

Wayne, Butler, and Stewart followed the mutineers and lodged in a Princeton tavern. Upon reaching Princeton, Wayne obtained the first specific statement of their demands, presented to him by the committee of sergeants. They were in summary: 1—all who had served for three years under the terms of enlistment that contained the disputed clause, whether the "three years" or the "duration of the war" had precedence in the contract, were to be discharged at once; 2—all who continued in the service were to receive the full enlistment bounty, the same amount as was given to the new troops, or be brought abreast it if they had received any bounty previously. Those who continued in the service were to have "real" pay, not depreciated currency; 3—payment was to be made at once of all arrears in pay and clothing, both to those who were to receive their discharges and to those who remained in the service by reenlistment.

The demands on their face were moderate. The unmilitary aspect was that they were presented not as a petition but in the form of demands. Wayne had strong sympathy for the men but utter lack of it for their method. Nevertheless, words had been unavailing with the authorities. Neither he nor Washington wanted to lose so many veteran soldiers when the American cause was in the doldrums. Most certainly they did not want to lose them to the British. That possibility, though remote, was always present.

Wayne did not feel empowered to make a settlement which was not an issue between the men and their military commanders, but between them and the civil authorities. The civil authorities were already in action. When news of the mutiny reached Philadelphia, Congress appointed a committee to act with President Reed of Pennsylvania. With a cavalry escort as protection against mutineers who were sprinkling the road between Princeton and Philadelphia, the Committee set out to negotiate with the ringleaders of the revolt. Reed sent ahead a letter to Wayne asking the general to meet him four miles out of Princeton.

When word of the mutiny reached St. Clair, he rode out with Lafayette to Princeton. He had to identify himself at the picket and await permission to enter the town, and at length the two generals got in. They were escorted to the "Board of Sergeants," now ruling body of the Pennsylvania Line, in session in Nassau Hall. The enlisted men were courteous throughout and Lafayette seems to have been received cordially. The men said they would be happy to fight under him in normal conditions and would die at his orders, but he was not acquainted with the manner in which they had been treated. Their first intention was to have redress from their government. Simple justice was what they sought.

After the arrival of St. Clair and Lafayette, Lieutenant Colonel John Laurens rode up to the picket and gained entry. This was a disquieting incident because the little town was becoming topheavy with high officers: the three newly arrived and the three, Wayne, Butler, and Stewart, who had traveled with the mutineers. Quickly their attitude hardened. The men were not fond of St. Clair. They told him to get out of town and gave him an hour to finish his dinner and leave. The situation was altogether novel, a division expelling its top commanding officer. Lafayette and Laurens were also required to depart but Wayne, Butler, and Stewart were permitted to stay. Those departing took their small cavalry escort along and by one of these horsemen Wayne sent a message to have the functionaries in charge of the accounts come out to Princeton so the matter of back pay and allowance for the depreciated currency might be calculated and settled.

When Clinton in New York heard of the mutiny he too swung into action promptly. He later explained it: "I immediately judged it probable that the least wrong step taken by the rebel rulers on such an emergency might be the means, with proper encouragement, of driving the mutineers in to us."

He ordered Major General William Phillips, commander of what he termed the "British elite," and the officers of the Hessian grenadiers and jägers, to hold themselves ready to march on notice. On the next day January 4, he transferred them to Long Island and thence to Staten Island, where they would be in a position to intervene in affairs in New Jersey. He sent three messengers by different routes to promise the mutineers protection, pardons for any past offenses against the King, and the acceptance of all their demands, including giving them the pay due them.

Clinton suggested to the revolters that they cross South River (the Delaware), which was exactly why Washington desired to put that barrier between them and Clinton in New York. Clinton's thought, as interpreted by the editor of his war narrative, was that they might pick up others disaffected in Pennsylvania, that their break with Congress would prove irreparable, and that they might be persuaded to go to the Chesapeake, where Benedict Arnold, who had been dispatched to that region in mid-December 1780, would take charge of them. How little Clinton understood the temper of the mutineers! He did say he had no special reason for optimism that they might join the British but it was impossible to judge and he felt the potentialities of winning them should be explored.[7]

One of Clinton's agents met the mutineers; the others lacked courage or dropped by the wayside. He reached Princeton January 5. He was John Mason, of Orange County, New York, leader of a band of freebooters. He had been checked in that predatory career and was about to go on a British expedition to Central America in lieu of prison, when Clinton used him as a spy to invite the mutineers to join the British. Enroute he picked up Benjamin Ogden, a young man from near Brunswick, New Jersey, who did not leave much of a record except that he was Mason's guide and companion and probably not otherwise a participant in the unfortunate event.

When they reached Princeton they were taken before the Board of Sergeants in Nassau Hall. They offered a paper that had been contained in a ball or square of lead, possibly to make it sink if they faced detection en route. The paper was Clinton's proffer to the mutineers. The treason of Benedict Arnold was still strong in the minds of some of the men, which caused one of the sergeants to exclaim, that they were no Arnolds, or, as otherwise quoted, to declare, "See, comrades, he takes us for traitors. Let us show him that the American army can furnish but one Arnold, and that America has no truer friends than we are."[8]

Whatever the wording, the sergeants took Mason, the spokesman, and Ogden, the guide to Wayne, whom they reached at 4 a.m. They aroused their old-time general and turned over the two men to him. This gave him a chance to employ his favorite term of contempt, "caitiffs," when he wrote to Washington that morning about it. The condition under which they were placed in his custody was that they be returned to the sergeants in case no accommodation could be reached with the Pennsylvania or Congressional authorities respecting their demands. Wayne said he would give fifty gold guineas to each of the two sergeants who brought in the "caitiffs." In his letter to Washington he said he, Butler, and Stewart had used every possible means to inflame the mutineers "against wretches who would insult them by imagining them traitors" and explained "had they thought them virtuous they would not have carried these overtures."

The condition that the spies be returned if the mutineers did not get a settlement out of Philadelphia authorities suggests that they were holding the Clinton offer as a threat that would speed the action of the Continental and state governments, and they might well have judged from past performance that some prodding of Congress and the Assembly would be necessary. Still, their eagerness to get the emissaries into Wayne's custody at such an early hour suggested paradoxically that they were firm in their loyalty and had no intention at present of turning to the British.

Wayne, who was something of a hostage himself in Princeton, concluded it was best to send Mason and Ogden toward Philadelphia on the road that the Philadelphia authorities would travel en route to Princeton, and to this the revolting sergeants assented. None seemed to want them or know what to do with them, so they were lodged in Trenton under custody of the Pennsylvania Executive Council.

President Reed stopped four miles outside of Princeton because he heard that St. Clair had been peremptorily, even rudely, ousted and Lafayette politely sent out of town. He did not want to subject himself, as the official representative of Pennsylvania, to such humiliation. Wayne had the foresight to have the sergeants assemble the men; then he read Reed's letter to them and it had a touching effect. Quite obviously all of them did not have their hearts in the mutiny. Some would not have participated except by coercion. They had gone through numerous sanguinary battles and now, in the end, they were distrusted by the chief executive of their own state. Nevertheless, the majority sentiment appeared to be that being now mutinous, they would carry it through to the end.

The attitude of the mutineers toward the spies Mason and Ogden reassured Reed. He was anything but cowardly. He had been at Washington's side at Trenton and through many other frays, but it helped to have Wayne's word that he could come into Princeton without fear of personal molestation. Wayne went out to see him and brought him in. Again the men were paraded, this time with all eyes dry. Their alignment was beautiful, their shabby uniforms a disgrace to a nation, large sections of which were prospering and feeling fairly gently the impact of war. Reed's attitude was standoffish. He returned the salute of the sergeants reluctantly. He was accompanied by Brigadier General James Potter, who had been at Mount Kemble when the mutiny occurred and had taken the news of it to Philadelphia, and Potter was named a delegate from the Pennsylvania Council sent to assist Reed.

Reed went into a period of considerable haggling with the sergeants, though he had been clothed by the committee of Congress and his own council with exemplary powers to make an adjustment. The sergeants in a spirit of compromise narrowed their demands to the simple condition that all who had enlisted at the early stages of the war, in 1776 or 1777, should be discharged and receive at once their arrears in pay and clothing with due consideration to the depreciation of the currency. Where a dollar was due they did not want to receive a Continental note worth two cents. But they recognized the shortage of cash and would take certificates from the state backed by suitable security.

Much discussion followed over the enlistment conditions prevailing at different times and under different circumstances; some soldiers had been held after their terms had expired; some had been, to all effects, coerced to remain because of the exigencies of the moment; some had never received their promised bounties of twenty dollars back at the beginning; some felt they had been cheated when the state made distributions of clothing and the like. Though he was a stickler, Reed was anxious to make a settlement.

At length he drafted an agreement, received a few suggestions for amendments from Wayne and the two colonels of the Line, and he and Potter signed these articles that recognized the soldiers' claims. The guiding thought was that soldiers should not be held beyond any period for which they had voluntarily intended to engage themselves, and any enlistment secured by coercion was void. Those who had enlisted for three years or the duration of the war were granted their immediate discharges with all arrearages. None would be punished for participating in the mutiny. This last was in accord with Wayne's promise.

Wayne and his officers were not altogether happy with some phases of the settlement. St. Clair, who had gone to Morristown to take charge of the bobtail end of the division that had remained there, was talking foolishly about using force and maintaining that the terms of the mutineers were out of all reason. Apparently because of his personal pique at being dismissed from Princeton, he would probably have lost for the army 1,300 of its top-grade soldiers. He was ignored.

The Congressional committee came out to Trenton to be ready for the result of Reed's negotiation. After heavy discussion, the mutineers went to Trenton, where there was an all-around acceptance of Reed's terms. The happy ending of the mutiny was that after the veterans had received their discharges, their certificates of back pay, and furloughs of forty days, two-thirds of them reenlisted and served out the war. They had been patriotic soldiers all along but had been neglected orphans of their government. What was done after the mutiny could have been transacted more easily before it. Whatever condemnation may be placed on the method employed by the men—the forbidding and sinister resort to mutiny—there was no doubt but that they had been allowed to reach reluctantly that desperate recourse by the failure of the authorities. The public cupboard was indeed bare but the principal function of Congress and the state was to finance the war. Neither had exhausted or drastically tapped the revenue-raising potential of the country.

Wayne's conduct throughout was prudent, courageous, and sincere. The men displayed their affection for him. He won Washington's commendation. He proved that while St. Clair was nominal commander, he was the *de facto* leader of the Pennsylvania Line.

The last sad phase of the affair had to do with the two waifs caught up in the play of circumstances—Mason, who had merely delayed passage to Jamaica and Central America to carry a message for Clinton; and Ogden, whose sympathies, whether British or American, none knew, who was hired simply to guide Mason over the New Jersey roads to Princeton. In Trenton they came under the guard of the Philadelphia Light Horse (later the First Troop Philadelphia City Cavalry), were tried by a court-martial presided over by Wayne, were judged guilty, and the sentence was approved by Lord Stirling, the ranking officer in Trenton. They were taken a short distance out of town and hanged.

Reed squirmed under the promise Wayne had made of fifty guineas to each of the two sergeants who brought in the emissaries. He thought the amount too large, the treasury too barren. He summoned the sergeants, claimed he did not understand the transaction, and wanted more light on it. Whether because of his niggardliness or because of the mettle of the sergeants, they relieved him of his discomfiture. They said they had not taken the men for gold but for their love of country and expected no reward. Pleased was Reed for having saved a hundred guineas.

FIFTEEN

Flash of Bayonets
at Green Spring

THE SOFT SETTLEMENT with the Pennsylvania Line was justified to Wayne and Washington because the men had been grievously neglected, but mutiny is like a virulent disease, and though a case may appear to have been cured by weak medicine, the poison abides and spreads. Both Washington and Wayne found that drastic punishment—death to the offenders—was in the end the most humane deterrent to revolt, else the entire army would degenerate into warring, leaderless bands, the cause would be lost, and the toll from internecine conflicts would be frightful.[1]

When Washington organized his mobile corps of New England troops, drawn chiefly from the Massachusetts Line, to intervene if the mutineers went toward the British or laid waste to the countryside, he designated to command them Major General Robert H. Howe, an early patriotic leader from the Cape Fear section of North Carolina, one of the two men of that colony proscribed by the British at the outset.

When clemency was offered all recanting rebels in 1776, he and Cornelius Harnett, known as the "Samuel Adams of North Carolina," were excepted. His soundness was beyond dispute; his military ability so manifest in the early Virginia campaigning, where he commanded the 1st North Carolina Infantry, that Congress made him a brigadier general of the Continental Army. Like Wayne, he was the butt of one of André's rhymes, the occasion being when he dueled with the South Carolinian, Christopher Gadsen, his detractor, and ripped Gadsen's ear with a pistol ball.[2]

Twenty days after the Pennsylvania Line mutinied, the whole affair seemed about to be reenacted by New Jersey troops stationed at Pompton. Washington was now satisfied that the army around West Point would be faithful in any emergency so he applied firmer methods to the Jersey revolters. He dispatched Howe's newly formed corps with orders to force them into unconditional submission and to execute the ringleaders. There were to be no parley and no terms offered.

Howe was the man for the task. He made a long night march, surprised the mutineers in their huts at dawn, forced them to parade without arms, required them to designate their three most incendiary leaders, had them tried by a drumhead court-martial, reprieved one as less guilty, selected the twelve most active offenders next to the two, and compelled the twelve to shoot the two on the spot. The mutiny was effectively quelled. Washington said to Congress: "I thought it indispensible to bring the matter to an issue and risk all extremities. Unless this dangerous spirit can be suppressed by force, there is an end to all subordination in the Army, and indeed to the Army itself."

Wayne's experience with still another mutiny came next. From time to time there had been suggestions that he should be sent to the South, apparently on no other account than the adage in the army that "Wayne was where the fighting was." As the war cooled in the North, Washington and Clinton merely watching each other, it flamed in hot fury and with varying fortunes in the South. Washington's devotion to the cause above any yearning for personal glory becomes apparent when one names the officers he was sending south. Among them were some of his most capable leaders—Greene, Wayne, Lafayette, Howe, Morgan, and Light Horse Harry Lee.[3]

Little more than a month had passed after the settlement with the Pennsylvania Line mutineers when Wayne was ordered to take them to Virginia to assist Lafayette.

Clinton at this time sent Major General William Phillips (whose artillery had killed Lafayette's father at Minden) with 2,500 Hessians and Loyalists to oppose the approaching Lafayette. Washington, hoping to clear Virginia of the enemy, now added Wayne's strength to that of Lafayette, who as a major general would retain command. As Lafayette marched through Baltimore he halted long enough to buy at his own expense new uniforms and undergarments for his entire force. For once, an American army would not be fighting in rags.[4]

Wayne ordered a concentration in York, Pennsylvania, as a step-off point, He could not outfit his soldiers so readily. Transportation was as urgent a requirement as uniforms, and wagons for hauling food and matériel were difficult to procure and assemble. Wayne's force has usually been placed at 800 men but was larger. The three regiments commanded by the three colonels, Butler, Walter Stewart, and Humpton, and the 4th Continental Artillery complement commanded by Lieutenant Colonel Thomas Forrest, who had been with Washington at the capture of the Hessians at Trenton, aggregated when finally collected upward of 1,100. That many were present when they finally reached Lafayette. Though Wayne received his orders to go south in late February, he was unable to move from York until May 20.

The men had been scattered after the mutiny. Most of them obtained furloughs and were slow to arrive and reenlist. But the principal delay was with the state auditors calculating what was owed to each man in arrearages and bounties and paying them in Continental notes, the best currency available. This and other causes prevented many from reaching the rendezvous on time. The Continental scrip caused bad spirits and grumbling, especially since all paper currency was on the toboggan and its true value, if it had much, was always difficult to determine. The men complained to Wayne that the money they received was not worth one-seventh of its stated value. As Wayne explained it: "This was an alarming circumstance. The soldiery but too sensibly felt the imposition, nor did the conduct or precept of the inhabitants tend to moderate, but rather inflame their minds, by refusing to part with anything for it; saying it was not worth accepting, and that they ought not to march until justice was done them."[5]

With the mutiny still fresh in their minds, this kind of talk, he felt, was about all that was needed to trigger off a new revolt. The men distinguished the paper from coin by calling coin "real" and paper "ideal" money. Over the issue of "real" versus "ideal" money, Wayne was about to sustain the shocking experience of another mutiny.

On the day before the march for Virginia was scheduled to begin, a group on the right of each regiment called out that they were not to be trifled with longer and wanted to be paid in real and not ideal money. When ordered into their tents they refused to go. Wayne was not prepared for any more temporizing. He had put the regimental officers on the alert. They knocked the ringleaders down to the ground, seized them, and put them under close confinement. Then Wayne ordered a court-martial to sit then and there in the open, in front of the little army. Like Robert H. Howe with the New Jersey mutineers, he believed in justice, but justice following speedily on the heels of the offense. As he stated it in a letter home: "The commission of the crime, trial, and execution, were all included in the course of a few hours, in front of the line, paraded under arms. The determined countenances of the officers produced a conviction to the soldiery that the sentence of the court-martial would be carried into execution at every risk and consequence."

He did not tell his wife and family the entire story of the execution. One of the men was not killed by the volley but lay writhing on the ground, and Wayne compelled one of the executioners, by holding a pistol to his head, to thrust a bayonet through the prostrate mutineer's body. The offender—Wayne called the mutineers "rogues"—could not be left in his agony and there was no reason to pardon him because the musket ball had not proved fatal. It would surely have been more humane to inflict the traditional *coup de grace* with another bullet; but this was a second mutiny, a special case requiring special action. Seeing the conspirator put to death with the same weapon which he and those watching knew and used so well to terrify the enemy, may have been what was needed to terrify out of them any thoughts of further mutiny.

Wayne did not distinguish whether it was by design or accident, but it could scarcely have been an accident that the special friends and messmates of the convicted men were the ones who did the executing. "Whilst the tears rolled down their cheeks in showers, they silently and faithfully obeyed their orders without a moment's hesitation. Thus was the hideous monster crushed in its birth, however to myself and officers a most painful scene."[6]

Wayne marched his brigade along the eastern slope of the Blue Ridge and thence eastward, and on June 7, 1781, joined Lafayette at Ely's Ford of the Rapidan River about twenty miles upstream from Fredericksburg. Meantime, Phillips had died, and on May 20 Cornwallis brought up the advance elements of his army from Wilmington, North Carolina, to where he had retreated after his stubborn battle with Greene at Guilford Court House. At Petersburg he picked up Phillips' force seven days after that officer's death, sent his cavalry leader Banastre Tarleton on a raid to Charlottesville, then turned on Lafayette, who, prior to his arrival, had been advancing on Petersburg. Cornwallis, the most active of the British generals, undertook unsuccessfully to interpose his army between Wayne, of whose approach he was aware, and Lafayette, but Lafayette retired as far as Fredericksburg while Cornwallis followed only to the North Anna River. Cornwallis had an army of about 7,200 men while Lafayette after his juncture with Wayne had less than half that number. Cornwallis had reassured Clinton that "the boy cannot escape me," but after Wayne joined the boy the British commander was content to send out raiding parties under Tarleton and Colonel John Graves Simcoe, each with their legions, not desiring to take his main army too far from water transportation on Chesapeake Bay and, thereby, contact with Clinton in New York.

When Steuben brought in some newly organized Virginia Continentals and other Virginia brigades joined him, Lafayette's force was increased to about 4,500, an army of sufficient size to maneuver with Cornwallis, though not to fight him except under highly favorable circumstances. Wayne here encountered his associate of Stony Point glory, Christian Febiger, now head of the Continentals Steuben had trained and a part of Steuben's Division.

Cornwallis returned from the North Anna to Richmond, then moved down the Peninsula to Williamsburg, where he rested briefly. He had marched, almost without rest, up through the Carolinas, north to Guildford Court House, then back to Wilmington, and up to Petersburg, a distance of about 1,500 miles, constantly maneuvering, marching and countermarching, and fighting battles. One even of his enterprise needed breathing time. But it was rudely interrupted by Clinton, who feared a combined attack on New York by Washington and Rochambeau and ordered Cornwallis to send him reenforcements of 3,000 men.

To board them on transports Cornwallis would have to cross the James River and go to Portsmouth, on the Elizabeth River near Norfolk. No sooner had he moved from Williamsburg than Lafayette was informed by his alert cavalryman, Lieutenant Colonel John Mercer, on July 5, that the British army had camped within nine miles of the ruins of Jamestown preparatory to crossing the river on the following day at Jamestown Island, on which the first English settlement in America stood. Lafayette and Wayne, believing an opportunity would be offered to fall on Cornwallis' rear while he was halfway over the river, crowded closer and took position on the early morning of July 6 at Green Spring planatation.

Cornwallis was apprised of Lafayette's position and deduced that he would likely be assailed at the crossing, which he intended to make at the Jamestown Ford. Very likely the man who described himself as a British deserter who came to Wayne that morning, accompanied by a slave, was sent by Cornwallis, though Tarleton claimed he, not Cornwallis, sent him to confuse Wayne. He reported that the British army already had begun to cross, that the main body was over the river, and a sizeable rear guard was exposed on the north bank.

Reconnaissance was difficult because the country was enveloped in an early morning fog. By noon it had lifted but a seething hotness made operations inadvisable. Lafayette brought up his army behind

General Lord Charles Cornwallis, by John Singleton Copley, now in Boston Museum of Fine Arts. *(Photo from National Archives)*

Wayne, who had at the outset 450 men, later brought to above 800 when his three regiments were up with two field pieces—guns which Wayne, a bayonet man, looked on as largely decorative, and more difficult to haul about than they were worth on the battlefield. In this instance, though, the two field pieces played their little part in the Battle of Green Spring Plantation, or, as it was sometimes called, Jamestown Ford, which Wayne with three regiments and a few auxiliaries fought on July 6 against the entire British army. Nearly always it has been rated deservedly as among Wayne's most brilliant achievements.

Wayne had been moving a few miles in advance of Lafayette as they came down from Fredericksburg, skirted Richmond, and closed in to watch Cornwallis at Williamsburg. From Green Spring plantation Wayne advanced toward Jamestown, near where he sighted the British when the fog lifted. Partly because of the oppressive heat he waited until 3 p.m. before feeling out the enemy, judging also that the late hour would permit a withdrawal in darkness if he were deceived about the size of the force in his front. The crafty Cornwallis had, in fact, set a trap for Lafayette. He had not begun any crossing of the James but had hidden his main body behind the heavy foliage and screened it with Tarleton's cavalry and some light infantry.

As was the case in several of his engagements, Wayne was hampered by a morass, this time one of the Chickahominy River swamps through which a causeway, built on a log foundation, connected with the firm ground on which the enemy waited.

Wayne threw two small rifle companies and a handful of dragoons to his front and followed with two cavalry troops, one under Lieutenant Colonel Mercer and a second commanded by one of the striking French officers drawn to the American War, Colonel Charles Armand, Marquis de la Rouarie. As Wayne moved toward the British, Lafayette came up in support, while twelve miles behind him Steuben remained in reserve at Byrd's Tavern. Wayne's force, though put at 800 probably aggregated more than 1,000 with his cavalry and rifle corps reinforcements. He crossed the morass and with his light troops and cavalry began an attack on a picket of Hessian jägers, at the time he was bringing up his three Line regiments, with Butler on the left and Humpton on the right, and Stewart in support. To the right of Butler was a battalion of Connecticut light infantry under Major John Wyllys. With this line he occupied a ditch, in front of which a rail fence gave good concealment, the two forming a strong position. Cornwallis, in preparation for his crossing the James River, had thrown up entrenchments for his rear guard but these were not in view.

Wayne's light troops and cavalry easily drove in the Hessian picket, which Cornwallis had ordered to fall back quickly to lure Wayne into his trap, then effectively pressed back Tarleton's cavalry, which was more of a lure than a determined combat force. For two hours the Pennsylvania Line regiments directed a persistent fire on what appeared to be the British rear guard in the woods. At that time Cornwallis, seeing that he could not draw on his attackers farther, began an advance that pushed in the light troops on Wayne's flanks and in front and quickly the long red line of British infantry broke from the woods. It was now, Cornwallis reported, sunset.

In a flash Wayne perceived that instead of assailing a rear guard at a time when Cornwallis already had his main body across the river, he was confronted by the entire British army that outnumbered him perhaps seven to one. On Cornwallis' right were the 43rd, 76th and 80th regiments that might be regarded among the most stalwart of British forces in America, commanded by Colonel Thomas Dundas. On his left was a part of the force Benedict Arnold had brought to Virginia to slash about around Richmond.

Cornwallis thought his chance was offered at last to fulfill his promise to Clinton that "the boy cannot escape me." Possibly the entire Virginia campaign rested on the decision of this minute. If Cornwallis, whose line was already overlapping Wayne's flanks, should bag the Pennsylvanian, Lafayette, close by, could scarcely extricate himself, and Steuben's small division, mostly militia and recruits, though it could probably escape, would be of little consequence. Considering the vagaries of warfare, it is strongly probable that had not Wayne been capable of quick thinking in an emergency, Cornwallis would never have been driven to the extremities of Yorktown, the French fleet would not have been attracted toward Virginia, and Washington would not have been tempted to make his long march from the Hudson highlands.

Wayne knew that if he retired, the withdrawal would become precipitate and likely degenerate into a rout. Instead of calling for a retreat he ordered his Pennsylvania regiments to charge the center of Cornwallis' army with the bayonet. Few instances as audacious are found in this bitter war, and likely few had such far-reaching significance.

When Wayne ordered his trumpeters to sound the charge, promptly the regiments of Stewart, Humpton, and Butler responded. Suddenly Cornwallis' center was hit by a compact, shouting mass of intrepid, hardy soldiers who relied on naked steel, and quickly the British line recoiled. Of Wayne it was said that his "presence of mind never forsook him, and, in moments of great danger, his judgment seemed the most astute and faithful." That was what happened at the crisis at Green Spring.[7]

Along with the Pennsylvania Line, the cavalry of Armand and Mercer, the light Connecticut troops of Major Wyllys, and the two little companies of Virginia riflemen rushed into the exciting melée and added to the amazement that swept down the British line. Wyllys and Humpton brought up the two field pieces and fired some rounds that caught the attention of the observant Cornwallis, whose curiosity, then concern, were aroused by the confident nature of Wayne's attack. Surely Lafayette's main army, not merely Wayne's advance guard, was in his front. Circumspection was called for. The firing of the cannon suggested it was not a hit-and-run affair. He pulled back his flanks and poured a heavy fire into Wayne's regiments. It was costly to Wayne, but it did not dislodge the attackers. The important fact was that the charge of the Americans halted the forward movement of the British and gave Wayne the chance he sought to disengage in an orderly manner.

Lafayette, watching from a promontory, took in the whole situation with a glance and was delighted. When he reported to Washington it was in terms of elation. But he could discern that Wayne, battling against such odds, was imperiled, so he sent back orders and had his own little army deployed in Wayne's rear to cover the retreat that was inevitable. His men crossed over the causeway and formed a line of battle half a mile back.

Wayne withdrew without great difficulty as dusk was settling over the field and the mists were beginning to rise from the James and Chickahominy swamplands. Cornwallis did not pursue. Here, again, good judgment had its reward. By not attacking until midafternoon; by devoting two hours to musketry against the British line; by the fight of the light troops; by the British advance; and by Wayne's counterattack, daylight had been expended. Night settled over the battlefield, over which Wayne could look with satisfaction. The main line of the enemy was halted. His little army stopped its retirement at Green Spring plantation, half a mile in the rear. Cornwallis did not molest their crossing of the causeway. He could renew the battle in the morning if circumstances were auspicious. They never were. Wayne's quick retreat had confused him and he feared an ambuscade. Tarleton criticised him for not following in the darkness.

Wayne saved all of his wagons but lost the two field pieces and 139 men killed, wounded, and missing, twice Cornwallis' losses. All of the artillery horses and most of the artillerymen had been killed or disabled and the guns themselves were rendered unserviceable. With all of his good fortune on this field, where he might have encountered disaster, Wayne was thinking not of how fate had smiled on him by the nature of his escape, but optimistically of his prospects of victory. He wrote on the following day: "From the mutual emulation in the officers and men of each corps, I am confident that, had the army been in force, victory would have inclined to our arms. However, every circumstance considered, our small reconnoitering party of horse and foot, who had the hardiness to engage Lord Cornwallis at the head of the whole British army, with the advantage of a powerful cavalry, on their own ground and in their own camp, are more to be envied than pitied on this occasion; and I trust that, in an equal contest, we shall produce a conviction to the world that we deserve success."[8]

Cornwallis reported to Clinton that all he needed was a little more daylight and he could have captured "the entire corps," meaning both Wayne and Lafayette. Possibly he could have defeated the Americans, but only after a desperate struggle, which he did not resume when he had a chance in daylight the next morning. Instead, he crossed the James River, marched south to Suffolk, crossed the Elizabeth River and moved north to Portsmouth. There he found that the order to send 3,000 men to Clinton had been countermanded, because Clinton had received troops from England. Not liking Portsmouth because he regarded it low, unhealthy, and exposed, as did Clinton from the reports he had about it, he suggested that Old Point Comfort, on the north bank of the James after it broadens into Hampton Roads, would be superior. He reconnoitered there, found it likewise unsuited, and selected what he judged the better campsite on the water, where he could await reinforcements, at Yorktown. He moved there unopposed and occupied as well Gloucester across the York River.

One battle at Green Spring, though minimized as unimportant by Cornwallis, elated the country and produced for Wayne much the same kind of applause he won from Stony Point. He knew how to handle troops in combat. Washington was generous in his commendation, but was already thinking of another assignment for Wayne in the South. He wrote: "I, with the greatest pleasure, received the official account of the action at Green Spring. The Marquis de La Fayette speaks in the handsomest manner of your own behaviour, and that of the troops, in action. I think the account which Lord Cornwallis will be obliged to render of the state of southern affairs, will not be very pleasing to ministerial eyes and ears. . . . I am in hopes that Virginia will be soon, if not before this time, so far relieved as to permit you to march to the succor of General Greene, who, with a handful of men, has done more than could possibly have been expected; should he be enabled to maintain his advantage in the Carolinas and Georgia, it cannot fail of having the most important political consequences in Europe."

Greene was equally enthusiastic: "The marquis gives you glory for your late conduct in the action at Jamestown, and I am sensible you merit it. It gives me great pleasure to hear of the success of my friends; but be a little careful and tread softly, for depend upon it, you have a modern Hannibal to deal with in the person of Lord Cornwallis. . . ."

Wayne made a good summary of Green Spring for Greene, who had not followed Cornwallis to Virginia but was busy trying to reconquer the Carolinas: "Among the choice of difficulties we adopted the manoeuvers of advancing and charging him [Cornwallis] which was done with such spirit and [obscure word] as to produce the desired effect by obliging them to halt their wings to consolidate their force, call back the flanks and form them in the rear. The door thus opened for retreat and we were not long in adopting it. . . . The few flankers we could afford were obliged to take to the woods to avoid a pass through deep swamps, so that when we came in contact our whole force was about 450 Pennsylvanians, opposed to many thousands. The enemy have had candour enough to acknowledge they were diverted from their original disposition."

Lafayette in his reconnoitering had inspired Wayne's admiration, for the marquis did not hesitate to go within musket shot of the enemy. In writing to Greene, of whom he had become increasingly fond, Wayne said of Lafayette that "if he has a fault it is an excess of bravery which if a crime it is of its nature the least to be reprehended in a soldier."

Another letter from his admirer, Robert Morris, showed an affectionate warmth both for Wayne and the Pennsylvania troops: "We have received a full report of the action at Green Springs. It is very flattering to find our troops arrived to that degree of discipline which enables them to face, with inferior numbers, that proud foe who have heretofore attempted to treat our army with such contempt. It is still more agreeable to find these handful of troops have been led to the your competitors for glory to enjoy the sweets, whilst you endure the conflict by officers revered for their public, and esteemed for their private, conduct through life. I do assure you, my worthy friend, that I shall think my present toils well rewarded when they enable you and toils of a military life."

SIXTEEN

Yorktown – but Not the End

THE UBIQUITOUS Allan McLane, who had disguised himself as a farm hand to reconnoiter inside Stony Point and sold the meat of dead cavalry horses to the British in Philadelphia during the Valley Forge winter, and scouted impudently almost everywhere, had been on a midsummer trip to the Caribbean, where the giant of an admiral, the Comte François de Grasse, intellectually strong as well as physically brawny, had the French fleet.

Under orders to cooperate with Rochambeau and the Americans, de Grasse determined that he could remain away from his West Indian station only until sometime in October. Washington and Rochambeau, who had talked again at Wethersfield, near Hartford, Connecticut, were planning a descent on Clinton in New York. De Grasse was expected to cooperate.

Everyone knew Allan McLane because he had assailed Philadelphia with his small band on the night of the Mischianza, the fete honoring Howe on his departure for England, and had almost broken it up by firing the abatis and creating such a din that it made the British prepare for an assault by Washington's entire army. McLane was one of the sharpest nettles to the British during the war.

Possibly it was no more than that McLane was large, hearty, and a thoroughly virile battler who crowded much into every day—qualities and traits common with those of the French admiral—that warmed de Grasse to him and made his conference fruitful. Their avoirdupois must have been about the same, though McLane's distribution was upward while de Grasse's was so horizontal that his walk was a waddle.

The result of it, according to McLane (and there is no reason to distrust the account of this able man), was that de Grasse was influenced to sail not to attack Clinton in New York, but to operate against Cornwallis in Virginia. In any event, de Grasse, whose orders from Rochambeau were discretionary, decided on the Chesapeake. The New York plans were scrapped—the attack there looked difficult—and Washington made his spectacular, surprise march from the Hudson River highlands to the Head of Elk, where his army boarded de Grasse's transports and was carried to Williamsburg. The genius of the movement was Washington's. French fleets had been along the coast from time to time without much significance, but he was willing to venture that if de Grasse could hold off reinforcements to Cornwallis by sea, he and Rochambeau could invest Yorktown and very likely capture another large British army and possibly end the war by that happy stroke.

Wayne was at Westover in Virginia, on the right of Lafayette's force, which extended across the peninsula from the York to the James River, watching Cornwallis. Lafayette wrote to Wayne on August 25, imparting the secret information that Washington was coming south. Though Clinton is alleged in many accounts to have been dumbfounded when he learned that Washington had left the highlands and had already crossed the Delaware, that general asserted emphatically that he was not surprised. Indeed, he had warned Germain against just such a move. He was most apprehensive of French naval superiority.

Washington did, in fact, slip away. Information of his probable intentions seems to have been passed around rather generously, but by his ruses he stole about three days' marches and was getting huzzahs as he passed through Philadelphia, with Rochambeau's 4,000 French troops close behind, while Clinton was still knitting his brows in New York.

Lafayette's letter to Wayne on August 25 was bubbling and irrepressible: "I am happy in this safe opportunity to open my heart to you. There is an important secret which I communicate to you alone, and which I request you to keep from every body's knowledge. There is great reason to hope for an immediate aid by water. In the last letter from the general, he communicates this intelligence, which I am bound upon honor to keep secret. He directs me to keep you here until further orders; and, above all, recommends that every measure may be taken to prevent the enemy's retiring to Carolina."

From his position at Westover, Wayne might cross the James river and interpose should Cornwallis cross and try to head south. One of Washington's main fears, as he marched toward Virginia, was that Cornwallis might be able to break through Lafayette and escape to the south. Lafayette continued to Wayne: "I would, therefore, wish you to take a healthy position near Westover; to make very preparation; to collect the means of helping to keep up the idea of a southern destination, and to improve your situation upon James' river, in having your men well supplied."[1]

Wayne replied, saying he had moved first to Malvern Hill, then, apparently to enforce the idea of a southern movement, had crossed the James "by persevering night and day, with a few bad boats without any hands, excepting soldiers unacquainted with water craft." He took a position at Cabin's Point and told Lafayette "that if I find Lord Cornwallis anxious to pass the river, I will endeavor to dissuade him from it by the most forcible arguments."

Washington and Rochambeau were on the Peninsula in front of Yorktown on September 25, in good season for de Grasse to cooperate and get back to his cherished West Indian base. Lafayette and Wayne then concentrated their forces at Williamsburg and joined the main army, helping to give Washington the largest army he had ever commanded. De Grasse drove off the British fleets under Admirals Graves and Hood, which sought to intervene. The curtain was run up for the last and greatest spectacle of the American Revolution.

When Yorktown was invested Rochambeau occupied the left of Washington's line, the American army the right, with Wayne's Pennsylvanians on the right close by Lincoln's division and near the York River, in the zone of the attack. Wayne was mentally alert, emotionally buoyant, but physically half-incapacitated during the early part of the siege. He had taken another wound, this his fifth in his country's cause. Like the others, it was happily not critical. It could not be called accidental but it came from a nervous, trigger-happy American sentry.

After Lafayette had imparted to Wayne the intelligence that Washington was coming, he called the Pennsylvanian to his headquarters at Williamsburg, a ride of two hours, which Wayne, made under darkness.

The oncoming French were light-hearted, debonair, fun-loving, wine-drinking but still excellent fighting soldiers and Lafayette now had some of them from the fleet. They had been putting on dramatic skits. One, the recently composed opera "Lucille," by André Grétry, was presented for American officers, once before and once after Washington came. Wayne went to Lafayette either to attend a performance, or for a glass with the marquis along with army business. Whatever his main purpose, he never had a chance to fulfill it.

Arriving at ten o'clock, September 2, he was challenged. He answered the sentry with the proper countersign, casually, for he was unsuspecting. Suddenly the man's musket belched a sheet of flame at close range and a sharp pain doubled Wayne across the saddle as the ball tore violently through his hip. It missed the bone but lodged in the flesh in the rear of the thigh. Severe as was the pain, to his surprise it set off an even sharper sympathetic pain in his foot, and that pain abided long after the hip wound had healed. The lower pain turned into gout that plagued Wayne through all of his later years. He always attributed the disease to the sentry's bullet at Williamsburg. Modern physicians might smile at his own diagnosis, but he went to his grave, when the gout finally conquered him, fully believing he was dying from the sentry's fire.

For a moment he was in extreme danger. The shot had brought the full guard running and they were about to blaze away at what they supposed were oncoming Tarleton raiders. Wayne's shouts quieted them. Lafayette, who heard his voice, came rushing out and carried him into headquarters, with Wayne's oaths still ringing out clamorously on the late summer air. The marquis put him to bed, got the surgeon, and kept him in bed for ten days. Fortunately they were days of inactivity, during the time when Washington was marching south, the French fleet had Chesapeake Bay corked between the capes, and Lafayette's troops and the three Pennsylvania Line regiments that Wayne left under Butler's command were guarding Cornwallis against any attempt at a breakout.

He wrote to Polly "lest you should receive unfavorable accounts." He told of his arrival at Lafayette's headquarters at 10 p.m., and the sentry's challenge, then: "But the poor fellow being panic stricken, and mistaking me for the British, immediately fired his piece and shot me in the middle of the thigh. The ball fortunately only grazed the bone and lodged pretty near the opposite side to which it entered. The whole camp was alarmed and I had some difficulty (wounded as I was) to prevent the whole advance guard from firing on me." Since he had never had gout before, he thought it extraordinary, as he told Polly, that the wound "brought it on me as quick as electricity, so much so that I thought I was wounded in the foot at the same instant." The foot, he said, continued much more painful than the thigh. At the time he wrote, on September 12, he said he was "much mended."[2]

By the time Washington arrived and surrounded Yorktown, Wayne was limping about in command of his brigade once more, and became a highly important element in Washington's method of throwing up parallel trenches that brought him nearer to the British works. Wayne's men would dig one night, then stand guard for the diggers the next night. Butler's journal, which recounts some of the activities of Wayne's command, gives evidence of the impatient wait for the heavy French fleet ordnance to be brought up from Williamsburg. On September 29 the allied army occupied a position in front of the enemy's works and the siege began.

The British opened a severe fire which the Americans, not yet having their guns up, could not answer. Butler counted the British artillery shots and arrived at 351 for October 2, between sunup and sunset, during which time Wayne's brigade was acting as the covering party. All night long the British shot fell from their works and about 10 p.m. the ships off Gloucester joined in the cannonade. "I reconnoitered the post at Gloster," Wayne's ranking colonel wrote, "and the shipping, which I compute at 10 sail; the Gloster port not strong—I think, by the size of the camp, 1,000 men; their works not regular, they have one good water battery on the York side; I observed a good work close by the bank with four embrasures, the ground very good for approaches."[3]

Then he reflected the difficulty of hurting Cornwallis at this stage: "In general our works go on slow, the heavy artillery hard to get up; not one piece of cannon as yet fired at them. Indeed, I discover very plainly that we are young soldiers in a siege; however, we are determined to benefit ourselves by experience; one virtue we possess, that is perseverence. . . ." Such was the spirit in Wayne's command, where the casualties were light despite the heavy British cannonading. Four men of one regiment in the covering party were killed on the next night, October 3, by a single cannon ball. Captain James Duncan of Wayne's Brigade bemoaned the loss of a private named Smith, "one of the finest men in the army," and told of another, a militiaman possessed of more bravery than prudence, who "stood on the parapet and damned his soul if he would dodge for the buggers." Luck was with him for a time— longer than anyone expected—and he became so foolhardy that instead of digging, he waved his spade at every cannon ball that passed. Then one hit him and the shovel waved no more.[4]

On October 4 Wayne limped beside Butler to reconnoiter along the York River, where the British were throwing up new defenses. Two deserters came over and reported to them, as Butler related it, that Cornwallis' army was puny, the sick in the hospitals numbering as high as 2,000, which would be about a fourth of his entire army. His force was calculated at 7,500 plus an indefinite number of Loyalists who aggregated into the hundreds. The British camp was tight, congested, according to the deserters, with insufficient acreage for so many men. That would mean enough muskets along the redans that it would be costly to take the place by storm. But, that night de Grasse landed 2,000 French marines on the Gloucester side, a welcome addition. Tarleton, now on the north bank, was urging, although the allies of course did not know it, that Cornwallis cross the river to Gloucester and cut his way out of the encirclement by marching northwest up the York and Matapony rivers. Washington had to guard against a breakthrough to the north as well as to the south. But could Cornwallis, wandering through Virginia and Maryland, have fared better than Burgoyne? Though a more resourceful general than the dapper gentleman of the gaming tables, and though he had a magnificent veteran army that had responded to him faithfully during the gruelling Carolina campaign against Greene, it is highly unlikely that he could have reached any haven where he could get contact with, and aid from, the indisposed Clinton. Already he seemed doomed.

He did, late in the siege, when faced with desperate last resorts, adopt the plan of crossing the York river, cutting his way through the French who invested Gloucester, and marching toward New York. He assembled boats and boarded his best grenadiers, and ferried the first consignment across. But the night darkened and the heavens smiled on the American cause through their gusty blackness. The effort had to be abandoned.

Yorktown was not an infantry or bayonet battle. Here at length was an action for the gunners, who gradually blew the British ramparts to bits. There was much night firing. The Pennsylvania and Maryland militia were busy making gabions, a sort of container of wicker, or sometimes a metal cylinder, filled with earth, used like sandbags to give greater strength to the works. Many of these were carried by Wayne's men the next night to near the York River, where the first parallel of trenches was formed in that area 400 paces from the British lines.

Thus the siege continued from day to day. On the 8th Steuben's Division, to which Wayne's regiments were now attached, completed a large battery on the extreme right, on the bank of the York River, mounting three 29-pounders, three 18-pounders, two 10-inch mortars and two 8-inch howitzers. A similar battery was completed by the

French on the extreme left, while a still larger battery was brought up in the center. Washington was on hand for the beginning of the American bombardment with the heavy guns. "The Commander-in-Chief paid the allies the compliment of firing first," wrote Butler. The French fired on the left, then Washington personally fired the first of the American guns.[5]

Thus continued the inexorable progress on the parallels at night, so that on near successive mornings the British, in spite of their tremendous night cannonades, could view the allied approach with fresh consternation. On the night of October 10, de Grasse threw red-hot shot into the British frigate *Caron*, and quickly her hull and sails were engulfed in a great, spectacular conflagration that lighted the river, the little towns of Yorktown and Gloucester, and the great camps of the two armies locked in their deadly struggle. Two transports were burned to the water's edge but others were preserved and most of the small boats remained intact for use in Cornwallis's last desperate effort to escape, which the storm frustrated.

Wayne normally would have led the main infantry action of the siege, had he not still suffered from his wound. Fresh daring was appearing under younger leadership. Colonel Alexander Hamilton, who had quit as Washington's secretary in a huff because the great man was brusque in his censure when Hamilton was a trifle slow responding to his summons, now sought glory in line duty. He commanded the American storming party which, under the general direction of Lafayette, took one of the two redoubts the British had pushed out 300 yards in advance of their works. The redoubt allowed them an enfilade fire against the second American parallel. A similar redoubt was taken by the French, on the same night, October 14.

Some days before the end, who should appear at headquarters but the stripped-down St. Clair. He had no soldiers. Wayne, who now again commanded Pennsylvania regiments, was still yielding to rank but was safely under another major general—Steuben. St. Clair had been left behind with the duty of defending Philadelphia. It was not an idle assignment because there was always the possibility that Cornwallis might be able to break away and form a juncture with Clinton there. But St. Clair wanted to be in on the kill. He gained permission and hurried south.

Cornwallis swept his eyes back and forth daily across the blue waters of the river and down the eleven miles to Chesapeake Bay, hoping against reason that Clinton would stir, waiting for the proud might of the British navy to assert itself. Finally Cornwallis capitulated on October 19 and the band by tradition played "The World Turned

Upside Down." Washington sent his aide Tench Tilghman racing on horseback to Philadelphia, where he arrived at the home of the President of Congress shortly before 3 a.m. The night watchman began crying repeatedly through the streets, "Three o'clock! Starlight night! Cornwallis is taken!" In London, when the news came, anguished Lord North strode dejectedly back and forth, echoing again and again, "Oh God! It is all over." The king demurred but Commons wanted no more of it and the measures were slowly set into motion for recognition of a new and independent nation.

After the surrender Wayne wrote to his friend Robert Morris describing it as an "event of the utmost consequence" which, "if properly improved may be productive of a glorious and happy peace." He added a warning against suffering that "unworthy torpor and supinity to seize us, which but too much pervaded the Councils of America after the surrender of Genl Burgoyne."[6]

But the war was not over. Washington, after a visit at Mount Vernon, went back to the highlands. Four important coastal cities remained under British occupancy—New York, Wilmington, North Carolina, Charleston, and Savannah. For Washington the humdrum of waiting and watching was resumed. Greene was busy rewinning South Carolina. Georgia remained. The assignment there fell quite naturally to Anthony Wayne.

Mad Anthony Recovers Georgia

ANTHONY WAYNE WAS richly entitled to a long leave and wanted it. He could well picture the disorder at Waynesborough, which missed the owner's directing hand. He longed to see his family—his wife, Polly, daughter Margaretta, his son Isaac. He wrote his request to Washington and confidently awaited the answer. But the determined commander in chief, seeing final victory within his grasp after Yorktown, had to ride heedlessly over all personal considerations in his hope to clear the thirteen provinces of the invaders as speedily as he could. He reluctantly told Wayne he had work in mind for him and could not let him go.

The assignment was to reinforce Greene, who sorely needed help in South Carolina and Georgia, where he had been fighting with a step-child army clothed in rags against some of the best British talent, including Lord Francis Rawdon, commander at Charleston. He worsted Greene at Hobkirk's Hill because of the meagerness and irresolution of the American militia, but Greene showed his qualities by writing, much in the spirit of the old Scotch ballad, that "We fight, get beat, and rise to fight again." That action was on April 25, 1781, at a time when Wayne was preparing at York, Pennsylvania, to march to Virginia. Then came bloody Ninety-Six, in May and June, where Greene besieged the last British post in the interior of South Carolina. He was repulsed and could not prolong the siege because Rawdon was coming toward it with relief.[1]

Next was the sanguinary battle of Eutaw Springs, a battle which had an influence on Wayne because Greene's losses were so heavy that he required more men. He told Washington it was "a most bloody battle—by far the most obstinate fight I ever saw."[2]

Of the 2,300 men he took into the combat, 522 were casualties, a rate of more than one out of five. Of these, 18 officers and 102 men were killed. Thus Wayne's reinforcements coming down from Yorktown did not do much more than bring Greene's small army up to the strength it had before this costly battle. Wayne moved slowly, his rate being controlled by a herd of 400 cattle that was diminished as beef was used for rations.

For the good of the service Wayne had to swallow his pride and accompany the "caitiff" St. Clair, who headed the Pennsylvania Line regiments being sent south. Because his wounded leg and gout were still causing him much pain, he had to ride in a carriage with one foot propped up on the front seat. He could not assert himself on the conduct of the march. St. Clair, in control, did not keep as tight a command as Wayne had done and lost a good many men on the march by straggling and desertion. Undoubtedly because Greene knew that Wayne would be happier in an independent department, away from St. Clair, the southern commander assigned him to the task of driving the British out of Georgia. That might not have been difficult had he not stripped the general of his cherished Pennsylvania Line regiments, that Wayne had trained and knew so well, and that knew him. Greene felt that because he was operating against a stronger enemy in South Carolina, now concentrated in Charleston, he would need the Pennsylvanians. Wayne consented tacitly: as John Armstrong stated, he offered "not a syllable of complaint." The admiration he had felt for Greene during the New Jersey and Valley Forge days was strengthened to a deep fondness and overriding sympathy during this southern campaigning, as he witnessed what Greene could accomplish with small numbers suffering great privation against some of Britain's best officers and soldiers. The truth was, no general ever did more with so little.[3]

St. Clair approached Wilmington, North Carolina, and the British garrison withdrew to Charleston. Then St. Clair got a leave and went north. As Wayne missed the Pennsylvania Line, so it missed his firm hand. The success of the mutiny at Mount Kemble misled a few of the unruly spirits in the ranks. Well before the British evacuated Charleston, some of Wayne's former soldiers, anxious to get home, became refractory under Greene. A sergeant named Gornell, who had been active in the Mount Kemble mutiny, thought he could get money from the British by kidnapping Greene and delivering him to the Charleston garrison. He communicated with the British about it. He and a few others were to call for a general mutiny of Pennsylvania and Maryland troops after Greene had been seized.

Sergeant Gornell must have forgotten Wayne's summary executions of the malcontents at York, Pennsylvania, before he marched south, or else he had decided the plot would be successful while Wayne was away. Greene learned about it, arrested Gornell, and hanged him, April 22, 1782. Four other sergeants involved were taken by guards and turned loose in the interior of the state. Some others escaped and went over to the enemy. That was the last flareup of mutiny in the Pennsylvania Line, or in Greene's other regiments. Strong measures were effective.[4]

The troops Wayne had available to take to Georgia were a detachment of 100 of Moyland's dragoons with whom he had operated often, and some artillery. The dragoons were commanded by a New Jersey colonel, Anthony White. The most important addition was a single young officer, Colonel James Jackson, twenty-four years old, who had emigrated from Devonshire, England, two years before the war, had become a Savannah bank clerk, and displayed such leadership qualities that he entered the provincial army as a captain in 1776, and helped to repulse the British that year at Savannah, at the age of nineteen. Soon he rose to be the leading military personality in Georgia, and eventually the commanding political figure in the days of peace, a representative in Congress, senator, governor, and again senator until his death.

Wayne and Jackson became friends. He fought under Moultrie and Pickens in South Carolina and took command at Augusta when the Americans recovered that town from the British in 1781. Then he joined Wayne with few troops but an ardent spirit such as this makeshift army needed.

Wayne crossed the Savannah above Augusta with a force augmented by 300 militiamen under General Wade Hampton of South Carolina—grandfather of the more distinguished Confederate general of that name—and moved to Ebenezer. There he was joined by Jackson and his small command known as the Georgia Legion, consisting of both infantry and cavalry, which Jackson had raised at the instigation of Greene. But with his several well-led units, Wayne could not muster a force of more than 500, and usually not more than 300; with these he faced three alert enemies, the first and most formidable being the British garrison of Savannah under the capable Lieutenant Colonel Alured Clarke, who would rise to become governor of Canada and a lieutenant general in the British army. In Savannah, Clarke had about 1,500 men. Wayne's two other enemies were a sizeable party of Loyalists in his rear and various raiding bands of Creek and Cherokee Indians whom the British had enlisted on the side of the king. At Ebenezer, up the river from Savannah, Wayne was able to keep a watch on the Savannah garrison and to prevent its union with the forces of Loyalists and Indians from the outcountry, a task that required continuous vigilance.

Wayne's assignment was to reinstate "the authority of the Union within the limits of Georgia," and the diligence with which he went about it could be seen from his letter to his former companion General Irvine, written February 24, 1782: "In the five weeks we have been here, not an officer or soldier with me has once undressed, excepting for the purpose of changing his linen. The actual force of the enemy at this moment is more than three times that of mine. What we have been able to do has been done by manoeuvring, rather than by force."[5]

Another glimpse at his situation is found in his letter to his long-time friend and associate Colonel Walter Stewart, to whom he wrote from Ebenezer on February 25, 1782: "I have completed the tour of the thirteen United States, made war in each of them, and now command in the sands and swamps of Georgia. The duty that we have performed on the present occasion was much harder than that of the Children of Israel; they had only to make brick without straw, but we have our army to form without men, provisions, forage and almost every apparatus of war; to provide without boats, bridges, etc., to build without materials except what we took from the stump, and what is yet more difficult than all, to make whigs out of tories, and with them wrest this country out of the enemy, all of which we have affected with the help of a few regular dragoons."

He was now, he told Stewart, in possession of all of the state except Savannah "but how to keep it with our present force is a matter that will require some address, as we have not only the British in front but the Savages in the rear." Then, harkening to earlier days with his old friends, he ejaculated a vain hope: "Would to God you were with us at the head of 1000 such fellows as used to parade with infantry caps decorated with flowing red hair, near the falls [of the] Passaick."

One of Wayne's first operations was to intercept ninety-three pack horses with skins, escorted by thirty mounted Indians and Loyalists. Colonel McCoy of Wayne's force captured three Indians and brought them into camp, where Wayne lectured them, declaring that the enemy was "wickedly and wantonly endeavoring to promote war between them and a people who had never injured them and would much rather make them friends than foes." The stolid Indians were unimpressed. The warfare of the tribes continued.[6]

Wayne at Ebenezer had returned to his reading: Sterne, Richardson, the campaigns of Charles XII of Sweden, and whatever was available in a camp devoted more to killing than culture. He rode alone on many afternoons on one of his handsome horses. Never had he lost his admiration of a beautiful mount. Apparently he reflected much and was at times moody. Where had the war led him? After trudging over the thirteen states that were just about to be free, what was his impression of a soldier's life into which fate had thrown him? Perhaps the closest expression of his conclusions was in a letter of March 2 to Polly: "Sterne's observation 'that a soldier is of a profession that tend to make bad men worse' is ill-natured and unjust; on the contrary I am sateate of this horrid trade of blood, and would much rather spare one poor savage than destroy twenty."[7]

He expressed a disgust of the type of warfare he was now witnessing: "The horrid depredation & murders committed in this country by one inhabitant upon another, i.e., by whigs and tories indiscriminately beggars all description."

Governor John Martin of Georgia had told Wayne in a letter in January, just after he entered the state, that: "I imagine we shall be able, by draft of one half of the militia, to bring about three hundred effectives into the field, exclusive of Jackson's cavalry and infantry, amounting to ninety men, and M'Coy's corps of volunteers to eighty." This was indicative of the small-unit warfare in which he was plunged in the sparsely populated state. Still, it was no less desperate than Washington's major battles. He received acquisitions of 300 men on April 4, consisting of former Loyalists who now were embracing the American cause. Yorktown was having its influence. That enabled him to keep the Savannah garrison in confinement.

Governor Martin tried to be helpful even though he had no supplies of shoes and clothing and some of Wayne's men, like Greene's, were reduced to little more than breechcloths. "Observing when in Camp," the governor wrote, "that your troops appeared to be in great want to Tobacco I shall purchase some as soon as possible & sent it down for their use, as nothing contributes more to health in this climate than that plant."[8]

The British commander Clarke managed to get word to the Indians and urge them to come to Savannah—two parties of Cherokee and one party of Creeks. As the warmth of the Georgia spring reached May, the Indians put on their war paint and moved over the trails toward the city. Wayne, alert, intercepted them. The Cherokee arrived first. By a skillful deployment he captured almost the entire party and adhered to the policy of compassion which he had expressed in his letter to his wife. He brought in the chiefs and treated them with a kindness to which they were unaccustomed. He had already written to Governor Martin in anticipation: "Had we not better make them our friends? and detach them from the enemy than to bring on an inevitable war, by murdering those in our power?" He suggested also that he intended to be lenient with the recanting Loyalists. The Assembly had opened the door and he favored "the reception of those deluded people who were the least obnoxious." Some Hessians also had come to his camp and he wrote to Greene that he planned a diversion that might bring in many more. He circulated a handbill in German offering them forgiveness and tracts of land.

Wayne's account to Irvine is the best explanation of his treatment of the party of Indians. He brought them before him and admonished them: "I briefly stated the ruin and progress of the present war. I informed them that I was no Englishman, but a plain open warrior, born upon the same great island with them—that all we asked of them was to remain quiet spectators until the war was terminated between us and our common enemy, after which our wise men and great warriors would be happy in assisting to open the path that led to the council fires to brighten the claim of friendship, but that if they were deaf to the voice of reason and wished to shed the blood of a people that never injured them: if they preferred the Hatchet to the Olive Branch, we possessed undaunted hearts, strong arms and keen cutting swords and were ready to meet upon their own ground."

The statement was a forecast of Wayne's successful policy with the Indians of the Northwest at a later day. A few of the chiefs were held as hostages, the warriors and braves were sent back to their home campfires and ventured toward Savannah no more.

That was not the case with the Creeks under their celebrated chief Guristersigo, one of the divisional leaders of a powerful and well-advanced tribe that spread over south Georgia and what became Alabama. Called Creeks by the whites because they lived on the waterways, they were properly the Muskogee, an ancient tribe that may have been pushed out of Mexico by the Aztecs. Aware of the approach of Guristersigo with 300 warriors, Colonel Clarke sent Lieutenant Colonel

Thomas Brown out of Savannah with a mixed command of British infantry and horse to join him at Ogeechee and bring him in with his warriors.

Wayne by this time had established a good information system; he learned speedily of Brown's intention and knew he would have to pass along a causeway leading through a marsh. On May 20, by forced marches and great fatigue, he reached the causeway near midnight and to his amazement found the British, who were likewise enterprising, advancing along the causeway at that late hour. He arrived just in time. He was heavily outnumbered because all of his force was not yet arrived. He had one company of infantry and one squadron of dragoons. But he had also his power of quick decision.

Knowing that numbers were not as important as initiative and well-handled blades in a night attack, he ordered a charge with the bayonet. Speedy action told the story. As he reported it, the attack was made with "vivacity and vigor." In the flash of a few minutes the British were defeated and dispersed. They were driven "without burning a grain of powder." Brown suffered forty casualties, a sizeable number for a night attack by two companies that did not fire a single round of ammunition.

The Creek chief and his 300 warriors remained to be dealt with. Guristersigo was no craven. He learned on May 22 that Brown had been worsted and would not reach Ogeechee. Bent on a reprisal, he moved stealthily to the attack through the swamps and forests. Approaching Wayne's camp at midnight on the 24th, he crawled with his warriors through the tall grass and managed to kill the first sentinel before he could fire or make an outcry. Then he fell on the small command of Colonel Thomas Posey, the Virginian who had been with Wayne at Stony Point.

The Indian attack was so frenzied that Posey was pushed back from the artillery park he was guarding. But Wayne's main body was now alarmed. Quickly the dragoons mounted and the infantry formed. Defense never entered Wayne's mind as he ordered the bayonet and saber charge. When it was delivered it broke the loosely formed Indians, who fought as individuals, and put them to flight. The dragoons were on their flanks and cut down those who resisted. Dead on the field was their chief Guristersigo and nineteen warriors who had been brave enough to stand with him against the steel, and fall together. The chief's bravery lasted to the end. While he was on the ground, mortally wounded, the American charge passed over him, led by Wayne. With his dying breath he pointed his pistol at the oncoming Wayne and pulled the trigger. The ball killed the general's horse under him but Wayne was brought down uninjured.

Some who did not know the Georgia swamplands, the long grass, or the wiles of Indian warfare caviled that Wayne had allowed the Creeks to get into his camp. But most who investigated the battle were impressed with the discipline and firmness of his troops the moment they were alerted. The Indians were not to be discounted as dangerous foes, as Braddock's men had found twenty-seven years before in the Pennsylvania woods and St. Clair would discover nine years later in the Ohio wilderness. Wayne's victories over Clarke and Guristersigo were further impressive examples of his mastery of warfare with the bayonet. None ever knew the full Indian casualties because the tribes carried off their dead. Wayne captured 177 pack horses loaded with peltry being taken to the British. His own loss was four killed and eight wounded.[9]

As he gradually grew nearer to Savannah his little army was conducting an investment of sorts which caused Greene to exclaim: "How strange to tell! That the enemy are pounded with less than one-third their numbers." Finally the British withdrew from Ogeechee and held precariously to Savannah, as they did Charleston and New York, waiting for what all knew was coming, the conclusion of peace in Europe.

The British evacuated Savannah on July 12, 1782. Earlier that month Wayne met a group of Loyalist merchants from the town who came out in anticipation of the British departure and were anxious about their status. Wayne said he would inquire of Governor Martin and asked them to return. He would assign to Major John Habersham, who had been one of his active and competent officers, the task of guarding the merchants when the British left. His own policy as he stated it would be: "That the merchants and traders, not citizens of the United States, nor owning allegiance to the state of Georgia, shall be allowed six months to dispose of their effects and adjust their concerns; at the expiration of which term, they will have a flag granted, to convey themselves, and such property as they may have received in exchange or payment for their goods, to one of the nearest British posts, should they request it."

He would make every effort to gain for them an act of oblivion for any offence except murder. For his moderation he gave his reason in his report: "In offering these terms, I had in view not only the interest of the United States, but also that of Georgia; by retaining as many inhabitants and merchants as circumstances would admit, and, with them, a considerable quantity of goods, much wanted for public and private use; but (what was yet of greater consequence) to complete your quota of troops without any expense to the public, and thus reclaim a number of men, who, at another day, will become valuable members of society. This also appears to me an act of justice, tempered with mercy; justice, to oblige those, who have joined or remained with the enemy, to expiate their crime by military service; and mercy, to admit the repentant sinner to citizenship, after a reasonable quarantine. By these means those worthy citizens [the Whigs], who have so long endured every vicissitude of fortune with more than Roman virtue, will be relieved from that duty." His policy was much more magnanimous than was the lot to common Loyalists in other provinces.

With James Jackson and John Habersham in the lead, Wayne's little army occupied Savannah as the British departed. They found the city peaceful, the bitterness of the war almost ended. The Georgia campaign had been most difficult for Mad Anthony. His gout bothered him continually. The disease has been held to be hereditary, which follows the long-standing belief that there are "gouty families." His father, Isaac Wayne's, irascibility and neighborhood quarrels could readily have been the result of gout, which is conducive of outbursts of extreme irritability. Wayne must have had a typical case. He was subject to paroxysms and sharp recurrences of pain in Georgia. He grew depressed at times and not infrequently was petulant. These were not qualities of his earlier, gayer army days.

On top of this annoying and peculiar affliction, he suffered from fever, drawn, it was supposed, from Georgian swamplands. He sickened after his return to South Carolina, where Greene prescribed rest and confinement in bed. His malady was taken for malaria. Probably it was in part sheer exhaustion, for none had given of his energy more wholeheartedly over a longer period than Wayne.

Georgia generously recognized his contributions and devotion, as well as Greene's. To Greene, who commanded the Southern Department, the state presented the estate of Mulberry Grove, fourteen miles above Savannah on the south bank of the Savannah River. It was the confiscated property of the royal governor Graham. As if to recognize the close attachment that had formed between the two generals, Georgia gave the adjoining plantation to Wayne, as a reward for his leadership in liberating the state. Both were magnificent properties which under normal circumstances would have made both generals secure for the rest of their lives, but for both they were to mean nothing more financially than misfortune and anguish.

EIGHTEEN

Top Command at Last

ON NOVEMBER 29, 1792 Anthony Wayne was at Legionville, Pennsylvania, a camp town he had named on the Ohio below Pittsburgh. Washington had called him again and he had responded. The decade that had elapsed since he cleared Georgia of British troops, pacified the Indians, and offered an accommodation to the Royalists who wanted to stay, had been a blending of high triumph and deep disappointment.

In front of Charleston, where he had joined Greene after liberating Georgia, his illness debilitated him for months. He remained resolutely with his friend until, on December 14, 1782, British Major General Alexander Leslie evacuated the city, leaving a Christmas present for Greene, Wayne, Gist, and the host of other officers and soldiers who had besieged and fought and waited long for the eventful hour.

Generous Nathanael Greene, who had accomplished so much by sheer perseverance in his Southern command, assigned to Wayne the pleasant duty of leading the advance into the city. With a detachment of the three arms, infantry, cavalry, and artillery, Wayne moved down King Street while the British were still boarding their transports. Greene, who followed Wayne, escorted the governor and civil officers to the Town Hall amid the outbursts of joy and celebration by a populace that crowded rooftops, windows, balconies and streets, while gradually receding might be seen the immense flotilla of 300 sail taking the British army and its followers home.

Wayne did not get the remaining stalwarts of his Pennsylvania regiments back to Philadelphia until the summer of 1783, more than two years after he had marched them from York to join Lafayette in a campaign which, in Lafayette's opinion, won the Southern part of the continent for the new republic. After the British left Charleston he went to Augusta to seal a better peace with the Creeks and Cherokee. Dr. Rush and Sharp Delaney, following the protracted nature of his illness from the reports reaching Philadelphia, urged him to come home. They were concerned about him after his long, rigorous campaigning. Each had plans; a trout fishing trip, an ocean voyage. Wayne did finally bring his troops back by water, sailing up the coast from Charleston and up the Delaware to the state that would always remember and honor his and their achievements, despite the mutinous flareup among a goodly portion of them.

St. Clair, Wayne's nominal commander, whose main talent after the first year of the war had not appeared to be fighting, had directed that he land his troops at Wilmington, Delaware and march them to Lancaster. That would mean avoiding Philadelphia. It was almost like sneaking home after years of gallant performance. The men were to be given, not discharges, but extended leaves of absence, a tricky method by which a final settlement of accounts with them might be avoided. The state coffers were empty and none had made the necessary preparation for the discharge of the fighting men. But they wanted no furlough on such conditions and the state government did face realities and square its obligations. Wayne bade them farewell at Lancaster. Most of them were proud for the rest of their lives to have served under Mad Anthony, the famed fighter of so many battles, in several of which they had won their part of the fray, even though the army as a whole had merely drawn or lost. Had he seriously sought a political career he would probably have fared better in his home section, crowded as Pennsylvania was with able statesmen, than in Georgia.

He had been eight years in the military service, the greater part of it away from home, with almost each day bringing its emergency; he had been in the hottest corner of most of the major battles of Washington's army and had led the attack in person in a host of lesser but nevertheless bloody affairs. Now the great war was over, independence was achieved, and he had not yet turned forty.

The crowning part of life, the leisures and slower accomplishments of peace, seemed ahead. First, he needed rest; instead of a fishing trip or ocean cruise, he hung his sword over the fireplace and took to his bed. He was too exhausted to go when Washington invited him to New York to be present at the final gathering at Fraunces Tavern, where the commander in chief, beloved above all other men of his day, took his farewell of his officers.

At first it appeared that Anthony would resume life much as he had left it before the war, and indeed, little had changed in the physical nature of things—in the long horseback ride into the city over the same roads, and in the city itself, where normal growth had been stunted by devotion to the emergencies of a bitter war. That fall he was elected to his old seat in the Pennsylvania Legislature and was appointed as well to a sort of executive committee called the State Board of Censors, which was not to suppress information, but rather to divulge to the people just what the other departments of the government were up to. Government even then was concerned with its public relations. One of Wayne's achievements that stands out as major during this brief legislative interlude was his liberation, or establishment, of the theater in Philadelphia. Plays and skits had been a diversion in both armies when the breaks in campaigning permitted. The theater was prohibited in sedate Philadelphia, where the restrained Quaker influence was dominant, but Wayne introduced a bill to take the shackles off of this form of artistic expression which through the centuries had been recurringly looked on as incompatible with religious expression, and shunned by many of the devout. With the cooperation of his friend and fellow legislator, Robert Morris, Wayne pressed his bill through the legislature and it took precedence over the Philadelphia city ordinance. A ramshackle old building in south Philadelphia had been used for plays and theatrical renditions during the British occupation, usually under the direction of Major John André. André had painted the scenery which was now shabby. The way was opened for the growth of the theater in Philadelphia and Wayne may be looked on as the father of it.

Still, he was restless in the old, prewar life. Heavily in debt as a result of his sizeable expenditures during his long military service and the drain from the mismanagement of his Waynesborough property, the Georgia opportunity beckoned him. The appreciative Georgia Legislature had spent an equivalent of about $25,000 in gold for the purchase of the plantation of 830 acres it had deeded to him as a gift. It was in a good rice area on the Little Setilla River, readily accessible from Savannah. It had been highly profitable when tended before the war. Neglect had given it back to nature and the swampland jungles had encroached. Money would be required to restore and operate it into some profitable crops. The yield before the war had reached toward 1,000 barrels of rice, or better than $12,500.

Wayne had never accomplished anything by holding back. He borrowed money at a time when money was scarce, obtaining 100,000 florins, or approximately $50,000, in Philadelphia. The loan was inadequate and he borrowed more, this time through the Dutch minister who put him in touch with Holland bankers, from whom he obtained about $20,000 on the security of his Waynesborough estate. Then he decided to move to Georgia, and left in the autumn of 1785. Polly Wayne, who had established a life for herself in Waynesborough, declined to go.

For both Wayne and Greene the Georgia ventures proved disastrous. Both were dragged down by debt. Greene's debts resulted from his expenditures and guarantees for rations and provisions he bought for his troops in the service of his country. While Congress eventually made a settlement of his claim, it acted after Greene had passed to the reward that awaits good and generous men. He died June 19, 1786, at the age of forty-three, worn out by campaigning hard enough to bring down in his prime this man of strong body, reared by his Quaker father, an iron master, at the forge.

Wayne, who had returned to Georgia, sat by Greene's bedside as he expired. He wrote to Colonel James Jackson, his political adversary but close friend and recent companion in the winning of Georgia, requesting that he make funeral arrangements: "My dear friend General Greene is no more. . . . He was great as a soldier, greater as a citizen, immaculate as a friend. . . . Pardon this scrawl; my feelings are but too much affected, because I have seen a great and good man die."[1]

With the assistance of Alexander Hamilton, Catherine Greene, the general's widow, obtained a payment of the accounts by Congress, in what seems at this late date an act of simple justice though General Thomas Sumter, a lesser figure than either Greene or Hamilton, whose brigade had given way at a critical time at Eutaw Springs, now a member of the House of Representatives, opposed it. Hamilton, whose good opinion any general of the war might prize, spoke of Greene in the following terms: "the vast, I had almost said the enormous, powers of his mind," and again, his "pervading genius which qualified him not less for the Senate than for the field." Among army comrades, save for Washington, Greene was closest to Wayne's heart.[2]

Wayne's failure as a Southern planter resulted from no more than that the rice crops did not bring in enough money to meet the payments of interest and principal due on his loans. He was greatly embarrassed but his lot was not extraordinary among those who were trying to develop a great new country and were willing to venture. He saved the Pennsylvania homestead.

Equally disappointing had been his brief political career on the national stage, which ended in a quick rebuff. When he decided to make Georgia his home, he looked forward to a long and pleasant association with the Greenes. Now Greene was gone, but he had made his decision; he became a citizen of Georgia. Georgia sent him to Philadelphia to help draft the new Federal Constitution. He became reacquainted with his family on the Pennsylvania visit. Isaac Wayne, his son, had begun the law course at Dickinson College. The Georgia plantation had drained the family of money and the pinch was being felt by his wife and daughter. Still, Polly did not complain; she rarely even wrote.

Wayne was a Whig before and during the war, a supporter of independence, and after it a Washingtonian, though party was only creeping in. Colonel James Jackson, who would become a Jeffersonian, was the first Congressman from Wayne's Georgia District. He was an easy talker who had a large following, and he was strongly opposed to the treaty Wayne had made with the Indians giving them 3 million acres of Georgia land. Wayne was urged by a number of Savannah acquaintances to run for Congress. The request was flattering and he consented but took little interest in it. When the returns came in he was declared winner by a handsome majority. He went to Philadelphia and began his service in the House. But the Jackson crowd would not hear of it and the ambitious young man contested Wayne's election. Whether or not some of the ballot boxes had been stuffed by anti-Jackson workers, Wayne's scrupulous integrity had been a byword in the army and his home friends knew it was ridiculous to charge that he had any part in it, if it occurred, any more than that Greene had profited personally out of the army contracts on which the supplier defaulted. Yet both generals had made enemies who were willing to villify them on any pretext.

One cannot go back now and recount the Georgia ballots, and writers have taken both sides of the question, but the House, which judges the qualification of its own members in contested elections, and at times has made one's political complexion the criterion for decision, decided to straddle and hold that neither Wayne nor Jackson had been properly elected. The vote in the House was so close that Speaker

Johnathan Trumbull of Connecticut broke the deadlock. Jackson had been a vigorous exhorter of troops but his speeches against a strong central government were looked on by many in the House as boring and he a fumer.

Wayne served from the opening session October 24, 1791, until March 21, 1792. When the seat was declared vacant it was awarded to John Milledge, a Savannah lawyer. The careful President Washington looked a little questioningly at Wayne at this time, a failure as a rice planter, now rejected as a politician. But Washington had known failure, too. Even now as President he was having severe trials growing out of war on the frontier.

Rejection by Congress proved one of the happy events of Wayne's career. Service in the House would have been drab indeed for one of his daring temperament. He was cut for the activity of the camp and field, not the humdrum of committee sessions and, in the discharge of most public issues, compromise, a word he scarcely knew and rarely if ever practiced. What great military leader ever made a patient legislator?—a good executive occasionally, as in the cases of Washington and Andrew Jackson, but not one willing to listen endlessly to the vaporings of politics and debate. Wayne's contest and his rejection by the House came almost at a time when couriers out of the Northwest carried distressful intelligence about the army of Governor Major General St. Clair.[3]

The Indian war was an aftermath of the Revolution and essentially a part of it. Great Britain had refrained from surrendering the forts held by her troops in the Northwest, maintaining principally that claims of Royalists had not been met by the Americans. The Indians were hostile to the oncoming tide of white immigration. Predatory Indian bands raided the settlements. When the Ordinance of 1787 created the Northwest Territory, one of Wayne's old army associates, Rufus Putnam, headed a company that settled Marietta, Ohio, named for Queen Marie Antoinette of France, consort of the patron of American independence. A settlement grew around Losantville, on the Ohio opposite the mouth of the Licking River, where Fort Washington was soon built. The location, a stepping off place for the campaigns up the Miami River, later became Cincinnati. Each year, during this period, 10,000 settlers were coming to Ohio and they required protection.[4]

Josiah Harmar, one of Wayne's officers at the storming of Stony Point, had remained in the army after the peace. Now a major general, he was given command of an army of 1,400, including 300 regulars, to pacify the Shawnee and Miami tribes in western and northern Ohio and northern Indiana. In 1790 he encountered the Miami Chief Little Turtle near the present city of Fort Wayne, Indiana. The Indian, gifted in strategy, caught Harmar with his force divided, defeated part of it under Colonel John Hardin, then the other under Harmar and sent the survivors back to the security of Fort Washington on the Ohio, with nothing more accomplished than the burning of some Shawnee towns. Harmar's killed numbered 183, wounded only 31, suggesting a lack of quarter. A court-martial acquitted him, but he resigned.[5]

The same year Major John Francis Hamtramck raided up the Wabash River, burned towns, but added nothing to the security of the white settlers. General Charles Scott, whose brigade had stood alongside Wayne's at Monmouth, led 800 mounted Kentuckians the next year up the Wabash to the area of present-day Lafayette, Indiana. He irritated the tribes and threw them into Little Turtle's growing concentration against the whites. These forays were followed by a movement in force under St. Clair. His army of 2,000 was impressive because it stepped off with 1,650 regulars and only 350 militia. The regulars were commanded by Major General Richard Butler, Wayne's old colonel of the Pennsylvania Line.

Already infirmities had broken St. Clair, who imprudently set out in late autumn against the Indians led by the crafty Little Turtle. Wrapped in flannel blankets and bundled amid pillows in a wagon, too weak to walk, he emitted groans each time the wheels struck a bump on the rough trail. He suffered from colic, asthma, and gout. Washington had warned him pointedly of the danger of surprise.

St. Clair reached the headwaters of the Wabash River in western Ohio, after suffering many desertions because of his loose command methods. He failed to patrol the forests effectively as he marched or when he slept. The result of it all was that he suffered overwhelming defeat, his army near annihilation.

Washington could not possibly have known the extent of St. Clair's infirmities or sluggish methods when he sent him against the resourceful Miami chief. Little Turtle had in his forces the Shawnee chief, Blue Jacket, one of whose alert followers was Tecumseh, now twenty-three years old. He led the Indian scouts, kept close watch on St. Clair's army, and reported its movements to the Indian leaders.

Wayne's friend, Major General Butler, was trying to form his men as the attack came but was shot down, gravely wounded. He was laid against a tree, where an Indian who had crept into the camp tomahawked and scalped him, then cut him to pieces and took out his heart. His death as the battle opened accounted for the completeness of the rout. One of his associates testified, "Personally Richard Butler knew no fear."[6]

St. Clair had 1,748 soldiers when attacked. Of these 629 were killed, 250 wounded. He had permitted 200 camp followers, some of them the wives of soldiers, to go on the hazardous march. Of them, 56 were killed.

Consternation spread over the West and into Pennsylvania and Virginia because of the disastrous nature of St. Clair's defeat. The story of Washington's anger was related by his secretary, Tobias Lear. Said Lear, "It was awful." Washington was not one to be baffled by defeat, though there was a considerable school of thought in favor of letting the Indians alone. Congress gave him authority in a "Bill to Protect the Frontiers" to recruit and equip up to 5,000 infantry and dragoons. He considered with great care the question of a commander. Initially at the top of his list was Henry (Light Horse Harry) Lee, now governor of Virginia, of whom he was personally fond. But Lee had held no higher rank than Lieutenant colonel during the war and had never operated with a large independent command. Officers who had been his senior might not care to serve under one they had commanded. Lee did rise to the rank of major general during the Whiskey Rebellion a few years hence, but his qualifications to command an army in action against an unseen and resourceful foe were questionable.[7]

Portly Henry Knox, who adored Washington, had become Secretary of War. While he was always ambitious, he was an artillery man, not a tried combat leader, and would not suit. Undoubtedly Alexander Hamilton would have done well as a military leader. Later, in the crisis with France, Washington picked him for his second in command. But he, too, was in the cabinet. Many were considered but everything pointed to Wayne.

This was the age of fastidiousness, of the Prince Regent and Beau Brummel. Wayne's love of ostentatious dress and his inability to suppress the swagger were in keeping with the times, but could not have appealed to the more reserved President, whose attitude seems to have been that the apparel did proclaim whether the man was a showoff or a performer. There were two negative considerations about Wayne; the first, Congress had rejected him in the contested election. It happens in politics in every generation, or perhaps every campaign, that some candidate's followers and managers do not toe the mark of virtue, but Wayne had not personally offended the proprieties. The second, his loss of the Georgia plantation, could not have been a recommendation to one of Washington's careful managerial practices. But with all the debits, here was the soldier who won his battles, who inspired in his men a certain élan and confidence. The President lingered over the name of—as he listed it—"Maj. Gen Baron de Steuben," whom he rated sober and brave and a disciplinarian. "High in his ideas of subordination—impetuous in his temper—ambitious—and a foreigner." Reflecting again and again over his list, Wayne's name always came to the top. His letter to Lee was almost an apology; the main purpose must have been to assuage him. It could not have been a studied expression of Washington's attitude toward the man he turned to at West Point when he asked, "Whom now can we trust?"[8]

Still, fourteen years had passed and the Virginia school, accustomed to dominate much of the new nation's thinking, was not Wayne-minded. Madison, then in Congress, recorded that the nomination was confirmed but went "rather against the bristles." George Hammond, the British minister, was doubtful from a fear growing out of the Mad Anthony name. He warned his home government that Wayne would likely attack the forts Great Britain had refused to transfer in the Northwest. He appraised Wayne as "the most active, vigilant, and enterprising officer in the American army," but judged his talents were altogether military.

Washington explained to Lee about Wayne: "He has many good points as an officer, and it is to be hoped that time, reflection, good advice, and, above all, a due sense of the importance of the trust which is committed to him, will correct his foibles, or cast a shade over them." The letter, not as generous as Washington might have written from his experience with Wayne, but addressed to a dissenter, must have considered as "foibles" Wayne's inordinate self-esteem, or cocksureness, a trait which displeased some, but which might be excusable in one who performs well. Success allows more than a modicum of vanity.[9]

Wayne was in good health except for the recurring attacks of gout, or what was diagnosed as such. He still carried in the back of his thigh the musket ball that had set off the pangs in his foot. He was battle-scarred and aging from hard service at forty-seven years, but the fire of combat still burned strongly within him.

He accepted, on April 13, 1792, only twenty-three days after his seat in the House had been declared vacant, the command of the United States Army, which, because of the aversion to a standing army that usually follows a protracted war, along with the abiding popular distrust of the military that was a heritage of the days of Cromwell (and which had expressed itself in different ways in the Constitution and the later Bill of Rights), was called the Legion of the United States.[10]

Long years after promotion had been due, Wayne received a major general's rank. He wrote in his letter of acceptance to Secretary

Knox: "I clearly foresee, that it is a Command, which must inevitably be attended with the most anxious care, fatigue, and difficulty, and from which more may be expected than will be in my power to perform. Yet I should be wanting both in point of duty, and gratitude, to the President were I to decline an appointment (however Arduous) to which he thought proper to nominate me."[11]

He put his affairs in makeshift order (Georgia had been his home in recent years), departed for Pittsburgh, reached there in June, and wrote on July 13 that farmers on the border of the frontier were harvesting their hay and grain without molestation from the Indians. No new troops had arrived, and (here the old story of the Revolutionary War was repeated) the situation of the First and Second regiments of the army that were being merged into the Legion, "with respect to Clothing is a disgrace to the service." The prospect for volunteers after St. Clair's defeat was not promising, especially since the country was experiencing an expansion of trade, industry, and agriculture. Jobs were plentiful. The hardy independents still preferred agriculture and sought the fresh, productive lands of the Ohio Valley. Old soldiers, especially Virginia veterans, wanted to settle in the Virginia Military Survey, a tract Virginia claimed by charter right in Ohio.

The country in 1791-1792 was bustling, expanding. Roads were deep-rutted with the heavy increases in haulage, the postal carriers overloaded with the rapid growth in the volume of mail. Undoubtedly Wayne's fame as a fighter, not any semblance of hard times, was what brought recruits, who trickled into Pittsburgh during the summer and fall of 1792. In November he moved them down the Ohio River and built a new town of huts which he named Legionville.

One of the early arrivals was a callow youth nineteen years old, William Henry Harrison, the youngest of fifteen children of Benjamin Harrison, Virginia patriot, friend of Washington, and signer of the Declaration of Independence. The young man, a protégé of Robert Morris after the death of his father, had thrown aside the beginnings of an education for a medical career to join the army, perhaps because there remained traces in his blood of the zeal of his forebear, Thomas Harrison, one of Cromwell's top cavalry leaders and the jailor of Charles I. Young Harrison was a graduate of Hampton-Sidney College and already an assiduous student of the Roman classics. He had such an educational background that Wayne, impressed, appointed him his aide-de-camp.

The recruits who came first to Pittsburgh and then to Legionville were not the type of stalwart veterans such as comprised Wayne's picked corps at Stony Point, but boys, ne'er-do-wells, drifters, along with some rugged fighters such as nearly always appear on the eve of combat. No greater misfortune could have befallen him than that sychophantic, intriguing James Wilkinson, who had moved earlier to Lexington, Kentucky, and had led a companion raid with that of Charles Scott against the Indians in west central Indiana, should arrive as a brigadier general and second in command. His principal role in the forthcoming campaign was that of a would-be marplot, who used anonymous letters and a glib tongue when they served his purpose. His career disclosed that in the course of American events a man can sometimes get ahead for a period by craft and underhandedness, but will eventually fall from those same methods.

Wayne at Legionville opened a potentially lucrative trade for bounty hunters by offering $40 reward for deserters, many of whom were darting over the western country after the rout of St. Clair, some perhaps innocently looking for a haven. A peculiar policy of the early government was that there appeared to be more money available in rewards for bringing in deserters than for paying the troops what was due them and depriving them of an incentive to desert. Similarly the Indians, who were offered large indemnities for peace, could not well understand why the sums were not given to the families migrating into the Ohio Valley, who must have been poor else they would not have left their homes in the East, so they would stay or return home and leave the tribes unmolested on their ancient domains. This was the burden of the answer given by the Northwestern chiefs to Washington's peace envoys sent out during the time Wayne was making his military preparations.[12]

No general in the army was a better drillmaster than Wayne and to the task he now gave his unremitting efforts. Drill in the morning, drill in the afternoon, all under his personal attention. He rode about supervising the methods and formations. He labored in Legionville to shape up his army from late November 1792 until late April 1793, carrying on a wordy correspondence all the while with Secretary of War Knox, reporting on virtually every detail about the personnel, equipment, and conduct of his command, and receiving Knox's voluminous letters of information, instruction, and advice. The unprepossessing recruits were gradually forged by practice and drill into stanch, disciplined, responsive soldiers. Wayne seemed happy about the caliber of many of the junior officers who joined him at Legionville or farther down the Ohio.

Some unusual men were with him. Solomon Van Rensselaer was shot through the lungs while serving with Wayne but survived to lead the Americans and take three wounds in the battle of Queenstown, where the much admired British commander, Governor General Isaac Brock was killed. Lieutenant Daniel Bissell of Connecticut and Cornet of Dragoons Leonard Covington of Maryland, both of whom became generals in the War of 1812, were there. Covington lost his life in Wilkinson's abortive invasion of Canada. He would distinguish himself in Wayne's defense of Fort Recovery and at Fallen Timbers.

Probably the most audacious, and the one who patterned his generalship the most clearly after Wayne's, was a young ensign from Connecticut, William Eaton, a wielder of the English language, especially in invective, that few military men have approached for vehemence and ornateness. He became a diplomatic representative to the Barbary States of North Africa, and leader of one of the most daring exploits of American history. With a handful of Marines and some irresolute Tripolitan auxiliaries, he marched across the northern arm of the Sahara from Egypt to Libya, captured Derna, and put the "shores of Tripoli" phrase in the Marine Corps hymn. After his observations in the Northwest he recorded one of the best firsthand estimates of Wayne the general: "He is firm in constitution, as in resolution; industrious, indefatigable, determined and persevering; fixed in opinon, and unbiased in judgment; not over accessible, but studious to reward merit. He is a rock against which the waves of calumny and malice, moved by the gust of passion natural to envy, have dashed; have washed its sides: he is still immovable on his base. He is in some degree susceptible of adulation, as is every man who has an honest thirst for military fame. He endures fatigue and hardship with a fortitude uncommon for a man of his years. I have seen him, in the most severe night of the winter of 1794, sleep on the ground, like his fellow-soldiers, and walk around the camp at four in the morning, with the vigilance of a sentinel. When in danger he is in his element; and never shows to so good advantage as when leading a charge. His name is better in an action, or in an enemy's country, than a brigade of undisciplined levies."[13]

Eaton in his military career had the same sleeplessness and attentiveness to detail that he observed in Wayne. Mad Anthony's influence might be felt each day as Eaton led his strange little army across North Africa, quelled mutinies, lived on wildcat fare, and stormed and captured one of the strong citadels of Tripoli, much as Wayne had stormed Stony Point.

William Clark, the youngest brother of George Rogers Clark, winner of the Northwest from the British in the Revolutionary War, had been too young to serve with his brother but became one of Wayne's lieutenants in the Legion. After the battle of Fallen Timbers, Wayne sent him on an exploration and reconnaissance down the Ohio

River to check on the activities of the Spaniards. His report showed he was an intelligence officer of merit. One of his subordinates was Meriwether Lewis, who became Thomas Jefferson's secretary. When President Jefferson purchased the Louisiana Territory in 1803, he selected these two to explore the vast territory, and the Lewis and Clark Expedition, 1804–1806, became one of the most fascinating stories of discovery and adventure of the history of the Republic.

Wayne had the opportunity to train still another soldier-explorer, Zebulon M. Pike, whom Jefferson later assigned to explore the headwaters of the Mississippi and still later the sources of the Arkansas and Red rivers. The lofty Colorado peak which he discovered bears his name, as do twenty-five towns and ten counties of the United States. As a general leading the attack on York (now Toronto) in the War of 1812, he was killed. He enlisted in his father's company when fifteen years old and was little more than that when first with Wayne.

George Rogers Clark had wanted the assignment that went to Wayne. Because of his successes in the Northwest during the Revolutionary War he thought himself entitled to it, but James Wilkinson, who likewise aspired to the command, so tarnished Clark with vastly exaggerated tales about his drinking that he lost all standing at the seat of government.[14]

He and his men had fought the Revolutionary War in the Northwest unaided, had captured Kaskaskia and Vincennes, and, in Clark's words, given the United States one-half of its territory, and nobody had yet paid them any money for doing it. His fate was like Greene's; he had spent his own money to clothe, feed and equip his soldiers. The country was pressing ahead and he was relegated to the rear as belonging to another age, the age of the winners and not the consolidaters.

Washington, Knox, and Congress were anxious to avoid an all-out, bloody war with the Indians even in the face of the slaughter of St. Clair's army and a long series of depredations against individual settlers along the frontier. Calculations showed that between the peace year, 1783, and 1790, in sparsely settled Kentucky alone, 1,500 persons—men, women, and children—had been killed or captured by the Indians. Not being a prolific race, the Indians were always anxious to capture and adopt white children, whom they might rear into warriors or the mothers of warriors.

In the fall of 1792 Washington sent three Revolutionary War officers—Benjamin Lincoln, Governor Beverly Randolph of Virginia, and Timothy Pickering of Massachusetts, whom he regarded as a good negotiator, as peace commissioners to the Miami. The commissioners traversed Lake Erie to the Detroit River, but all they accomplished was to gain a reiteration of the Indian demand that the whites stay south of the Ohio River, the old-time border agreed on in the Treaty of Fort Stanwix in 1768. During several unsuccessful attempts by Washington for a peace by negotiation, Wayne kept waiting at his post on the Ohio, impatient to be unleashed. Though he had been guilty of no overt act against the Northwest Indians, unless his position at Fort Washington might be regarded as such, the peace commissioners protested that the Indians were provoked by his preparations, while the British likewise, by some peculiar process, regarded them as "unfair and unreasonable."[15]

The commissioners did decide later that Wayne had not hampered them. They thanked him for withholding his bolt while they sought peace by parleys. Finally in late August 1792 the three commissioners concluded that they were making no headway with conversation; they returned and reported that the negotiations had collapsed. Thus Wayne, waiting patiently on the Ohio, was freed of restraints.

NINETEEN

The Northwest Subdued
at Fallen Timbers

WAYNE HAD MOVED DOWN the Ohio to a campsite he named "Hobson's Choice," a mile below Fort Washington, which he reached on May 5, 1973. There he continued his intensive drill, in recognition that the best answer to surprise is discipline. He drilled the men on reloading their muskets while rushing forward, an operation that became much easier with practice and one that was all-important to an army on the offensive, intent on establishing and maintaining fire superiority over the foe.

He explained to Knox his choice of the unusual name for his camp. There was no good ground for maneuver in the neighborhood of Fort Washington, added to which, "the village of Cincinnati is filled with ardent poison & Caitiff wretches." Further, "there is no ground between the two Miamias, in the vicinity of the Ohio, suitable for an encampment, except near some dirty Village," and "I have therefore called this place Hobson's Choice."[1] The term came from an innkeeper, Thomas or Tobias Hobson of the days of James I, who had many horses in his stable but always required the hirer to take the one nearest the door. Thus Hobson's Choice, as noted in *The Spectator* of Addison and Steele, meant that there was no alternative.[2]

The restraints imposed by the peace negotiations were not lifted in time for Wayne to begin a summer campaign but, on October 6, he marched to the branch of Great Miami near Fort Jefferson; then, on October 23, he built a stockade he called Fort Greene, named after his late beloved friend, Nathanael Greene, and established the settlement Greene Ville, which became Greenville, Ohio. The fort was near the juncture of two clear, bubbling streams, one Greenville Creek and the other now bearing the uninspiring name of Mud Creek.

Behind him he had left a series of forts connecting with Fort Washington and the Ohio River. His position was secure. He reported to Knox that his movement had been made in "perfect order". He had marched with 3,630 well-drilled regulars. Generously he named one of the forts in his wake after the unhappy Arthur St. Clair; another, that grew into the Ohio city north of Cincinnati, after Alexander Hamilton. Just before Christmas he sent Major Henry Burback, an engineer officer from Massachusetts, ahead from Greenville with eight companies of infantry and dragoons to erect a fort on the site of St. Clair's defeat. Appropriately he named it Fort Recovery.[3]

Wayne's cautious, well-patrolled advance was not without influence on the Indians, who, as they had with St. Clair, observed every movement. Tecumseh, again their leading scout, adhered to the Shawnee chief, Blue Jacket. The Shawnee had been pushed back by George Rogers Clark and others to a string of settlements along the Aix Glaize River in northwestern Ohio. Blue Jacket was for war to the finish. As the Indians watched the American general coil stealthily ahead, they gave him the name of "the Blacksnake."

Little Turtle, the most astute chief in the Northwest, was having doubts. On a raid into Kentucky he had captured a white boy twelve years old, named William Wells, whom he had adopted and reared, and who married his daughter. Wells, with a knowledge of the whites retained from boyhood, had been an able assistant to Little Turtle in the Harmar and St. Clair campaigns, but more recently had been given to introspection and reflection. His decision had distinct bearing on Wayne's fortunes. As he reviewed the events of the slaughter of St. Clair's men, the thought came that he was fighting his own people, and that some he had killed might indeed have been of his own blood and kin. He asked Little Turtle, to whom his attachment had become strong, to go with him to what was called the "Big Elm," a council tree two miles east of Kekionga, or present Fort Wayne.

There he poured out his heart to his foster father, saying it was now time that he left the tribe and returned to his native people. He pointed to the sky, said he and the chief would be friends until the sun reached that position, and thenceforth they would be enemies. If Little Turtle wished to kill him thereafter he could, and if he at some time wished to kill the chief, he had that privilege. Such was the parting. Little Turtle watched the younger man, of whom he had grown immensely fond, cross over the Maumee River and disappear into the forest. The unfathomable old chief shed no tears but his emotions were deeply stirred—so deeply that he never again lifted his hand against the Long Knives.[4]

Wells traveled eastward in order to reach Wayne's army. The general, accepting his story, made him his chief scout, in a position called "captain of the Spies," a title that became so fixed that when Wells after the war settled on a little stream near Fort Wayne it became known as "Spy Run." He was faithful to the whites and later became Indian agent for the government. He operated at first in Wayne's army under the direction of Captain Richard Sparks of the 7th United States Infantry, who likewise had been captured by the Indians when a child and taken to the leading Shawnee village. He was reared as an adopted son by the warlike chief Blackfish, and treated with great kindness. As a boy he was a companion of another of Blackfish's adopted sons, Tecumseh.[5]

Wells's defection from the Miami was a severe loss to the Indians because of its effect on Little Turtle. The tribes held council a little later on August 19, as Wayne drew near the Maumee River rapids, and the chiefs spoke, among them representatives of the Delaware, Miami, Shawnee, Ottawa, Wyandot and scatterings of Chippewa and Potawatomi. Little Turtle had been looked to as the leader in the impending battle. When he rose, however, it was not to lift his *kukewium*, or battle standard, but to sound the call for peace: "We have beaten the enemy twice under different commanders [Harmar and St. Clair]. We cannot expect the same good fortune to attend us always. The Americans are now led by a chief who never sleeps. The nights and the days are alike to him, and during all the time he has been marching on our villages, notwithstanding the watchfulness of our young men, we have never been able to surprise him. Think well of it. There is something whispers me, it would be prudent to listen to his offers of peace."[6]

The Turtle's advice went unheeded; it was roundly denounced by some of the other chiefs. Unrelenting Blue Jacket of the Shawnee called him a coward to his face, a charge he did not stoop to answer, for any fair-minded red man knew he had exhibited his personal bravery on many fields.

Wayne advanced his army, which was being weakened as he left garrisons at the forts in his rear. On reaching newly built Fort Recovery, he recognized that Washington's first desire was for peace, and issued what the Indians always termed a "speech"; it was an invitation for negotiation and it probably would have been accepted then or a little later had not the Indians come to place unwarranted reliance on British intervention in their behalf.

As has been noted, the British in Canada, smarting from their failure to hold the colonies, retained possession of forts south of the Great Lakes, in violation of the treaty that ended the war. This was a settled British policy resulting partly from chagrin but more because of the contention that issues were not yet adjusted between the two countries, among them the claims of British subjects for debts owed by Americans incurred before the Revolution; the disputed eastern border between the United States and Canada; control of the Indian fur trade; certain navigation rights; losses to American shipping from captures by British warships; and impressments of seamen. These issues were being negotiated at the time by John Jay and Lord Grenville on behalf of the two governments and it was not the tought of the British ministry that war should be invoked while the negotiations were in progress, however strongly the Indians might lean to that impression. Jay sailed for England on May 12, 1794.

One of the main obstacles to a better understanding between the Americans and Canadians on the border was John Graves Simcoe, Wayne's old opponent at Germantown, Monmouth, and on other fields. Simcoe during the course of the war developed an intense dislike of the Americans, which abided after he became a leading factor in shaping conditions in the Northwest. After the war and after a sampling of Parliament, he was returned to North America to serve under the Governor General, Lord Dorchester, formerly General Guy Carleton, whom Wayne had opposed in Canada and upper New York. Simcoe was instrumental in bringing about the division of Canada into two provinces, Upper and Lower Canada, which Dorchester opposed. He became governor general of Upper Canada, and in July 1792 made the little town of Newark, on the Niagara River, his capital. A year later he transferred the capital to York (now Toronto) on Lake Erie, and was the father of that great city.

His moves for the development of Canada were commendable but he managed to step across the border and take renewed concern over the area south of Lake Erie. Instead of being content with holding the old forts until their status could be determined by negotiation, he surprised the frontier by building and garrisoning a new fort at the Maumee rapids, called Fort Miami. The fort was looked on by the Indians as their haven and was a decisive factor in their determination to give battle to Wayne close by it.

Governor General Dorchester, hitherto well disposed toward the Americans but anxious to save what he could for the Crown out of the North American wreckage, had adopted the plan, long seriously discussed when the colonies and Canada were being torn apart, of creating an Indian buffer state occupying a fringe of land south of the Great Lakes, leaving those prized waterways British. Often representatives in the field are more ardent in their nation's cause than the cautious foreign departments that see dangers in the broader picture. That is what happened with Dorchester in Canada. Relations between the United States and Great Britain in the early 1790s became strained, but not belligerent. Dorchester thought a conflict was imminent and dropped more than a hint to the Indians in a speech that excited the border. On February 10, 1794, when Wayne was wintering and drilling at Greenville, Dorchester's welcome to a delegation of chiefs contained inflammatory remarks and predicted a new war between Great Britain and the United States.[7]

While Wayne drilled and Jay negotiated, Dorchester sought to elicit from the Indians an understanding of their grievances against the Americans so that the buffer state might be made a consideration during discussion of new treaty terms. The tribes were concerned primarily that the Ohio River be maintained as the border, a situation that would allow the creation of a semi-independent red nation under the suzerainty of Canada or Great Britain. These conditions eventually reached the American government in Philadelphia through the British minister, George Hammond, but of course could not be inserted, willing as Jay was to make reasonable concessions, in the treaty. Jay's Treaty did not reach Philadelphia until March 5, 1795, and therefore could have had no bearing on Wayne's campaign. But had Wayne been defeated, the British likely would have claimed the border strip and the forts and solidified their position as custodians for the Indians; this disputed territory might well have become a part of Canada, not the United States. Thus Wayne's was no trivial campaign. He was marching, in truth, for the control of the meeting place of corn, coal, and iron, destined to become the breadbasket and forge of a great nation.

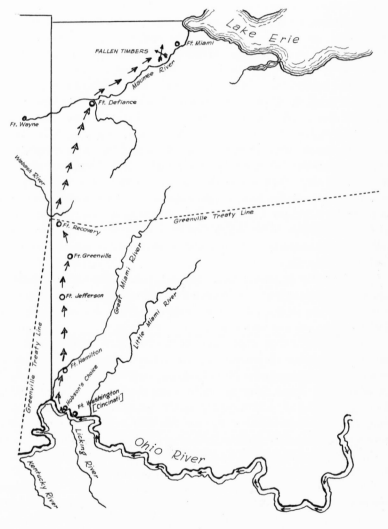

WAYNE'S MARCH TO FALLEN TIMBERS
Battle fought August 20, 1794

Wayne's men had their first heavy encounter with enemy tribes-men at Fort Recovery, where St. Clair had been surprised. There Tecumseh and his scouts, in June 1794, observed food and provisions being carried into the fort by 300 pack horses convoyed by ninety riflemen under Captain Asa Hartshorne, of Connecticut, and fifty dragoons under Lieutenant Edmund H. Taylor of Virginia, the whole commanded by Major William McMahon. All were Regular Army officers. Judging that the escort would return south quickly, the scouts sent out a call for the tribes and on June 30, the following day, when the convoy left the fort, 1,500 to 2,000 Indians had assembled. The red warriors viciously attacked McMahon's detachment of 140 infantry and horsemen before they had gone a scant quarter of a mile from the fort.

Hartshorne's riflemen, surrounded, returned the fire as best they could, being beset from every direction, while McMahon, Taylor and Cornet Daniel Torrey charged with their dragoons. Cornet Torrey was killed at the outset and a number of saddles were emptied. Major Hartshorne had his thigh broken and was killed. Perceiving that they were hopelessly outnumbered, the party turned to cut their way back into the fort, helped by a detachment of twenty volunteers who sallied out under Lieutenant Samuel Drake. The troops of the convoy at length got inside but the loss suffered was heavy. As Wayne reported it, twenty-two were killed and thirty wounded, casualties that aggregated well over one-third of the little force. The manner of Captain Hartshorne's death was uncertain. Lieutenant Drake was carrying him into the fort when he was dropped by a musket ball in his groin. Hartshorne fell, Drake was carried inside, and Hartshorne either succumbed from his wound or was tomahawked.

The Indians then began an attack on the fort and carried it on throughout a night that was dark and foggy. From inside the warriors could be seen carrying off their dead by torchlight and occasionally the garrison fired in the direction of the torches. The tribesmen continued the attack the next morning but drew off about noon. Wayne, who was back at Greenville, was high in his praise of Captain Alexander Gibson, a Virginian, of the 4th Sub Legion (a term Wayne employed in place of regiment) who commanded Fort Recovery during the attack.[8]

Wayne was confident that the Indians were abetted by whites, presumably British. Some of Wayne's Indian scouts who were outside reported "that there were a considerable Number of armed white men in the rear, who they frequently heard talking in our language & encouraging the Savages to persevere." The faces of these men were generally blackened except for three British officers in scarlet. These appeared to be men of distinction because the others were so attentive to them.[9]

In Wayne's opinion, the effort was a *coup de main* by which the Indians hoped to carry the fort. He did not think they had time to assemble such a force after seeing McMahon's arrival, but the Indians did move with great speed. He gave interesting information about the artillery St. Clair had lost in 1791. The Indians after defeating St. Clair had hid the cannon they captured by turning over the trunks of fallen trees, placing the cannon in the hollows inside, and turning the trunks back to their former position. When Wayne's army reached the scene the men, versed in Indian methods, were shrewd enough to discover and haul off the cannon. During their attack on the fort the Indians could be seen going through the woods turning over logs and searching for the guns. Wayne reported that the guns were mounted in the fort the Indians were attacking and were being used against them.[10]

Major General Charles Scott reached Greenville on July 29 with 1,600 mounted volunteers from Kentucky, which balanced off the garrisons Wayne had been compelled to leave in the forts behind. Two days later the little army took up the march toward the Indian villages concentrated on the Maumee River near Simcoe's guardian Fort Miami. The fort was garrisoned with 450 British soldiers under the command of Major William Campbell.

Never did Roman legion move with greater circumspection than Wayne's in its penetration of the Indian heartland where Harmar had met defeat. Scouts were thrown far ahead and patrols guarded the flanks as the army marched. Each night the first duty was to entrench. Discipline was severe, desertion virtually nonexistent. Where could a deserter go except to the tomahawk and scalping knife? Mindful that liquor had not been an unimportant factor in the defeats of Harmar and St. Clair, Wayne issued stern orders against drinking.

Twenty-four miles north of Fort Recovery he built Fort Adams, named for the Vice-President. On August 8 the army reached the juncture of the Aux Glaize River with the Maumee, where a stronger stockade was erected to which he gave the challenging name of Fort Defiance. Around him stretched the beautifully cultivated fields of the Indians; grainlands and gardens, which reflected that the tribes were gradually turning—as Jefferson hoped they might—from a hunting to an agricultural people. He reported that he had never observed anywhere in America, from Canada to Georgia, such immense cornfields as were in the bottomlands of the rivers flowing into the Great Lakes. He wrote to Knox that the Indians had abandoned their towns "with such apparent marks of surprise and precipitation, as to amount to a positive proof that our approach was not discovered by them"—not until a lone deserter from his quartermaster department went ahead with a warning.

Wayne skillfully concealed his objective. He made demonstrations toward the Miami town, Kekionga (Fort Wayne) on his left, and toward Roche de Bout (foot of the rapids) on his right, and caused the Indians who had now gathered in his front to concentrate in these directions, while he approached by what he called "a devious, i.e., in a central direction." All was in readiness now, August 14, 1794, to advance on the main body of the Indians, but mindful of the President's wishes, he extended his hand once more in friendship: "I have thought proper to offer the enemy a last overture of peace; and as they have everything that is dear and interesting now at stake, I have reason to expect that they will listen to the proposition mentioned." The proposal was in a speech dispatched the day before "which may eventually spare the effusion of much human blood. But should war be their choice, that blood be upon their own heads. America shall no longer be insulted with impunity. To an all-powerful and Just God I therefore commit myself and gallant army."

The speech, a frank offer of peace and conciliation and a warning to the Indians not to be "led astray by the false promises and language of the bad white men at the foot of the rapids," was sent to the Delaware, Shawnee, Miami, and Wyandot. The answer returned was that if Wayne would remain where he was for ten days they would treat with him but would give him battle if he advanced. Ten days was too long but still Wayne was not impetuous. He moved cautiously to the foot of the rapids and there on August 18 began building Fort Deposit (near present Waterville), so named because it was where he could protect his baggage and commissary stores and maneuver more freely without them. Seven miles ahead was the British Fort Miami and between the two the concentration of Indian tribes with whom it now appeared inevitable a battle would be fought.

With Little Turtle holding aloof, command of the Indians went to the Shawnee chief, Blue Jacket, a hard fighter but a less resourceful leader. How many tribesmen he had is not known because the Indians gave no enumeration. The best available figures show there were 450 Delaware, 275 Wyandot, 275 Shawnee, 225 Ottawa, 175 Miami, unknown but smaller numbers of Seneca, Potowatomi and Chippewa, and an indefinite number of whites, estimated at 500. The whites, mainly from Detroit, fought under Captain William Caldwell, an Irish soldier of fortune who had migrated to Pennsylvania, then Detroit, married a beautiful Indian maiden, a sister of Blue Jacket, and became a British officer in the Northwest, and eventually colonel in the Canadian Indian Department. Other white leaders in the action were Simon Girty, despised by frontier Americans, and the Indian agents and traders Matthew Elliott and Alexander McKee. Probably Blue Jacket took about 2,000 redmen and whites into battle. Wayne's force aggregated about 3,000, divided about equally between the Legion and the Kentucky militia under Scott. The action was fought mainly by the legionnaires.

He resumed his march at 8 a.m. on August 20 and after moving five miles was almost within the shadow of Fort Miami. His advance, consisting of a select party of dragoons under Major William Price, of Kentucky, felt resistance, then encountered a heavy fire of musketry. Wayne's dispositions were; the Legion on the right with its right resting on the bank of the Maumee River, the right wing being commanded by Brigadier General James Wilkinson; he left, under Lieutenant Colonel John Francis Hamtramck of the Regular Army, consisting of a brigade of mounted volunteers from Kentucky under Brigadier General Robert Todd, and a second volunteer brigade in support, under Brigadier General Thomas Barbee of Kentucky.

Not until the firing on Price sounded from the woods and heavy grass was it known that the Indians intended to give battle. The Legion advanced in two lines with fixed bayonets. The main line of Indians was discovered in an area along the riverbank through which a tornado had apparently ripped a few years before, leaving the ground strewn with the trunks of great trees. These formed a defensive position, protected almost as though secured by abatis.

Wayne had practiced a minor stratagem before the battle. The custom of the Algonquin warriors was not to eat food on the morning of a battle. Consequently, Wayne sent the Indians a warning from Fort Deposit that he meant to fight, but did not name the day, so for three days many of the tribesmen ate sparingly or not at all, and were weakened at the hour of combat.

Always the Indians of that era fought as individuals and were not amenable to battle formations. Blue Jacket arranged them in three lines but gave them too much elbow room. His line extended for more than two miles at a right angle to the river. Though it was three ranks deep it was grievously thin everywhere. Some estimated it to reach for five miles, but that would have meant no more than a warrior for about every five yards, and less if he retained a reserve, which would have amounted to no line of battle at all, or merely a skirmish line.

Wayne quickly discovered from their firing the extent of their line and the vulnerability of their flanks. He ordered Major General Scott to take his mounted Kentuckians by a circuitous route and fall on the

Indian right flank. Without awaiting the result of this operation, he ordered the Legion to advance with its arms at the trail, bayonets fixed, and on encountering the foe behind the fallen timbers to charge with the bayonet, then, when face to face with the foe, to deliver a close and well-directed fire. This was to be followed by another brisk charge that would not allow the Indians time to load again. The commander of the Legion's hussars had the unusual name of Captain Robert Mis Campbell. Wayne ordered Captain Campbell to charge the enemy along the line of the river, penetrate between them and the riverbank, and turn their left flank. Thus Wayne's plan was to attack with the bayonet in the center and turn the two flanks with his cavalry.

As would happen, the gout had struck him like a bayonet thrust that morning and he had to be helped into the saddle, but he took a position where he could personally direct perhaps the most responsive army he had ever commanded. Certainly it was as thoroughly drilled and disciplined as any that had appeared on any battlefield of the Revolution. His orders were obeyed precisely, not only with promptness but with the highest enthusiasm. With both bayonet and fire superiority the legionnaires drove the warriors from their cover and pursued them impetuously over the logs without losing their own formations. The army was always well in hand. Captain Campbell and his horsemen, at times jumping the logs, but finding also good ground for a charge along the river, plunged through the weak Indian line, sabering and scattering the braves and warriors, and shattered what flank the Indians possessed. They joined in the pursuit, but not Captain Robert Mis Campbell, who lay dead on the field. Unhappily for Scott, who had ridden all the way from Kentucky for this hour, the Legion had cleared the ground before he was able to deliver his bolt on the enemy's right flank. The battle was won and Blue Jacket, his warriors, and their white supporters were driven from the field in half an hour. Years of drill and preparation narrowed down into a decision in minutes.[11]

Now occurred an episode that broke the charm the British had come to hold for the Indians of the Northwest. The defeated tribesmen, hotly pursued, rushed up to the walls of Fort Miami, which had been built presumably to give them protection. The gates were barred and, though hammered upon, Major William Campbell, the British commander, would not open them. Tecumseh, who had fought as gallantly as an Indian could in a battle so poorly managed by his chief, was the last to leave the field. With a small party of braves he conducted a rear guard action of sorts back to the fort. Never did he forget, or ever forgive the fact that the British, from whom aid was expected, would not let him and the others enter. Twenty years later at Fort Malden, in the War of 1812, when exhorting the British General Henry A. Procter not to abandon Malden, he denounced with his flaming oratory his British allies of another day as faithless: "At the battle of the Rapids in the last war, the Americans certainly defeated us; and when we retreated to our father's fort at that place, the gates were shut against us."[12]

Why did Campbell keep the gates closed? A general's reputation is a weighty factor on the battlefield. He knew that if he let the Indians in, Mad Anthony would storm his weakly garrisoned fort and capture it, and bring either censure to him from London, or else set off another war.[13]

The battle of Fallen Timbers broke the Indian power in the Northwest. Discouraged by defeat, disheartened by being abandoned by the British, the survivors of the tribes were on the way home while a horseman was racing through the forest trails taking the exhilarating news of victory to Washington in far-off Philadelphia.

The Chiefs Assemble and Sign at Greenville

IN ALL QUARTERS there was applause, reaching its height when Wayne paraded the army at Greenville in December and read a message from President Washington, conveying the unanimous thanks of the House of Representatives to General Wayne, the Legion of the United States, and to the Kentucky volunteers.

Secretary Knox gave his own comment: "This approbation the most exalted and precious which could be offered by a grateful Country must be highly gratifying to all included therein." Then he added words which though ponderously expressed, must have been sweet indeed to one who, through the long, trying war for independence, had never failed to look on Washington, understanding his trials, with the highest admiration and deep affection: "In addition to this approbation. . . . it is but justice to say that the President has formed the most favourable judgment of your incessant industry in diciplining the troops for the mode of Warfare incident to the service in which they are engaged and for your judicious arrangements and vigilance in marching and encamping the Troops and for your care in obtaining the necessary supplies for an army in a wilderness."

He went on to express hope that peace might be achieved with the tribes on liberal principles and: "This would be closing the scene of hostilities in your quarter most satisfactorily indeed to the President and the great portion of the good Citizens of the United States."[1]

He included the interesting intelligence that Lord Dorchester had written indicating a desire for peace among the Indians and giving the expectation that Major Campbell's garrison at Fort Miami would be withdrawn. The repercussions of Fallen Timbers were beginning to be felt. Wayne's battle was far less grisly than St. Clair's—33 Americans killed, 100 wounded—and its impact on the settlement of the Northwest was profound.

Immediately after the battle he sent out detachments to burn the grainlands over a wide stretch through the Maumee Valley, the area he had described as one of the fairest he had ever gazed upon. His destruction of crops and homes seemed wanton to some, but behind it was the belief commonly held on the frontier that it was a necessary part of the pacification of the tribes. Destroying the corn would force the warriors to hunt for game that their families might survive, and therefore they would have little time for warfare.

Still, Wayne demonstrated to them by the burnings the futility of opposing the Long Knives (a term handed down from Wolfe's army at Quebec because the Scotch Highlanders carried broadswords). His destructiveness was systematic, appalling and well near complete. They had rejected the hand of friendship and must now see it waving the torch of enmity. The tribes had dispersed and pursuit was well near futile, nor could he scatter his best troops over the country and leave a potentially hostile British garrison in Fort Miami in his rear.

During the three days while he rested his triumphant army around the battlefield and while conflagrations raged in all directions, consuming hut, wigwam, and grain, the British inside the fort were baffled spectators of the wholesale destruction. The flames did not spare the trading post nearby, conducted by the British Indian agent, Alexander McKee, where the Maumee River Indians had long left their pelts and procured their supplies. The dwelling houses of the establishment likewise were razed.[2]

The country around was indisputably a part of what had been ceded to the United States in the Treaty of Paris in 1783. By what right was the British commander entitled to intercede? Objections from the Indians on humane grounds would have been more valid, but they had chosen the tomahawk deliberately when offered peace. The devastation continued for fifty miles, marking the course of Wayne's march back to Fort Defiance.

In the three days after the battle Wayne and Major Campbell, the British commander, exchanged a spirited correspondence. It was set off by Campbell, who asked why the American army approached His Majesty's fort when no war was known to exist between the two countries. Wayne waded in with a sharp rejoinder: "Without questioning the authority or the propriety, sir, of your interrogatory [the big words where a smaller would serve suggest that Lieutenant William Henry Harrison may have been his amanuensis] I think I may, without breach of decorum, observe to you, that, were you entitled to an answer, the most full and satisfactory one was announced to you from the muzzles of my small arms, yesterday morning, in the action against the horde of savages in the vicinity of your post, which terminated gloriously to the American arms; but, had it continued until the Indians, etc, were driven under the influence of the post and guns you mention, they would not have much impeded the progress of the victorious army under my command, as no such post was established in the commencement of the present war between the Indians and the United States."[3]

Campbell found this in some manner an insult to the British flag and said he would open his guns if the Americans continued to approach in a threatening posture. The correspondence then began to lose sparkle, with Wayne saying he knew of no war between the two countries and ordering the British to retire peacefully, the Briton refusing until so ordered by his own government. So it ended; neither desired to fire the first hostile shot.

The only discordant American note came from Wilkinson, who, the day after Fallen Timbers, when all the country was about to begin celebrating Wayne as the hero of the 1790s and winner of the Northwest, wrote a mean little letter to the Kentucky senator, John Brown, denigrating his commander as ignorant and boastful. Wayne's handiwork, the precision of the battle, disproved the first adjective. He did not gasconade, but was self-assured, positive, forthright, where Wilkinson was devious.[4]

But what if he did gasconade? If he could win battles like Fallen Timbers in the far-off forest over foes who had badly worsted Harmar and destroyed his predecessor St. Clair, was it any more than a venial shortcoming? Wilkinson's strictures were intemperate; he had found the procedure effective against George Rogers Clark, and now put Wayne in his sights. The jealousy was apparent. Wilkinson would be a nonentity in American history were he not such a striking example of one who got far by the most reprehensible methods.

His letters to his Kentucky friend and lawyer, Harry Innes, abusing Wayne excessively, seem bordering on irrationality. Yet Wayne, with an ill-timed generosity Wilkinson probably could not even understand, mentioned him first in his commendations to Secretary Knox after the battle. He was the senior subordinate and an oversight would have led to controversy.

Knox was disturbed about the letters Wilkinson was writing and wondered if a compromise were not possible "for discussions of that sort afford no pleasure but to the malevolent." A more vigorous secretary of war might have cashiered Wilkinson and saved the country grief in the War of 1812, or tried him for insubordination for writing behind his commander's back. His attempted invasion of Canada in the War of 1812 fully exposed his incompetence.

Secretary Knox thought Wayne might get Wilkinson off his back by granting him leave of absence for a "handsome term . . . I suggest this only for consideration." Wilkinson then filed charges against Wayne and asked a court of inquiry, an absurd request which Knox brushed aside, saying the charges should be more specific. Knox sent a copy to Wayne, who condemned them as being "as unexpected as they are groundless, and as false as they are insidious; and had I not known the real character and disposition of the man, I should have considered the whole as the idle Phantom of a disturbed imagination." He capped it by saying that if he were guilty of all Wilkinson charged he ought not to be court-martialed, he ought to be hanged! Baffled, Wilkinson wrote a public letter changing his tune, saying his lips were now sealed and his pen "dismissed from depicting well founded grievances." Wayne thereafter pushed him out of sight, gave him no part in future dealings with the Indians, thought that "if he had any modesty he would resign." But Wilkinson went on to greater and more disturbing quarrels and intrigues with others elsewhere.

Wayne's policy was to starve the Indians to the council fire. He reported to Knox from the Miami villages at the Maumee headwaters a month after the battle that the Indians "are certainly sore from the late General interview with this Army." He continued: "Nor can they support themselves but by the aid of the British Magazines, which probably can not well supply from seven to Eight thousand, additional mouths, including men women & Children now thrown upon [the British], belonging to the different Hostile tribes, whose Towns Villages & provisions are totally destroy'd & laid waste, & whose hunting grounds are now in our rear, so that their future prospects must naturally be gloomy and unpleasant."[5]

Work progressed on a blockhouse and stockade at the Miami villages where the St. Joseph and St. Mary's rivers met to form the Maumee, to which the army made a diversion before returning to Fort

Defiance. Wayne had reached the site on September 17 and on October 22, 1794, Lieutenant Colonel Hamtramck took command of the completed and permanent post. A salute of fifteen guns was fired and Hamtramck christened the post Fort Wayne. The army, leaving a garrison with Hamtramck in command, marched to Greenville and arrived November 2.

The longer the Indian tribes studied the more clearly they recognized the futility of war against "the chief who never sleeps." All through the winter they reflected. The last to waver and succumb to the lure of peace and the prospect of ready money were the Shawnee, due partly to Tecumseh's resolution never to part with the land. But Blue Jacket was the chief. He overruled the younger and more spirited man and the Shawnee finally capitulated. The tribesmen and their leaders began the slow movement toward Greenville. With the chiefs came the squaws.

When spring turned to summer, ninety-two chiefs and their squaws were encamped around the little army post and village. Scattered about on the little streams were 1,000 warriors, receiving food, waiting for the opening of the whiskey casks, anxious for the distribution of the promised money. When they asked Wayne continually when they would get the distribution, his invariable answer would be, "Tomorrow," the simplest word he had for saying, later. It won for him a new name. At Greenville he became known as "Wabong," meaning "Tomorrow."

Wayne's negotiations were furthered by an achievement across the Atlantic. John Jay completed his negotiations with Lord Grenville. The British agreed to vacate the Northwest Territory forts. Jay brought home a good treaty, though the public could not discern yet that it was such, and rallied against it. Washington had to use his full influence to get it ratified by the Senate, June 24, 1795. Wayne was able to tell the chiefs that they now stood alone—they could look for no help from the white father across the sea. With the hungry Indian warriors the intelligence was effective.

The conversations went on from June 16 until August 10. The Indians were not a hurried people and it was pleasing to be close to the American commissary supplies. When the conference was convened, everyone, as was the Indian custom, spoke. Stragglers arrived. Wayne was not dallying. The treaty money had to come under escort all the way from Philadelphia. He had no professional peacemakers to grow impatient and hamper the proceedings. He was commissioner plenipotentiary on behalf of the United States government.

Engaging in the discussions were the leading chiefs of the Northwest. Most of the tribes of what became Ohio, Indiana, Michigan, Illinois and lower Wisconsin were represented: the Miami, Delaware, Wyandot, Shawnee, Ottowa, Chippewa, Potawatomi, Wea, Piankashaw, Kickapoo, and Kaskaskia.

What the United States got was not so much an empire, but the stepping-stone to an empire. What the Indians got was pitifully small—goods to the value of $20,000 and a scattering of promised annuities amounting collectively to $9,500 a year. The British minister may have said that Wayne was a general and nothing more, but he surely showed here that he was a bargainer. Perhaps the most important consideration for the whites was that they broke the barrier of the Ohio River established at the Treaty of Fort Stanwix. It is true that the United States obtained title to the Northwest Territory from King George III, who in turn had obtained it from the French after Wolfe's capture of Quebec. But how valid were the titles of the French and English kings? Now the title was made secure. The Greenville Treaty line ran across Ohio from Fort Recovery to the Cuyahoga River, and on the west from Fort Recovery to the Ohio River opposite the mouth of the Kentucky River. This included a segment of southeastern Indiana.

The only Indian of importance who held aloof from the signing was Tecumseh, who denounced the chiefs who signed and broke relations with his father's friend and head of his own Shawnee, the venerable Blue Jacket. Tecumseh held that the land belonged to the Indians in common, like water and air, and could not be sold or traded away by any chief or group of chiefs. He watched the proceedings from a cabin near Urbana, Ohio, then moved to east central Indiana and gradually developed the confederation of tribes that led to later hostilities and merged into the second war with Great Britain in 1812. When it came to the distribution the wily Little Turtle managed to get a double share. He succeeded in classifying the Eel River Indians as a separate tribe, when they were no more than a sidepocket of the Miami. But the Turtle was a decided peace factor in the Northwest and was entitled to special consideration.[6]

The land ceded to Wayne and the pacification of the tribes which followed in Ohio stimulated a heavy tide of immigration. Eight years after the Treaty of Greenville, Cincinnati was becoming a flourishing city and Ohio was admitted as a state. The winning of the Northwest was the achievement of Wayne's generalship and statesmanship—his and the combat ability of the army he had forged out of the same kind of material as was surprised and butchered under St. Clair. Well might a latter-day warrior-peacemaker, Theodore Roosevelt, rate him at the top of American combat generals.

TWENTY-ONE

Mary Vining Says Yes, Destiny No

MAJOR GENERAL ANTHONY WAYNE, commander of the Army of the United States, was riding home, his work of pacifying the Indian tribes of the Northwest finished. Things would be different, with Polly no longer at Waynesborough. She had died while he was away drilling his men intensively before his march into the Ohio wilderness. Of course he could not return for the funeral; it would naturally have been held before the horseman could made the long ride over the Pennsylvania mountains from Eastown to Pittsburgh and thence to Legionville. Moreover, those were the times when all personal considerations had to yield to the country's cause.

His daughter Margaretta, now grown to a lady of twenty-four years, and Isaac, his son, twenty-two, would be there. Margaretta was married to William Atlee, and had a new baby, Anthony's first grandchild, while his son Isaac was preparing for the law in Philadelphia, though he would live mainly throughout his life as a country squire in Waynesborough.

Behind him, coming to greet him after his arrival, was the intelligence that Winthrop Sargent, who had survived the horrors of the St. Clair massacre and the wound he had taken there and was now secretary and acting governor of the Northwest Territory, had drawn off a section of Michigan containing the post and town of Detroit, and named it Wayne County. It is now one of the most heavily populated counties in the country. There Wayne, the assiduous reader, would later be honored along cultural lines by having a great university bear his name.[1]

As he now approached Philadelphia, at the old Welsh settlement of Radnor, he saw ahead on the pike a body of mounted troops, drilling perhaps, after his own teachings. On nearer view they were seen to have an artillery complement. They were three companies of the Philadelphia Light Horse Brigade, the elegant City Troop, organized in 1774, already celebrated as the oldest military organization in the United States, though a North Carolina Company and perhaps others might claim that distinction. At the head of one of the companies was Captain John MacPherson, commander of what became known as the "MacPherson Blues," who had left the British army when the colonies revolted to become one of Wayne's companions in arms.[2]

This time Anthony Wayne was not to be allowed to slip around Philadelphia as he had been required to do on returning from rewinning Georgia. Escorted by the three troops, he was ferried across the near-frozen Schuylkill River. He heard the firing of guns and ringing of bells. It was February 6, 1796, brisk and clear, the ground snow-covered, but the waiting people were on the streets while the salute guns sounded from Center Square. The impressive companies of cavalry, the Stars and Stripes at their head, moved down Arch Street to Ninth, where dinner was set at Richardet's Tavern, the leading assembly place of the city, with most of the distinguished of Philadelphia on hand. Outside, though it was day, fireworks and rockets streamed through the air.

Wayne's return from the pacification of the Indians had been awaited as an occasion for the broad celebration of peace in all quarters, an event for which one of the enterprising Philadelphia manufacturers, Ambroise & Co. (quite incidentally the makers of fireworks!), had solicited and procured a public subscription for the erection of an imposing Temple of Peace, in Arch Street between Seventh and Eighth, close by Richardet's Tavern. While the toasts were being drunk to Wayne on a generous scale and to all friends of liberty and democracy inside, the fireworks sounded and screamed through the air for the throng without.

The peace edifice, a triumphal arch twenty-six feet high, was designed to show the gratification of the people that war attended them no more. The United States was at peace with Algiers (temporarily, it proved, and not permanently until the Philadelphia-reared Stephen Decatur enforced it by his frigate's cannon); with the elector of Hanover, the title chosen for King George III, peace between France and the Republic of Holland; and finally, through Wayne's ability as general and statesman, peace with the Indians of the Northwest. All the world momentarily was at peace!

The Peace Temple rested on four pillars; the cornice bore the legend of peace and supported a globe of the earth atop which was the dove with the olive branch in her beak. There was much else—the statue of a woman symbolizing the Union of the States; statues of Peace, Plenty, Liberty, Justice, and Reason. The last showed the French influence, for the Revolution there had enthroned the new god. The ornamentation continued with vases and baskets, but mainly, it revealed to all the world that Anthony Wayne was the cherished idol of his home city. Gout-ridden, bullet-laden, battle-scarred Anthony Wayne loved it all.[3]

That night the reception brought together the notables of the government and city, entering into the more formal tribute to the general. Wayne's daughter and her husband, William Atlee, his son Isaac, his friends Delaney, Peters, Rush, were there. He gave each his attention— the courteous gentleman, the Pennsylvania squire and dapper dresser, as well as the frontier general making the ground his bed. In the line passing to speak their warm thanks, a feminine face and figure caused him to start, then give to her his complete attention, for he was gazing again into the brown eyes of Mary Vining. More than eighteen years had passed since the effervescent Lafayette, nineteen, whose heart was almost always on his sleeve and to whom all womankind seemed fair and desirable, had introduced him to "the most beautiful girl in America."

Mary Vining he would now see often. Tributes were lavished on all hands, from old friends, and from the generation that had arisen since he marched off to war. Newcomers were in the government. Knox, who had felt the need to repair his personal finances after faithful service in war and Washington's cabinet, had resigned as secretary of war, to be followed by Timothy Pickering and then by James McHenry. Wayne had coveted the assignment to be secretary of war after Knox and had been mentioned for the post widely, and deserved it more than McHenry.[4] Wayne might have fit the duties well; none knew the army better, none was a more diligent provider for the troops, none could reflect better the viewpoint of the enlisted men, or merge their needs into the broader picture of the public interest.

The peace festivities continued. Captain Morrell's cavalry corps, the Vermont Greens, was in the city and on February 25 gave a dinner for Wayne in Weed's Tavern at Gray's Ferry, which commanders of some of the local cavalry troops attended. Brigadier General Thomas Proctor, who had managed the guns for him at Chadd's Ford at Brandywine, had a chance to shake his old commander's hand.

Always somewhere among the welcomers was Mary Vining, middle-aged but strikingly beautiful. In some respects she looked little more than the girl with whom Anthony had been enraptured in Wilmington. Through years that had passed, for those inscrutable reasons known only to women who love deeply, she had never married. Scarcely ever or for long had she permitted the companionship of other men, though her alert mind and beauty had drawn many to her.[5]

Almost before they had known again the warmth of their affection, the consuming call of duty began to rear itself between them. Before February 1796 wore into March, Secretary McHenry was writing about the disposition of forces and garrisons in the Northwest, and asking the number of troops necessary for taking possession of the forts that under Jay's Treaty the British would surrender. Did not these inquiries arouse a presentiment? Would Anthony have to make the long journey on horseback again to the remote Northwest?

But for the moment there was happiness such as he had not experienced before. For six months they were together almost constantly. The proposal would not have had to be spoken, but was. They rode about Philadelphia in the sleigh, visited Wilmington, Newcastle, and Dover, prepared for the wedding. She was thirty-nine, he fifty-one, not too wide an age gap for them to have many companion interests and future years together.

The general reached Waynesborough from the Philadelphia fetes in late February. After an absence of about four years he could sleep in his own bed, look over his own acres, see what amounted to the virtual wreck of his handsome plantation and thriving tannery of former years. These were happy days. In the long quest he had attained at last the things he sought most, achievement, glory, recognition, applause, and now, the love of a beautiful woman. Life could just be opening to its fullest.

Many of his companions of the gruelling campaigns had passed— Butler perhaps the one most missed. Greene was gone. His congratulations over Fallen Timbers would have been the warmest. Lafayette had been a top figure in the great revolution in France which had been triggered off by that in the United States, and Wayne and Washington would see him no more. Lord Stirling had died in Albany at fifty-six, as the Revolutionary War closed; he was rarely brilliant, always reliable. The hardihood of the old generals had been sapped by poor food, lack of sleep, arduous living conditions during the nine years between Lexington and the final hauling down of the British flag and the raising of the Stars and Stripes as the last of the British forces left New York.

Good-by to politics, good-by to the army also, with its jealousies and frictions, its contemptible Wilkinsons and caitiff St. Clairs, its call for eternal vigilance which a good general could not delegate to others! Good-by to inspecting the pickets at three o'clock in the morning, then riding with a bandaged leg to watch and guide the bayonet practice! In most respects, nevertheless, it had been a grand life. The most handsome rewards undoubtedly were the pleasant commendations coming with each new feat from the great man of the age, whom it was a privilege to serve because he too gave of himself so unsparingly.

Wayne would wed Mary Vining, he fancied, and enter into a new happiness. The amours of middle age are sometimes the strongest. He lavished her with gifts—a set of Lowestoft china that may still be seen in the Ridgely house in Dover. This china, made in the English North Sea town after which it was named, had a vogue in America and on the Continent during the post-war period, before the coming of Wedgewood.

In this season of happiness Jay's Treaty, which pleased Wayne because it marked the last vestige of British claim on the Northwest Territory he had won, had to be put into full operation. Washington had proclaimed it. Wayne's great work in preserving for the United States the vast prairie stretches of the present-day Mid-West and near Northwest seemed completed; the repose he longed for on his estate, the happiness with Mary Vining enthroned there, seemed at hand.

Then something happened. Washington called once more, and the faithful Anthony Wayne again responded. The British were about to surrender the Northwest forts under the terms of Jay's Treaty and who could receive them for the United States more appropriately than the man who had pacified the Northwest—whose victory at Fallen Timbers had been something of a shock to the negotiations between Jay and Grenville, and had told Britain that the Northwest could not be held as a buffer state by Indians alone, but would call for a great new army and a new war. Who but Wayne should represent the Republic in the formal proceedings of transfer?

Wayne was in the saddle in early June. Love would have to wait again. In reasonable time the trip could be completed by the following February, when he would be fifty-two, Mary Vining forty. The commander of the Army of the United States, in handsome new uniform from the best Chestnut Street tailor, accompanied by a small staff, rode once more over the successive ridges of the Pennsylvania mountains. The trip was made rapidly. He was writing Secretary McHenry from Philadelphia on June 7 as he departed, and from Pittsburgh on June 24, saying he would descend the Ohio on the 27th.

The repossession of the forts proceeded amicably. Wayne did not have to make personally the long journey to Michilimackinac. Acting Governor Winthrop Sargent went there in September with Major Henry Burbeck, received the post, and sent to Wayne a sketch of the works and minutes of the proceedings. Finally, on September 20, 1796, Wayne was able to write to Secretary McHenry of the complete possession of all the posts "on the American side of the Demarcation" specified in the treaty. These were mainly Michilimackinac, Detroit, Miami, Niagara, and Oswego, "with their dependencies inclusive." All had been surrendered to American troops by the British commanders "in the most polite, friendly & accommodating manner;—without any injury or damage—other than what time has made."

There was a significant farewell statement in a paragraph of the long report of the transactions he sent to Secretary McHenry: "An event that must naturally afford the highest pleasure & satisfaction to every friend of Order & good Government, & I trust will produce a conviction to the World—that the measures adopted & pursued by that great and first of men the President of the United States,—were founded in Wisdom, & that the best interests of his Country have been secured by that unshaken fortitude, Patriotism & Virtue, for which he is so universally & justly celebrated (a few *Democrats* excepted—& even they in their hearts must acknowledge his worth)."[6]

Wayne over the years had been anything but a sycophant, but more a prodder of Washington. Could it be that the rigors of the Fallen Timbers campaign and now those of the days in the saddle, and the recurring severity of his gout, were giving him a premonition that he would never see Philadelphia or his old commander again? Or was it that Washington, being under abuse from the radicals who wanted to plunge the United States in some manner into the French Revolution, which seemed running its course on its own blood, made him desire to add this small note of support to his chief, knowing that his final report on the acquisition of the British forts would command national attention? Perhaps it was much of both.

Could Wayne at fifty-two be thinking ahead to the Presidency? It seems unlikely. The statesmen—Adams, Jefferson, Madison, were ahead of the generals, with Washington, the statesman-general, standing apart. Politics had dealt with Wayne badly; it is doubtful that he would have sought another brush with it. The future seemed placid at Waynesborough, with a delightful companion in Mary Vining.

His mission happily concluded, Wayne turned toward home. The discomforts of riding with his irritated leg caused him to seek lake transportation.

He wrote on November 12 that he was leaving Detroit—a post too remote for general army headquarters—for Pittsburgh, which could be reached in a week's time by fast courier from Philadelphia. He recommended the change in headquarters. That was the last letter of Anthony Wayne to the War Department.

Five days later he was aboard the sloop *Detroit*, going down Lake Erie to Presque Isle (Erie, Pennsylvania), where he planned the journey overland to Pittsburgh and from there to Waynesborough. Perhaps it was the letdown, after the activity of field and garrison, perhaps the accumulation of strains over the years, that caused him to weaken on shipboard. All phases of his illness were attributed to gout, which, true enough, can be devastating. His leg became badly swollen. Whiskey, the common remedy of the frontier, did not help. Apparently it only aggravated the disorder.

There was no physician on the sloop, nor one present when he landed at Presque Isle. The fort that was being built there during his Fallen Timbers campaigns, but on which Secretary Knox had halted work so as not to further inflame a tense situation with the British and Indians, had now been completed. One of Wayne's junior officers from the Ohio campaign, Captain Russell Bissell, was in command. When Wayne was carried off the boat, Bissell immediately put him to bed, in the second story of the newly completed blockhouse. He dispatched a messenger for the general's old physician, Dr. J. G. Wallace at Fort Lafayette, who had been on the Maumee River campaign and at Fallen Timbers. But Wallace never completed the long overland journey; while enroute he was intercepted by another courier who told him that Anthony Wayne was dead. One of Wayne's requests, seeing the gravity of his condition, was for Dr. Benjamin Rush, but Rush was far away, and the news of the general's death came ahead of the summons.

The only physician who reached him before the end was the army surgeon, Dr. George Balfour. He resorted to the conventional practice of bleeding, at least twice in one day, which appeared to comfort the patient by putting him to sleep, but weakened him. When he awoke his first request was for a stimulant and again received whiskey. He spoke occasionally. Finally, he reached his hand to Bissell and said, "I am dying. Bury me on the hill, at the foot of the flagpole."

On the morning of December 15, 1796, sixteen days before he would be fifty-two years old, Anthony Wayne breathed his last. Never again would the "blacksnake" coil. The "Chief Who Never Sleeps" was asleep at last.

An undisturbed rest was not to be the lot for this restless man. Wayne is the only personage of American history known to have two graves. He was buried as he had wished at the foot of the flagpole, in the Great Lakes corridor that had been obtained for his state by the legislative activity of his old subordinate, Irvine. The site was called "Garrison Hill." In 1809 the Society of the Cincinnati decided to monument Wayne in his home area, in St. David's Churchyard in Radnor, where his forebears were buried. Because of this the general's son, Isaac Wayne, drove over the mountains to Erie in a one-horse sulky to get the body for reinterment.

He departed with the impression that he could transport his father's remains readily, though the country was rough and many streams were bridgeless. He enlisted the help of Dr. J. G. Wallace, the physician who had been at Fallen Timbers and had tried to reach Presque Isle before the general's death. When they opened the grave they found the body in an almost perfect state of preservation and it was therefore impractical to reduce it to small packages that would fit into the back of the sulky. In early writings about the misadventure the doctor is credited, or charged, with providing the solution, which was to separate the flesh from the bones by boiling. The flesh, when thus softened, was stripped from the bones, and it, the viscera, and the knives that had been employed, were replaced in the coffin and restored to the old grave.

Isaac Wayne took the cleaned skeleton in the sulky back to Radnor. There, on July 4, 1809 the funeral was attended by a great outpouring of people from Philadelphia and the surrounding towns, with the famed City Troop serving as the guard of honor. In front of the hearse in the procession from Waynesborough in Chester County to St. David's Church in Delaware County, walked Samuel Smiley, one of Wayne's veterans of the Pennsylvania Line, a distance not great for one who had tramped through his campaigns.

None could more appropriately deliver the funeral oration than the Reverand David Jones, the chaplain who had followed George

Rogers Clark, had joined Wayne before Brandywine, passed the winter with him at Valley Forge, marched with him to Virginia and Georgia, then accompanied him to Fort Defiance and Fallen Timbers. Unhappily none preserved his remarks but it is written that the chaplain, then seventy-three, was "of heroic mould" and known as "Old Man Eloquent."

The grave at Presque Isle, which perhaps had by weight the greater part of Wayne's body, was forgotten for many years, then eventually was rediscovered by an enterprising Erie doctor, Edward G. Germer, and marked by a restoration of the old blockhouse that had burned. Thus Wayne does, in fact, have two graves.

Notes

INTRODUCTION—*A Glimpse at Mad Anthony.* 1. H. N. Moore, *Life and Services of Gen. Anthony Wayne*, 132–3. Later biographers have followed the story of Jemy but taken sharp exception to any implication that the name denotes instability. 2. Henry B. Carrington, *Battles of the American Revolution*, 167. 3. John R. Spears, "A Sane View of Anthony Wayne," *Harper's Monthly Magazine*, Vol. 105—Pg. 885 (Nov. 1902). 4. At a preliminary council with seventeen officers present, only Wayne and Cadwalader favored attacking Clinton on the march. Cadwalader was absent a week later when Wayne alone voted favoring battle. Lafayette kept the minutes. 5. Charles Janaway Stille, *Major General Anthony Wayne and the Pennsylvania Line*, 28. Stille, provost of the University of Pennsylvania, educational leader, author, president of the Historical Society of Pennsylvania, was Wayne's substantial biographer in the latter part of the nineteenth century. Joseph J. Lewis, 364n, tells of the incident at the grave. 6. Edward J. Lowell, *Hessians and Other German Auxiliaries in the Revolutionary War*, 226–227. Lowell cites Ewald's *Belehrungen*, Vol. II—pp. 284–293.

ONE—*Assignment from Dr. Franklin.* 1. Stille, 23, commenting on Wayne's reading of Caesar and Saxe, pointed out that many of the officers were ignorant, "but a large fund of common sense, experience, and perfect coolness in emergencies, rather than books on the art of war, tempered the zeal of Wayne. . . ." 2. Moore, 7; Moore is the principal source followed on the family history, his facts having been obtained from the general's son, Isaac. 3. Thomas Allen Glenn, *Some Colonial Mansions*, 288. 4. Moore, 8–10. 5. Joseph Granville Leach, *History of the Penrose Family of Philadelphia*, 32–33.

TWO—*Committeeman and Continental Colonel.* 1. John C. Miller, *Origins of the American Revolution*, 325–329. 2. The account of the coming of war to Philadelphia is summarized from John Scharf and Thompson Westcott, *History of Philadelphia*, I—293ff. 3. *Ibid.*, I—293f. 4. Alexander Graydon, *Memoirs of His Own Time*, 282. His conversation with Wayne was just before the battle of Brandywine.

THREE—*Confidently In, Hurriedly Out of Canada.* 1. Members of the commission were of mixed religious persuasions. They were Charles Carroll of Carrollton, wealthy Maryland Catholic; John Carroll, a Jesuit priest of Maryland; Samuel Chase, Maryland Protestant; and Franklin, chairman, a deist leaning in later life to Presbyterianism. 2. Sources used in the Canadian campaign include Garrington, 166–7; Moore, 18–19; William Hunt, *The History of England (1760–1801)*, 130; 151–52, 155–56; Commager and Morris, I—214–17; Lossing, I—127ff.; an apt characterization of Ethan Allen noticed was in *En. Br.*: he was "a back woods strategist untrammeled with military pedantry." *Wayne Papers*, Historical Society of Pennsylvania (hereafter *Wayne Papers* Pa.). For inoculation in American army, Lossing I—307 and 307n; Christopher Ward, *The War of the Revolution*, 2 vols., I—463.

FOUR—*Winter Ordeal at "Old Ti."* 1. The Trumbull paintings in the United States Capitol are *The Signing of the Declaration of Independence*, *The Surrender of Burgoyne*, and *The Resignation of Washington*. More than fifty are in the School of Fine Arts at Yale. 2. F. J. Hudleston, *Gentleman Johnny Burgoyne*, 155–7. British General William Phillips is quoted as saying, "Where a goat can go a man can go, and where a man can go he can haul up a gun." 3. *Wayne Ms. Collection*, New York Public Library (hereafter *Wayne Papers* N.Y.). 4. Commager and Morris, I—221. 5. William Henry Smith, editor, *The St. Clair Papers*, I—407–8; Commager and Morris, I—552. 6. Hunt, 177. Huddleston, 177, varies the quote slightly. George III has been somewhat rehabilitated in later-day literature and opinion, which have tended to relieve him from some of the odium cast by historians of both sides for the better part of two centuries. See J. H. Plumb, *The First Four Georges* (1956), who uses the phrase "a convenient scapegoat," and R. J. White, *The Age of George III* (1968), 4ff. for a fresh picture of the era of the maligned monarch.

FIVE—*Sparring with Howe in New Jeresy.* 1. While Lord Stirling, Wayne's commander at times, is listed under that name in some British reference works, he is called William Alexander as frequently in American biographical sketches. He was born in 1726 in New York City, where his Scot father, James Alexander, had found refuge in 1716 after the cause of the Old Pretender, James Stuart, whom he ardently supported, had collapsed. His mother was the daughter of fabulously wealthy "Ready-money" Provost of New York, who won his fortune from smuggling. William Alexander enlisted for the French and Indian wars and soon was aide-de-camp to Governor William Shirley of Massachusetts, who, after Braddock was defeated and killed in western Pennsylvania, became the admired supreme commander of the British forces in North America, as he had been the best liked of the colonial governors sent out by Great Britain. When Shirley returned to England, young Alexander accompanied him. His intelligence and delightful personality won him the acquaintance of political leaders, some of whom suggested that he try to establish a claim to the earldom of Stirling. He began litigation on the ground that his father had been the presumptive heir to the title when he fled to New York. An Edinburgh jury supported him; it declared that William was the nearest heir to the last recognized earl of Stirling. The claim won no further official confirmation and while he was sometimes called Earl or Lord Stirling in England, the disposition there was and has been to treat him as titular earl, not recognized by the court, cabinet, crown or House of Lords. When he returned to New York in 1761 he assumed the title of Lord Stirling and as such was accepted and addressed in the American army. 2. Moore, 25. John Armstrong, *Life of Anthony Wayne*, says Washington remarked at the time of Wayne's appointment that his command "could not fail under his direction to be soon and greatly distinguished." 3. Wayne to Rush, June 3, 1777. *Wayne Papers* N.Y. 4. Wayne to Washington, Sept. 2, 1777. *Wayne Papers* Pa., IV—2. 5. *Ibid.*, III—121. 6. Mrs. Henry G. Banning, "Miss Vining, a Revolutionary Belle." Paper read before Colonial Dames of America, May 30, 1894, and published in *The American Historical Register and Monthly Gazette of the Patriotic Heriditary Societies of the United States of America of the State of Delaware*, May 1935. Pgs. 1190–1205. Some engaging articles about Mary Vining were written in 1902 after much research by Edward Robins, president of the Historical Society of Pennsylvania. Interesting material is in Elizabeth Montgomery, *Reminiscences of Wilmington in Familiar Village Tales, Ancient and New*, 133ff. and Scharf and Wescott, II—903–4.

SIX—*Brandywine—The Battle Rolls off to the Right.* 1. A consensus exists on most of the major points about Brandywine. The principal guidance was obtained from Carrington's *Battles etc.*, 366ff.; Washington Irving's *Life of Washington*, Vol. III—Pgs. 235ff.; the original source excerpts in Commager and Morris, Vol. I—Pgs. 606ff.; Scharf and Wescott's *Philadelphia*; John Armstrong's, Moore's, and other Wayne biographies, and the *Wayne Papers*.

2. The ford is spelled both Chad's and Chadd's in early accounts. The writer has used the present post office spelling, which appears to have been that of John Chadd, whose home was nearby. 3. Lossing, II—371. 4. Irving, III—247. Brand Whitlock, *Lafayette*, 2 vols., I—90. 4. What apparently excited Cheney was that he overheard someone of Washington's staff say he "looked like a Tory." 5. Related in William Darlington letter, Commager and Morris, I—616. Freeman, IV—481, thought the remarks did not sound like Washington and questions the story. 6. A fair estimate of Howe at Brandywine was made by Carrington, 373–74. This historian was highly approbative of Washington's plan to cross the Brandywine with Wayne, Greene, and others, and to attack Knyphausen, when he learned that the British had divided their forces. 7. A by-product of the battle was that it closed the only Sunday school being conducted south of New England. This had been established in 1740 by Dunkers at Ephrata. The schoolhouse was turned into a hospital and the school was ended. Not until 1790, under the stimulus of Bishop Francis Asbury, was the next southern Sunday school opened in Hanover County, Virginia. John Bach McMaster, *A History of the People of the United States*, 7 vols., Vol. II—Pg. 83.

SEVEN—*At Paoli—The Surprisers Surprised*. 1. The main sources followed in this chapter are Wayne's report, letters, and defense at his court-martial; Moore, 303ff.; Sparks, 78–83; Joel Tyler Headley, *Washington and His Generals*, 2 vols., Vol. I—317–318; John Armstrong, 20–23; and S. Paul Teamer and Franklin L. Burns, two Easton, Pa., residents who made a study over five or six years of the terrain and literature of the Paoli "Massacre" and Valley Forge, only to have their accounts published obscurely in the *Tredyffrin-Easttown History Club Quarterly*, in mimeographed sheets, in 1937–1939.

2. The bayonet accounted for some of Wayne's later victories and was especially impressive against the Northwest Indians at Fallen Timbers. Theodore Roosevelt, discussing Wayne and the bayonet, wrote: "This was always his favorite weapon; he had the utmost faith in coming to close quarters, and he trained his soldiers to trust the steel." Roosevelt and others have cited a number of Wayne's successful uses of the weapon: at Germantown, Monmouth, Stony Point, against Cornwallis in Virginia and against the Indians in Georgia. See Theodore Roosevelt, "Mad Anthony Wayne's Victory," *Harper's New Monthly Magazine*, Vol. 92—Pgs. 707–708, April 1896.

3. Pennsylvania tradition. 4. Irving, III—257–58. Moore, 36. Headley, 317. Armstrong, 19–20. 5. *Wayne Papers* Pa., IV—9. 6. Scharf and Westcott, I—298. Lossing, II—269n–270n. 7. Wayne to court-martial, *Wayne Papers* Pa, IV—20. Moore, 32. Spears, 78–79. 8. Grey has been absolved of much of the obloquy found in early Revolutionary War literature. See Ward, I—469 and his citations correcting misstatements about the Paoli affair. 9. Major John André, *Journal*, Commager and Morris, I—621–22. 10. *Wayne Papers* Pa., IV—11.

11. Teamer and Burns, conceding that Grey did not fight battles delicately, pointed out that the "rules of war" then prevailing (if war ever has rules) were that prisoners not be taken in night attacks. These students of Paoli awarded to the attackers high daring, courage, and skill for making such a successful night assault over unfamiliar ground against one of the best American divisions. They placed Wayne's casualties at nothing like the 300 often given, but at 100 or less.

12. *Wayne Papers* Pa., IV—11. 13. Major Samuel Hay to Irving, Commager and Morris, I—622–23. 14. John Marshall, *Life of George Washington*, 2 vols., I—161. In his summation of this chapter Marshall uses the phrase "General Wayne Surprised." Armstrong, 22n–23n goes into detail to defend Wayne against the charge of being surprised. 15. *Wayne Papers* Pa., IV—16. 16. John Fiske, *The American Revolution*, 2 vols., I—314. 17. Spears, 83. 18. *Wayne Papers* Pa., IV—26.

EIGHT—*Driving Ahead Through the Germantown Fog.* 1. For a discussion of Lafayette's relations with Conway, see Woodward, *Lafayette*, 61ff. 2. Lossing, Vol. II—Pgs. 313n–314n. 3. *Wayne Papers* Pa., Vol. IV—Pg. 25. 4. Wayne's men quite obviously gave little or no quarter in this attack with the bayonet. The troops in memory of Paoli took no prisoners, despite the cries of their officers for moderation. That is the burden of Wayne's own wording when he said the "cries for mercy were of little purpose," and "the Rage and fury of the Soldiers was not to be restrained for some time—at least until a great number of the enemy fell by our Bayonet." *Wayne Papers* Pa., Vol. IV—Pg. 31. As Wayne rode at the head of his column a musket ball grazed his head, another, largely spent, hit his foot, still a third wounded his hand, while a fourth dropped his handsome horse with wounds in the head and flank. Wayne jumped from the saddle as the mount fell and dashed forward on foot calling on his men to follow. He was astonished when two days after the battle his roan steed, not severely injured, reached his camp after apparently searching for him over the battlefield. Headley, 321. 5. *Wayne Papers* Pa., Vol. IV—Pg. 31. 6. Diary of Lieut. Sir Martin Hunter, *Historical Magazine*, Vol. IV—Pg. 347; Commager and Morris, Vol. I—Pgs. 625–725. 7. *Ibid.* 8. This didactic command, a high point of the battle, is widely attested to, as in Irving, Vol. III—Pg. 333; Lossing, Vol. II—Pg. 337, and other accounts. Of Knox's axiom, John Armstrong, who after his military service was Madison's secretary of war during part of the War of 1812, wrote: "The maxim alluded to is of old date, and, during feudal wars, had great authority and extension from the fact that baronial castles formed the principal if not the only objects of attack and defense . . . at no time would a few men, taking refuge in a dwelling-house, neither constructed nor prepared for defense, destitute of cannon and having only a small supply of ammunition, be permitted to stop the march or otherwise disturb the operations of an army of Ten thousand men." It is clear that Wayne, in by-passing Chew Mansion, was more calculating in his methods

than Knox in his rigid adherence to precepts. Wayne was following a necessity in battle of never giving a fleeing enemy in time to regroup. 9. *Wayne
Papers* Pa., Vol. IV—Pgs. 31ff.; Moore, 42–46.

NINE—*Hardships and Capers at Valley Forge.* 1. *Wayne Papers* Pa., Vol.
IV—Pg. 43. 2. *Ibid.*, 50–51. 3. Priscilla Walker Streets, *Lewis Walker of
Chester Valley and His Descendants 1686–1896*, 74–76. 4. *Ibid.*, 76–77.
5. *Tredyffrin-Easton Quart.*, 56. 6. Franklin L. Byrne, *Ibid.*, 57. 7. Wash-
ington's correspondence during the winter is filled with similar statements.
Selected samples are in Commager and Morris, Vol. I—Pgs. 637–651.

TEN—*Named for Gallantry at Disappointing Monmouth.* 1. Sketch of Lee
and his subsequent actions are from extensive discussion of him in Freeman's *Washington*, Vol. IV; Moore, Chapter IV; Carrington, Chapters LV–
LVI; Irving, Vol. III—Pgs. 465ff.; Lossing, Vol. II—Pgs. 352n and 223n;
Commager and Morris citation of Benjamin Rush *Papers* (Conner, ed),
Vol. I—Pgs. 276–277. 2. Palmer, 148. 3. Spears in *Harper's Magazine*, Nov.
1902, calls this "the greatest speech known to the records of the American
councils of war." 4. The account and incidents of Monmouth are based
largely on Carrington, 412–445; Moore, 54–71; Irving, Vol. III—Pgs. 477–
512; William B. Willcox, Editor, *The American Rebellion, Sir Henry Clinton's Narrative of his Campaigns, 1775–1782*, 85–98; Ward, Vol. II—Pgs.
570–586; Lossing, Vol. II—Pgs. 353–368; *Wayne Papers* Pa.; Woodward,
Whitlock, and Morgan biographies of Lafayette. 5. Willcox, editor, Clinton's
Narrative, 91. 6. Lossing, Vol. II—Pgs. 363–363n, gives one of the best
stories of Monckton's death and burial and describes the grave as he saw it
in 1850. 7. Willcox, editor, Clinton's *Narrative*, 97. 8. Washington's praise
in his report to Congress was made the basis for W. H. MacVeagh's address
delivered on the Centennial anniversary of the battle of Paoli. Published
address, pg. 21. 9. Justin Winsor, *Narrative and Critical History of America*,
Vol. VI—Pg. 400, considers that Lee's conduct would have passed unnoticed
had he not written his letter to Washington. 10. The full Wayne-Lee correspondence is published in Moore, 65–68.

ELEVEN—*Demotion and a New Challenge.* 1. Stille, 149, 160–162. 2.
Moore, 81–82. 3. Perhaps the main count held against his prospective suc-
cessor was Wayne's belief that St. Clair had spread the impression he was
derelict at Paoli. When Wayne heard this he was irked above forgiveness.
St. Clair's sneers at the court-martial that acquitted Wayne hurt St. Clair
more than the object of his scorn, for Wayne by that time had fought at
Germantown and made his reputation before the country secure. 4. Headley,
218, 224. Headley was author of numerous biographies and his books were
influential in creating public attitudes respecting Revolutionary War generals. His most successful books were *Napoleon and His Marshals*, which
went through fifty editions, and *Washington and His Generals*, which sold

almost as well. He was correct in suggesting that St. Clair's main military asset was Washington's attachment to him resulting from the Trenton-Princeton campaign of 1776, when Washington rode much with his brigade. 5. Moore, 75. 6. *Ibid.*, 84–85. 7. Charles Jared Ingersoll saw a peculiarity of life in Hull's career: how the young are fearless yet the aged cling desperately to their last uncertain years. Hull fought gallantly in nine battles of the Revolutionary War but was palsied with fear when the British shells began to drop into Detroit at the outset of the War of 1812. Of him Ingersoll said: "In 1777, he would have fought or died without care; in 1812, with not much of life left, he was fearful of losing that little." So it is, that the young must fight the wars.

TWELVE—*Stony Point—The Capture That Turned the Tide.* 1. The principal sources used for Stony Point are Henry B. Dawson's paper, "The Assault on Stony Point," read before the New-York Historical Society, July 24, 1863; Wayne's letters and report to Washington (transcript copy in Revolutionary War Papers, # 2194, Southern Historical Collection, Univ. of N.C., Chapel Hill); Lossing, Vol. II—Pgs. 174ff.; Frank Moore, *Diary of the Revolution*, Vol. II—Pgs. 192ff. (this citation of Frank Moore is not to be confused with more frequent citations of the early Wayne biographer, H. N. Moore, cited throughout as Moore); Headley, 323–329; Irving, Vol. III—Pgs. 572–579; Willcox, editor, Clinton *Narrative*, 129ff.; Freeman Vol. V—Pgs. 108ff; Ward, Vol. II—Pgs. 596–604; Commager and Morris, Vol. II—Pgs. 722–725. 2. Irving, Vol. III—Pg. 572n, treats this as a tradition, while Headley, 324, puts it in the realm of hearsay, though Spears, *Harper's*, Nov. 1902, Pg. 886; Banning, 1197, and others use it as historical though without documentation. 3. The importance of the "Blue Book" is seen in Palmer's *Steuben*, 202ff. 4. Though Wayne was not the first to employ this method of surprise, he did bring to the fore, in latter-day tactics, methods employed in great battles of World War I and the American Civil War, of effecting a concentration far behind the point of intended attack, and moving troops forward rapidly under cover of darkness. 5. Lossing, Vol. II—Pg. 176–176n. Dawson in his comprehensive paper discredited the story, a ground being that one of Washington's letters showed indisputably that the intelligence on which the attack was planned came from a deserter from the fort; another, that Wayne had given orders that none in the country around the fort was to be trusted in any manner; and finally, Wayne's statement that Colonels Stewart and Fleury, during their mile and a half advance from Springsteel's, relied on the personal knowledge they had gained about the terrain. These citations do not disprove the story, or even in themselves cast serious doubt on it. The Negro could still have been the guide over the last lap on the moonless night, and one would have been useful, even to those who had reconnoitered the approaches. 6. Apparently first quoted in New Hampshire *Gazette*, Sept. 7, 1799. The words vary in different accounts. Irving, Vol. III—Pg. 575; Headley, 327. 7. Lossing, Vol.

II—Pg. 181n. 8. Wilcox, editor, Clinton *Narrative*, 133. 9. Commager and Morris, Vol. II—Pgs. 724–725.

THIRTEEN—*Bull's Ferry and Succor for West Point*. 1. Moore, 115n. 2. *Ibid.*, 110–111. 3. The description of the attack follows in the main Wayne's report to Washington in his letter from Tonoway, N.J., July 2, 1780. 4. Moore, 115. 5. Washington's own account, followed here, recorded by Tobias Lear, is republished from Lear's *Diary* and Richard Rush, *Occasional Productions*, Commager and Morris, Vol. II—Pgs. 756–758.

FOURTEEN—*The Mutiny—Wayne's Supreme Trial*. 1. Among the sources followed in this chapter are Carl Van Doren's fascinating and detailed study of the revolt in his *Mutiny in January*, a definitive account; Moore, 199ff.; Marshall, Vol. I—Pg. 420ff.; Lossing, Vol. I—Pgs. 310ff; Irving, Vol. IV— Pgs. 251ff.; Freeman, Vol. V—Pgs. 235ff. 2. Lossing, Vol. I—Pg. 312; Moore, 127n. 3. Van Doren, 46. 4. Moore, 119ff., gives this and other correspondence with Washington, including citation of the biography in the *Casket* written by Wayne's son, 453. 5. Washington's reactions at this stage are shown in Freeman, Vol. V—Pgs. 237–238, and Irving, Vol. IV—Pg. 254. 6. Irving, Vol. IV—Pg. 255. 7. Willcox, editor. Clinton *Narrative*, 240–241. 8. Moore, 129; Irving, Vol. IV—Pg. 259. Van Doren avoids (Pg. 41) the Irving tendency to refer to Wayne as "Mad Anthony," and points out that on Wayne's thirty-sixth birthday (Jan. 1, 1781) he was not yet known by the "Mad" sobriquet. That came to be applied during the Virginia campaign later in the year.

FIFTEEN—*Flash of Bayonets at Green Spring*. 1. The main sources used in this chapter are Headley, 300ff.; Carrington, 602ff.; Moore, 130ff.; Wayne *Correspondence*, Bancroft Collection, N.Y. Public Library and Hist. Soc. of Pa., Philadelphia; Irving, Vol. IV—Pgs. 359–369; 425–442; Lossing, Vol. II—Pgs. 507ff. 2. Hugh F. Rankin, *The North Carolina Continentals*, 173, says they both missed at eight paces and quotes a version that Howe had been recalled because of some matter of "private armours," in South Carolina. Washington employed Howe until the end of the war, being impressed with his military abilities. 3. Washington's greatness was disclosed in his readiness to part with his best officers in an emergency elsewhere, as he had with Morgan to reinforce Gates when Burgoyne threatened, or when earlier he sent Morgan and Benedict Arnold to Montgomery in Canada—all in contrast with a practice not uncommon in armies of sending culls when help was requested. To the list in the text may be added Lord Stirling, one of Washington's main reliances, who declined to go south and for whom Wayne was substituted (Gaine's Mercury, Dec. 6, 1779, cited in Frank Moore's *Diary of the American Revolution*, 248), and Steuben, whom Washington had come to trust, and who was sent south to organize and drill the Virginia Continentals. 4. W. E. Woodward, *Lafayette*, 91. Lafayette's personal outlay for overalls, shorts, hats, underwear, and shoes for every man in his command was repaid to him later by the United States. 5. Wayne explained the difficulties of organizing the expedition and matters over money in a detailed letter home, Moore, 130–133, to which he affixed a P.S. explaining the absence of Jemy the Rover, as noted in the Introduction of this book. 6. *Ibid.* Wayne has been severely condemned, as in Woodward's *George Washington*, 381, for soldiers being made to shoot their comrades, and in particular for commanding a soldier to bayonet his friend who had been merely wounded. When the soldier at first refused, Wayne put a pistol to his head and got obedience by threatening to blow out the soldier's brains. Woodward thought the country had traveled far since the "People's Revolution," but he published his book in 1926, well before the later-day excesses and cruelties in much warfare. 7. Lossing, Vol. II—Pg. 467. Similar references to his conduct at Green Spring are by Carrington, 608, "His self-possession and daring were never more conspicuous, and the Pennsylvania troops under his command fought on equal terms with the best troops of Cornwallis," and by Headley, 331, "At this critical moment the hero of Stony Point needed all his presence of mind, for a single false movement would insure his ruin. But with his usual promptness and decision, he instantly took his determination. . . . The charge was sounded and that gallant little corps moved steadily forward. . . ." 8. Wayne's exchange of letters are in Moore, 135ff.; to Greene, *Wayne Papers*, Bancroft Collection, New York City Public Library; to Robert Morris, Bancroft Collection; from Washington and Greene, in Moore.

SIXTEEN—*Yorktown—but Not the End.* 1. *Wayne Papers*, Bancroft Collection, New York Public Library, Case 6-210, Pg. 59. 2. *Ibid.*, 75. 3. Butler's account. Commager and Morris, Vol. II—Pg. 1228. 4. *Ibid.* 5. *Ibid.*, 1230. 6. Bancroft Collection, 79.

SEVENTEEN—*Mad Anthony Recovers Georgia.* 1. Francis Vinton Greene, *General Geene*, 242. 2. *Ibid.*, 275. 3. Armstrong, 62. The offer of a force so inadequate for the task would have caused most men to regard it a hardship or insult, Armstrong wrote, but with Wayne, "The command was accepted, not merely with professional submission, but with the utmost alacrity. . . ." 4. Greene's *Greene*, 288. 5. Armstrong, 62. *Wayne Papers* Pa., Vol. 3, Pg. 167. Armstrong, 62ff. gives an adequate account of Wayne's Georgia campaign, as does Headley, 332ff. 6. *Wayne Papers* Pa., Vol. 3, Pgs. 135, 175. 7. *Ibid.*, 191. 8. *Ibid.*, 235. The governor's observations about the healthy quality of tobacco for soldiers is of interest in the 1970s. The succeeding correspondence is from *Wayne Papers* Pa., Vol. 3, Pgs. 145, 170, 417. 9. Headley, 335, says Wayne cut down Chief Gunistersigo (variously spelled) with his sword, and, though Wayne was completely surprised by the attack, "he was not staggered for a moment; and in the very midst of the panic his quick mind took in the whole extent of the danger, and planned his defense."

EIGHTEEN—*Top Command at Last.* 1. Green's *Greene*, 313. 2. *Ibid.*, 298, 315–316. 3. Wayne, with his magnetic leadership and wide following, might well have attained high political office had he survived his Northwest campaigning, though, as has been mentioned, he probably would have been irked by the routine of being a legislator. 4. The chief sources followed in this chapter are the Wayne correspondence with Secretaries of War Knox, Pickering, and McHenry, compiled and edited by Richard C. Knopf, entitled *Anthony Wayne, A Name in Arms* (hereafter Knopf, Wayne corres.); Dale Van Avery, *Men of the Western Waters*, an engaging account of the Indian wars in the near Northwest, *passim*; Theodore Roosevelt, *The Winning of the West*, Vol. IV—Pgs. 54ff., and article in *Harper's*, April 1896; Lossing, *Field Book of the War of 1812*, 37 pp.; Henry Howe, *Historical Collections of Ohio*, Vol. I—Pgs. 223ff., 530ff.; Freeman's *George Washington*, Vol. V, *passim*; Tucker's *Tecumseh*, 58ff.; Brice's *History of Fort Wayne*, 145ff.; Moore, 204ff. 5. Little Turtle (Misch-e-can-o-quoh) was born about 1747 about twenty miles west of present Fort Wayne, on the upper Eel River. 6. Another account of the manner of Butler's death was that a surgeon was dressing his five wounds when an Indian dashed in and dispatched him. One son, Lieutenant William Butler of the U.S. Navy, was killed in the War of 1812 while another, James, was captain of the Pittsburgh Blues in that conflict. Probably no other loss in his military career bore more heavily on Wayne than that of this faithful subordinate during the trying war years. 7. McMaster, Vol. II—Pg. 44ff., 71. 8. Palmer's *Von Steuben*, 389. 9. Lee's name had been mentioned earlier, at the time Harmar was selected. 10. He departed on the long, toilsome campaign at a time when many believed the Northwest Territory, where the bones of St. Clair's soldiers were bleaching in the Ohio wilderness, was not worth the effort to reclaim it from the Indians, termed "savages" in the literature of the day. Political opposition sometimes engenders strange obsessions: one of the fairest sections of the globe, thinly utilized by one race, needed by the vast populations breaking out of their old-world confines, not worth another campaign when it had been ceded in the Treaty of 1783! 11. Knopf, Wayne corres., 17. 12. The best latter-day account noticed of the events at Legionville is that of Dale Van Avery, *Men of the Western Waters*, 182ff. The 3rd U.S. Infantry organized and trained by Wayne had a splendid record in later fighting. Andrew Jackson led it against the Creeks and it helped him defeat the British at New Orleans. With it, Colonel Henry Leavenworth built the fort on the Missouri River that bears his name, while some who rose during the Civil War were earlier junior officers in it. Charles M. Cummings, *Yankee Quaker Confederate General*, 77, 84. 13. Tucker, *Dawn Like Thunder*, 347. 14. Van Avery, 170, gives a good picture of Clark at this period when he was in eclipse and disappointed with the failure of Virginia to settle his Revolutionary War accounts. Virginia did allot to him a tract of land in southern Indiana opposite Louisville, Kentucky. For Wilkinson's strictures, Van Avery, 102. 15. Of this Theodore Roosevelt wrote: "This was a preposterous complaint; throughout our history, whether in dealing with Indians or other foes, our Peace Commissioners have invariably shown disadvantage when compared with the military commandants, for whom they always betray jealousy. Wayne's conduct was eminently proper; it is difficult to understand the mental attitude of the commissioners who criticised it because the British found it 'unwarrantable.' " *The Winning of the West*, Vol. IV—Pg. 54.

NINETEEN—*The Northwest Subdued at Fallen Timbers.* 1. Knopf, Wayne corres., 234. 2. George Stimpson, *A Book About a Thousand Things*, 250. 3. Knopf, Wayne corres., 278. 4. The rather gripping story of Wells severing relations with Little Turtle is told by Wallace A. Brice, *History of Fort Wayne*, 147–148. 5. Tucker, *Tecumseh*, 30. 6. Brice, 148. 7. While this speech was Dorchester's attitude at the time the Treaty of 1783 as affecting the near Northwest was in dispute, it was not representative of British policy between the period of Jay's Treaty and the outbreak of the War of 1812. For a discussion of the British attitude during this period see Tucker, *Tecumseh*, Chapter 14, "The British Restrain Tecumseh." 8. Benjamin Drake, *The Life of Tecumseh and His Brother the Prophet*, 80–81. 9. Lyman C. Draper in his Ms. collection about Tecumseh (microfilm at Library of Congress) has an item from the *Western Star*, Stockbridge, Mass., Dec. 9, 1794: "At Fort Recovery a great number of British soldiers faces, blackened, assisted in the attack. Three British officers kept at a distance behind the assailants and directed the operations." Wayne declared that the three British officers appeared to be "men of great distinction" and that a number of white men in the rear were heard to be speaking English. Knopf, Wayne corres., 348. 10. *Ibid.* 11. The account of the battle follows Wayne's report to Knox, Aug. 28, 1794, Knopf, Wayne corres., 351–355. Other accounts followed are Lossing, *War of 1812*, who reports Wayne's final overtures and "speech" to the Indians, 53–57; Brice, 149ff., who relates Tecumseh's participation; Headley, 33–338; and the latter-day account of John Anthony Caruso, *The Great Lakes Frontier*, 177ff. In addition to the gout, Wayne was suffering bruises caused when his mount brushed him across the branches of a beech tree. Both arms and legs were bandaged before the battle began but in the excitement of the fray he jerked off these impediments to free motion and commanded the firing line in person as in the days of Green Spring and Stony Point. 12. Tucker's *Tecumseh*, 69–71, 300. 13. Wayne explained to Knox in his report that the British garrison had to remain "tacit spectators" to his devastation of the Indian country after this victory.

TWENTY—*The Chiefs Assemble and Sign at Greenville.* 1. Knopf, Wayne corres., 365. 2. *Ibid.*, Aug. 28; Pg. 354. 3. Brice, 152. 4. Van Avery, 102. 5. Knopf, Wayne corres., 383. After calling Wilkinson a "vile assassin," Wayne said, "Was a peace once Established with the Indians no consideration wou'd induce me to remain a single hour longer in the service shou'd that worst of all bad men belong to it." *Ibid.*, 35. Wilkinson was long on a secret Spanish payroll. 6. Tucker's *Tecumseh*, 72–73; 76. Rivalry was keen among the Indian chiefs who signed at Greenville. Wayne, writing to Secretary McHenry, Oct. 3, 1796, about a delegation of chiefs who were embarking for Philadelphia, said: "Among whom is the famous Shawanoe Chief *Blue Jacket*, who, it is said had the Chief Command of the Indian Army on the 4th of November 1791 against Genl St. Clair, The *Little Turtle* a Miami Chief who also claims that honor, & who is his rival for fame & power—& said to be daily gaining ground with the Wabash Indians—refuses or declines to proceed in company with *Blue Jacket*." Knopf, Wayne corres., 532. Wayne made a pleasant address to the Indians after the treaty was signed, during the days while it was being engrossed on parchment: "We will eat, drink, and rejoice, and thank the Great Spirit for the happy stage this good work has arrived at." Lossing, *War of 1812*, 57, gives an account of the final council and Wayne's affectionate farewell to the tribesmen. The aftermath of Fallen Timbers, the Treaty of Greenville, and the settlement of Ohio are well related in Caruso, *Great Lakes Frontier*, 183ff.

TWENTY-ONE—*Mary Vining Says Yes, Destiny No.* 1. Winthrop Sargent, a Revolutionary War soldier from Massachusetts, a Harvard graduate, was St. Clair's secretary and often governor of the Northwest Territory in St. Clair's absence, and served as governor for a number of years after St. Clair's defeat. Later he was governor of Mississippi Territory. His grandson of the same name was a historian and biographer of the middle nineteenth century. 2. The main source for Wayne's homecoming is Scharf and Westcott, *Philadelphia*, Vol. I, *passim*. 3. Wayne still carried in his leg the sentry's bullet he had received shortly before Yorktown. 4. Richard C. Knopf, editor of the *Wayne-War Department Correspondence*, says, 477, that Wayne was chagrined that he was passed over for the appointment and was unimpressed with McHenry. So general was the belief that Wayne would get the cabinet post that Commodore Thomas Truxton, then supervising completion of the *Constellation* at Baltimore, wrote to Wayne, bringing him up to date on the situation. The Navy Department had not yet been established and the Navy was under War Department management. Eugene S. Ferguson, *The Life of Commodore Thomas Truxton, U.S. Navy*, 123–124. 5. The sources of the Mary Vining account are those used in Chapter Five of this book, among them Banning and Edward Robins, an earlier-day president of the Historical Society of Pennsylvania. The Robins collection contains stories he wrote about Mary Vining for the Philadelphia *Bulletin*. Part of the Vining story as at times embellished is no doubt shadowland but Robins believed the essentials faithfully. The Robins collection contains a letter he wrote October 27, 1941, to Professor Louis Gottschalk, History Dept., Univ. of Chicago, some lines of which are: "My family brought me up on the story of Mary Vining. She was a cousin of Caesar Rodney, who was my great, great grandfather. . . . You may depend on it that her story is historical—not merely legendary, although of course it may have been embroidered a bit." Elizabeth Montgomery in her *Reminiscenses of Wilmington* tells the story of Mary Vining's life as a recluse in poverty after the passing of Wayne until her death in 1821 at the age of sixty-three, pgs. 135–137. 6. Knopf, Wayne corres., 525–526.

Bibliography

Adams, Henry. *A History of the United States of America.* New York. 1890.

Armstrong, John. *Life of Anthony Wayne.* (Jared Sparks Library) New York. 1854.

Arnold, James Oliver. "Fort Greenville Traditions." *Ohio Historical Society Publications.* Vol. XVII, 1908.

Ashworth, Mary Wells, and Alexander Carroll. Vol. 7 completing Douglas S. Freeman's *George Washington: A Biography.* New York. 1957.

Atwater, Caleb. *A History of the State of Ohio, Natural and Civil.* Cincinnati. 1838.

Banning, Mrs. Henry G. "Miss Vining, a Revolutionary Belle." *The American Historical Register and Monthly Gazette of the Patriotic Heriditary Societies of the United States of America of the State of Delaware,* May 30, 1894. Philadelphia, 1895.

Bemis, Samuel Flagg. *Jay's Treaty: A Study in Commerce and Diplomacy.* New York. 1923.

Boyd, Thomas. *Mad Anthony Wayne.* New York. 1929.

272

Brice, Wallace A. *History of Fort Wayne.* Fort Wayne. 1868.

Burne, Franklin L. "New Light on the Encampment of the Continental Army at Valley Forge, Dec. 19, 1777–June 21, 1778." *Tredyffrin-Easton History Club Quarterly,* July 1939. (Additional Burne articles written with S. Paul Teamer are listed under Teamer.)

Carr, Albert Z. *The Coming of War: An Account of the Remarkable Events Leading to the War of 1812.* Garden City. 1961.

Carrington, Henry B. *Battles of the American Revolution.* New York. 1876.

Carroll, Alexander, and Mary Wells Ashworth. Listed under Ashworth.

Caruso, John Anthony. *The Great Lakes Frontier.* Indianapolis. 1961.

Clinton, Sir Henry. *Sir Henry Clinton's Narrative of His Campaigns 1775–1782.* Edited by William B. Willcox. New Haven. 1954.

Commager, Henry Steele, and Richard B. Morris. *The Spirit of 'Seventy-Six: The Story of the American Revolution as Told by Participants.* 2 vols. Indianapolis. 1958.

Dawson, Henry B. *Gleanings from the Harvest Field of American History. Part X. The Assault on Stony Point by General Anthony Wayne, July 16, 1779.* Morrisenia, N.Y. 1863.

Dodge, Jacob R. *Red Men of the Ohio Valley.* Springfield, Ohio. 1860.

Drake, Benjamin. *Life of Tecumseh and His Brother the Prophet.* Cincinnati. 1841.

Drake, Francis S., Editor. *Indian Tribes of the United States.* 2 vols. Philadelphia. 1883.

Drake, Samuel Gardner. *The Aboriginal Races of North America.* New York. 1880.

Ferguson, Eugene S. *Truxton of the* Constellation. Baltimore. 1956.

Fiske, John. *The American Revolution.* 2 vols. New York. 1896.

Freeman, Douglas Southall. *George Washington: A Biography.* Vols. 4, 5, and 6. New York. 1951.

Glenn, Thomas Allen. *Some Colonial Mansions, and Those Who Lived in Them.* Philadelphia. 1900.

Greene, Francis Vinton. *General Greene.* (Great Commanders Series) New York. 1897.

Greene, George Washington. *Life of Major General Nathanael Greene.* 3 vols. New York. 1867–1871.

Griswold, B. J. *The Pictorial History of Fort Wayne, Indiana. A Review of Two Centuries of Occupancy of the Region about the Head of the Maumee River.* Fort Wayne. 1914.

Headley, Joel Tyler. *Washington and His Generals.* 2 vols. New York. 1948.

Howe, Henry. *Historical Collections of Ohio.* Cincinnati. 1851.

Hudleston, F. J. *Gentleman Johnny Burgoyne.* Indianapolis. 1927.

Hunt, William. *The History of England from the Accession of George III to the Close of Pitt's First Administration (1760–1801),* London. 1905.

Irving, Washington. *Life of George Washington.* 5 vols. (New Hudson Edition) New York. 1880.

Jacobs, James Ripley. *Tarnished Warrior. Major General James Wilkinson.* New York. 1938.

———. *The Beginning of the U.S. Army 1783–1812.* Princeton, N.J. 1947.

Johnson, Henry P. *The Storming of Stony Point on the Hudson, Midnight July 15, 1779.* New York. 1900.

Jones, C. C. *History of Georgia.* Boston. 1883.

Knapp, Frederick. *The Life of John Kalb.* New York. 1884.

Knapp, H. S. *History of the Maumee Valley.* Toledo. 1872.

Knopf, Richard C. *Anthony Wayne: A Name in Arms.* (The Wayne-Knox-Pickering-McHenry correspondence transcribed and edited by Richard C. Knopf) Pittsburgh. 1960.

Leach, Josiah Granville. *History of the Penrose Family of Philadelphia.* Philadelphia. 1903.

Lee, Henry. *Memoirs of the War in the Southern Department of the United States.* Washington. 1827.

Lodge, Henry Cabot. *The Story of the Revolution.* New York. 1903.

Lossing, Benson J. *The Pictorial Field Book of the Revolution.* 2 vols. New York. 1851.

———. *The Pictorial Field Book of the War of 1812.* New York. 1869.

Loth, David. *The People's General: The Personal Story of Lafayette.* New York. 1951.

Love, N. C. B. "Me-She-Kim-Nogh-Quak, or Little Turtle." *Ohio Archeological and Historical Society Publications.* Vol. XVIII, 1909.

Lowell, Edward J. *The Hessians and the Other German Auxiliaries in the Revolutionary War.* New York. 1884.

McGee, James E. *Sketches of Irish Soldiers in Every Land.* New York. 1872.

McMaster, John Bach. *A History of the People of the United States from the Revolution to the Civil War.* 7 vols. New York, 1907. (Vol. 1)

MacVeagh, W. Y. *Anthony Wayne: An Address Delivered at the Centennial Anniversary of the Massacre of Paoli.* Philadelphia. 1877.

Marshall, John. *The Life of George Washington.* 2 vols. Philadelphia. 1835.

Miller, John. *A Twentieth Century History of Erie County Pennsylvania.* 2 vols. Chicago. 1909.

Miller, John C. *Origins of the American Revolution.* Boston. 1943.

Montgomery, Elizabeth. *Reminiscences of Wilmington in Familiar Village Tales Ancient and New.* Wilmington. 1872.

Moore, Frank. *Diary of the American Revolution.* 2 vols. New York. 1860.

Moore, H. N. *Life and Services of Gen. Anthony Wayne, Founded on Documentary Evidence Furnished by His Son, Col. Isaac Wayne.* Philadelphia. 1845.

Morgan, George. *The True Lafayette.* Philadelphia. 1919.

Morris, Richard B., and Henry Steele Commager. *The Spirit of 'Seventy-Six, etc.* Listed under Commager.

Palmer, John McAuley. *General Von Steuben.* New Haven. 1937.

Penman, John Simpson. *Lafayette and Three Revolutions.* Boston. 1929.

Plumb, J. H. *The First Four Georges*. London. 1968.
Preston, John Hyde. *A Gentleman Rebel: The Exploits of Anthony Wayne*. London. 1928.
——. *Revolution 1776*. New York. 1933.
Randall, E. O. "Tecumseh the Shawnee Chief." *Ohio Archeological and Historical Society Papers*. Vol. XV, 1906.
Rankin, Hugh. *The North Carolina Continentals*. Chapel Hill. 1971.
Robins, Edward. *Romances of Early America*. Philadelphia. 1902.
Roosevelt, Theodore. "The Battle of Fallen Timbers." *Harper's Monthly Magazine*. April 1896.
——. *The Winning of the West*. 6 vols. New York. 1905.
Scharf, John Thomas, and Thompson Wescott. *History of Philadelphia, 1609–1884*. 2 vols. Philadelphia. 1884.
Schouler, James. *United States 1783–1865*. Vol. 2, World's Best Histories Series. New York. 1898.
Spears, John R. *Anthony Wayne*. New York. 1905.
Stille, Charles Janaway. *Major General Anthony Wayne and the Pennsylvania Line*. Philadelphia. 1893.
Streets, Priscilla Walker (Collector and Compiler). *Lewis Walker of Chester Valley and His Descendants 1686–1896*. Philadelphia. 1896.
Teamer, S. Paul. "Wayne's Last Great Service to His Country."
——. "The Morale of the Continental Army During the Pennsylvania Campaign." (With Franklin L. Burns).
——. "The Paoli Massacre." (With Franklin L. Burns). All three articles in *Tredyffrin-Easttown History Club Quarterly*, April 1937, April and July 1939.
Trevelyan, George Otto. *The American Revolution*. (One volume condensed from original six). Edited with notes by Richard B. Morris. New York. 1964.
Tucker, Glenn. *Tecumseh: Vision of Glory*. Indianapolis. 1956.
——. *Poltroons and Patriots: A Popular Account of the War of 1812*. 2 vols. Indianapolis. 1954.
Upton, Emory. *The Military Policy of the United States*. Washington. 1917.
Van Avery, Dale. *Men of the Western Waters*. Boston. 1956.
Van Doren, Carl. *Benjamin Franklin*. New York. 1938.
——. *Mutiny in January*. New York. 1943.
Waln, Robert. *Life of the Marquis De Lafayette*. Philadelphia. 1826.
Ward, Christopher. *The War of the Revolution*. 2 vols. New York. 1952.
Wayne, Anthony. Correspondence of General Anthony Wayne (including Bancroft Collection). New York Public Library, New York.
——. Manuscript and correspondence collection. Historical Society of Pennsylvania. Philadelphia.
Weighley, Russell V. *Toward an American Army*. New York. 1962.
White, R. J. *The Age of George III*. New York. 1968.
Whitlock, Brand. *Lafayette*. 2 vols. New York. 1929.

Bibliography

Wildes, Harry E. *Anthony Wayne: Trouble Shooter of the American Revolution.* New York. 1941.

Wilkinson, James. *Memoirs of My Own Times.* 3 vols. Philadelphia. 1816.

Willcox, William B., Editor. *Sir Henry Clinton's Narrative.* Listed under Clinton.

Winsor, Justin. *Narrative and Critical History of America.* 8 vols. Boston. 1889.

————. *The Westward Movement. The Colonies and the Republic West of the Alleghenies 1763–1798.* Boston. 1897.

Woodward, W. E. *George Washington: The Image and the Man.* New York. 1926.

————. *Lafayette.* New York. 1938.

————. *Tom Paine, America's Godfather 1737–1809.* New York. 1845.

WPA Federal Writer's Program. *Delaware: A Guide to the First State.* New and Revised Edition by Jeannette Eckman. Edited by Henry G. Alsberg. 1938 and 1955.

Index

277

Stirling, Lord (William Alexander), 57, 60; at Brandywine, 70–77 passim; at Germantown, 92–104 passim; at Valley Forge, 106–113 passim
Stony Point, capture of, 143–163
Storm King, 144
Sullivan, Brig. Gen. John, at Brandywine, 70–77 passim; at Germantown, 94–104 passim; at Three Rivers, 38–44 passim
Sumter, Gen. Thomas, 221
Susquehanna River, 25
Swede's Ford, 79, 89, 107

T

Tappan, N.Y., 144
Tappan Zee, 143
Tarleton, Lt. Col. Banastre, 193
Taylor, Lt. Edmund H., 238
Taylor's Tavern, 127
Tecumseh, 142, 233
Temple of Peace, Philadelphia, 251–252
Tennessee, 92
Thermopylae, 133
Thomas, Brig. Gen. John, 38
Thompson, Brig. Gen. William, captured, 42; at Three Rivers, 38–44
Three Rivers, Canada, campaign and battle, 37–44, 48, 69, 78, 138
Thunder Mountain, 144
Ticonderoga, *see* Fort Ticonderoga
Tilghman, Lt. Col. Tench, 208
Todd, Brig. Gen. Robert, 241
Torrey, Cornet Daniel, 238
Townsend, Joseph, 74
Tredyffrin, Pa., 84
Trenton, N.J., 58, 64, 115
Trumbull, Col. John, 47–49; 53–54
Trumbull, Jonathan, as governor of Connecticut, 51; as speaker of the House, 223

V

Valley Creek, 114
Valley Forge, 12, 79, 90, 114, 115, 116; believed haunted, 117, 118, 121, 135–136; winter encampment, 105–113

Van Rensselaer, Solomon, 228
Varnum, Brig. Gen. James M., 127
Vauban, Sebastien de, 48
Vermont, 48
Verplanck's Point, 143–144
Villars, Marshal, 35
Vining, Mary, 17, 66–67, 139; betrothed to Wayne, 254; Wayne's courtship of, 252; Wayne introduced to, by Lafayette, 17
Virginia, 12–13; campaigns in, 190–208; House of Burgesses, 30
Vulture (sloop of war), 146, 161

W

Walker, Joseph and Sarah, 107–108
Walker, Lewis, 108
Wallace, Dr. J. G., 256–257
Warren's Tavern, 80, 85
Washington, George, 12; admires Wayne, 14; announces recognition of Colonies by France, 115; appoints Wayne to command U.S. Army, 226; at Brandywine, 68–77 passim; decides on battle at Monmouth, 118; education of, 24; favors creation of Light Corps, 139–140; fortifies West Point, 144; at Germantown, 91–104; Hudson headquarters of, 144; instructions to Wayne re Stony Point, 146; maneuvers near Philadelphia, 80–81; at Monmouth, 113–131; at Morristown, 156; moves army to Williamsburg, 202; moves on West Point, 166; New Jersey maneuvers, 53–67; opposes invasion of Canada, 33; orders Arnold to West Point, 170–171; orders Gen. Howe to Pompton, 191; orders Wayne to the assistance of Gen. Greene, 199–200; orders Wayne to Stony Point, 143; orders Wayne to West Point, 171–172; personally thanks men, 160; plans for attack on Stony Point, 149–150; prepares New York defenses, 33–34; pursues Clinton, 116; recalls Wayne to duty, 165; receives report from Wayne on mutiny, 181–182; reorganizes army, 55–56; sacrifices men for invasion of Canada, 33; sees public interest in war wane after Colonies' recog-